T0058018

ALSO BY CHRISTOPHER J. OLSEN

Political Culture and Secession in Mississippi: Masculinity, Honor,
and the Antiparty Tradition, 1830–1860

THE AMERICAN CIVIL WAR

CHRISTOPHER J. OLSEN

THE AMERICAN CIVIL WAR

A Hands-on History

HILL AND WANG

A DIVISION OF FARRAR, STRAUS AND GIROUX

NEW YORK

Hill and Wang
A division of Farrar, Straus and Giroux
18 West 18th Street, New York 10011

Printed in the United States of America
Published in 2006 by Hill and Wang
First paperback edition, 2007

The Library of Congress has cataloged the hardcover edition as follows:
Olsen, Christopher J.
    The American Civil War : a hands-on history / Christopher J. Olsen.— 1st ed.
      p.   cm.
    Includes index.
    ISBN-13: 978-0-8090-9538-4 (hardcover : alk. paper)
    ISBN-10: 0-8090-9538-6 (hardcover : alk. paper)
    1. United States—History—Civil War, 1861–1865. 2. Reconstruction (U.S. history,
1865–1877)   I. Title.

  E468.O57 2007
  973.7—dc22

                  2005033184

Paperback ISBN-13: 978-0-8090-1640-2
Paperback ISBN-10: 0-8090-1640-0

Designed by Lisa Stokes

www.fsgbooks.com

For Jennifer Ann, Emma Catherine, and Charlotte Ann,
the wonderful women who run my life, and
for Ross Christopher—good luck, you'll need it

★ CONTENTS ★

Northwest Ordinance	1787
Constitution ratified	1788
Missouri Compromise	1820–1821
The Liberator published first edition	1831
Nullification Crisis	1832–1833
Wilmot Proviso	1846
U.S.-Mexican War ended	1848
Uncle Tom's Cabin published	1852
Kansas-Nebraska Act	1854
Republican Party formed	1855
Lincoln-Douglas debates	1858
Lincoln elected	1860
	1861
Deep South secession	December (1860)– January
Confederacy formed	February
Lincoln inaugurated	March 4
Fort Sumter surrendered	April 13
Upper South secession	April–June

First Battle of Bull Run   July 21
First Confiscation Act   August 6

1862

Forts Henry and Donelson captured   February 6–16
Legal Tender Act   February 24
New Orleans captured   February 25
Battle of Shiloh   April 6
First CSA Conscription Act   April 16
Jackson's "Valley Campaign"   May
Battles around Richmond   May–June
Second Confiscation Act   July 12
Second Battle of Bull Run   August 29–30
Battle of Antietam Creek   September 17
Preliminary Emancipation Proclamation   September 22
Battle of Stone's River   December 31–January 2
    (1863)

1863

Emancipation Proclamation   January 1
Union Enrollment Act   March 3
Richmond Bread Riot   April 2
Battle of Chancellorsville   May 1–3
Battle of Gettysburg   July 1–3
Vicksburg captured   July 4
New York City Riots   July 13
Attack at Fort Wagner   July 18
Battles around Chattanooga   September–November
Lincoln announced Reconstruction plan   December 8

1864

Grant appointed general-in-chief	March
Battles in northern Virginia	May–June
Siege of Richmond and Petersburg	June–April (1865)
Wade-Davis Bill passed	July 2
Siege of Atlanta	July–August
Atlanta captured	September 2
Lincoln reelected	November
Sherman's "March to the Sea"	November–April (1865)

1865

Sherman's Field Order 15 issued	January
Thirteenth Amendment passed	January 31
Hampton Roads Peace Conference	February 3
Army of Northern Virginia (Lee) surrendered	April 9
Lincoln assassinated	April 14
Joseph Johnston's army surrendered	April 26

Southern states formed new governments	Summer 1866
Black Codes passed	Fall–winter 1865–1866
Freedmen's Bureau extended	February 1866
Civil Rights Act	March 1866
Military Reconstruction Act	March 1867
Fourteenth Amendment ratified	1868
Grant elected president	1868
Fifteenth Amendment ratified	1870
Southern states "redeemed"	1866–1877

THE CIVIL WAR WAS the greatest crisis in American history, and produced its greatest economic, political, and social revolutions when the Union won and slavery ended. It helped redefine the American federal system, subtly but permanently making the national government superior to the states. The war years also tested American families and social beliefs about men and women like never before. With so many men off fighting the war, women in both the Union and the Confederacy had to adapt and assume new responsibilities that men normally fulfilled. By the end of the fighting nearly every family had been affected by its massive, unexpected level of death and destruction. Emancipation, expansion of the federal government's power and responsibility, more than one in ten adult white men dead, massive constitutional changes, and the lingering sectional hatred resulting from the war and postwar years left a collective legacy that largely defined American life into the mid-twentieth century, and even today.

The American Civil War: A Hands-on History examines the coming of the war, the war years, and Reconstruction. It is designed for readers who want to understand the most important events, individuals, issues, and consequences of the Civil War era, and to get a sense of what Americans of those years said and thought. Therefore, the book combines a narrative of critical moments and topics with primary source documents that take the reader into the minds of nineteenth-century American men and women. The documents offer insights into a great range of topics and perspectives, drawing on a diversity of materials: newspaper editorials, cartoons, public and private letters, photographs, government documents and legislation, poetry, and music. Through the narrative and documents, readers will also live through the uncertainty of the war years, when hundreds of individual decisions determined the course of events and the fate of the nation. Why did the war begin in 1861? What convinced Abraham Lincoln to issue the Emancipation Proclamation? The answers lie in the individual and collective beliefs, thoughts, and actions of American men and women.

A Note on the Documents

The primary documents are reproduced as originally written, including misspellings and errors in grammar, in order to maintain authenticity.

THE AMERICAN CIVIL WAR

Political Sectionalism
Before 1850

WHEN THE MAJORITY of white Southerners opted to secede from the Union in 1860 and 1861 it signaled a failure of the American political system and its renowned ability to compromise difficult problems. For most of the antebellum period, nearly all politicians tried to avoid a national discussion of slavery or slavery expansion, believing such a debate would be too divisive for the country. At times, though, the questions were unavoidable, and threatened to destroy the Union. In turn, Northerners and Southerners negotiated a series of compromises, a practice that stretched back to the Constitutional Convention of 1787 and that over the decades engaged the efforts of George Washington, Thomas Jefferson, Henry Clay, Andrew Jackson, John C. Calhoun, Daniel Webster, Stephen A. Douglas, Jefferson Davis, and others. These well-known figures effected compromises at the national level, but the debate over slavery eventually reached into America's communities and entered the conversations and feelings of ordinary folks, too. Most men and women across the country ultimately took positions on the growing sectional divide, and those individual choices determined the coming of the Civil War.

What provoked these moments of national crisis? First, it is important to acknowledge that the vast majority of white Americans considered the practice of slavery a very different political or legal issue from slavery's expansion into territories where it nominally existed or did not exist. There was widespread agreement that slavery in the individual states was a local issue to be decided by residents of those states. In other words, even if the national government—that is, the majority of the voting public acting through Congress—wanted to abolish slavery, it could not, because abolition was not permitted under the Constitution. But the expansion of slavery was something else. Territories were governed directly by Congress, and therefore the issue of whether or not slavery would be allowed to expand was a matter for the national government in Washington.

Even before the Constitution was written, in fact, slavery in the West was an issue for the national government. America's earliest governing body, the Confederation Congress (constituted under the Articles of Confederation), approved the Northwest Ordinance in 1787, barring slavery from the Northwest Territory. In 1784 the Congress had considered a proposal from Thomas Jefferson (as part of his ordinance to grant early statehood) that would have prohibited slavery in all western lands, including the Southwest. When the antislavery provision failed by one vote, Jefferson famously lamented that "the fate of millions unborn" hung "on the tongue of one man, and heaven was silent in that awful moment." In the mid-1780s, Jefferson, like many of the Founding Fathers, was in the flush of revolutionary rhetoric about equality and liberty, and whatever antislavery impulses he had ever felt were at their most intense.

The expansion of slavery caused heated division for a variety of reasons. For some it was a matter of morality—slavery was wrong and therefore should be limited as a first step toward abolition; others saw it as an economic matter, part of the competition for good land and resources; many Northern whites wanted to restrict slavery in the hope of creating an "all-white" society in the West. All of these factors, and others, helped to energize Northerners and Southerners and made the question of slavery expansion an explosive national issue. Ultimately, the compromises effected in Congress between the North and South involved basic questions of political power in the national government—votes in the House and the Senate, votes in the Electoral College, votes to help decide the makeup of the Supreme Court. Thus—and this is the critical point—for the large majority of all whites, whether or not slavery expanded to the West involved a series of questions unrelated to the fate of black people. In short, the expansion of slavery was a vital and urgent issue for whites, even while most of them did not care whether or not slavery itself continued in the South. This explains why the Civil War was "somehow" about slavery, as

Abraham Lincoln said, even though the vast majority of whites had no interest in abolition—and neither cared nor probably even thought much about slaves.

In the Constitutional Convention of 1787, delegates from Northern and Southern states discovered that two issues related to slavery divided them. First was the question of counting slaves for representation and taxation. Most Southerners wanted to count slaves as people when it came to proportional representation in the House of Representatives and Electoral College, but not when figuring each state's tax liability. Most Northerners wanted it the other way around. In the end, it was primarily a matter of finding an acceptable ratio that counted slaves as a portion of a person, for both representation and taxation, with delegates finally settling on 5:3— each slave would count as three-fifths of a person. The question of slavery's legitimacy was not part of the discussion, which was strictly a political debate.

The other issue at the Constitutional Convention, which had far more potential to divide the new nation, was the international slave trade from Africa. The trade was still legal, although abolitionists in Great Britain were already turning public opinion against the practice as unchristian and immoral. Most of the constitutional delegates also opposed the overseas trade, including many slaveowners such as Virginia's George Mason, who spoke passionately against it. The trade was easier to attack than slavery itself: the death rate was appallingly high; often mothers and children were separated; slaves were torn from their families and culture. On the other hand, most whites believed that slavery itself "uplifted" black men and women by bringing them in contact with Christianity and "civilization." If they survived the trade and made it to the United States, the argument ran, slaves were infinitely better off than they would have been in Africa. However, many Southerners considered opposition to the international trade a slippery slope, and any discussion that included words such as *immoral* in the same sentence as *slavery* made them uncomfortable. Representatives from Georgia and South Carolina insisted that the international trade remain open for economic reasons: their economies were just beginning to take off, and the planters in those states believed they needed a reliable, fresh supply of workers straight from the Old World. They even threatened to leave the new country if the international slave trade was disallowed. True to form, the Founders compromised: the overseas trade could not be banned in fewer than twenty years (in 1808, Congress did outlaw it). In those two decades, planters from the Deep South imported tens of thousands of men and women from Africa.

These compromises largely removed the issue of slavery from national politics for more than three decades. In that time, free and slave states were added to the Union in nearly matched pairs: Indiana (1816) and Mississippi (1817), and Illinois (1818) and Alabama (1819), for instance. In 1819, however, the population of Missouri Territory exceeded sixty thousand, the minimum required for statehood. The land was part of the Louisiana Purchase, in which slavery was legal under French and Spanish laws, and many Southerners had settled there after coming down the Ohio River Valley and through St. Louis. In 1819, slaves constituted about one-sixth of the territory's population. While considering legislation to allow Missourians to write a constitution, an obscure New York congressman, James Tallmadge, offered an amendment that provided for gradual emancipation of all enslaved residents of Missouri in about thirty years. To the surprise and horror of most white Southerners, Tallmadge's amendment passed the Northern-dominated House of Representatives, after several vitriolic debates. Gradual emancipation, though, was defeated in the Senate, where Southerners had parity with the North. The debate over Missouri's application and Tallmadge's amendment sharpened sectional differences and revealed an undercurrent of moral opposition to the spread of slavery. The aging Thomas Jefferson declared the controversy a "fire bell in the night" that "filled me with terror."

The crisis lasted nearly two years as Northern and Southern politicians searched for common ground. Southerners asserted their constitutional argument for the legality of slavery in all U.S. territories, which was based on the Fifth Amendment. The territories, they maintained, were the common possession of all American citizens, and slaves were property like any other kind of property. Therefore, if the federal government denied planters the right to own slaves in any territory, then it was a violation of their due process rights under the Constitution. This argument remained the cornerstone of the "Southern position" on slavery in the territories for the rest of the antebellum years—during which time more and more Northerners expressed a strong desire that slavery not spread beyond its present borders. The reasons for this ranged from political jealousy to hatred of Southern planters to moral antipathy for the South's "peculiar institution."

Some Northerners argued that as the free states now enjoyed a much greater, and fast-growing, population, they should also have a majority of votes in the Senate. To Southerners this idea was particularly threatening, since the debate over Tallmadge's amendment underscored how important their equality in the Senate was, and how much power they had lost in the House of Representatives. In 1820, just over 40 percent of congressmen came from slave-owning states. Much more offensive to Southerners were comments such as those from New York's Rufus King, who declared slavery against the "laws of God." Lastly, others suggested that slavery violated the provision that each state have a republican form of government. Men from Virginia and the rest of the South—like all nineteenth-century Americans obsessed with their revolutionary heritage—were livid.

After months of deadlock, the young Speaker of the House, Kentucky's Henry Clay, helped win approval of compromise legislation that admitted Missouri to the Union and solved the question of slavery in the remainder of the Louisiana Purchase territory. Often called "Handsome Harry" or "Harry of the West," Clay was known for his love of bourbon, cigars, and poker. He ran for president and lost—three times—but he helped engineer three major sectional agreements to earn his most lasting moniker, "The Great Compromiser." To solve the deadlock, Maine (formerly a part of Massachusetts) was admitted as a free state, paired with pro-slavery Missouri. Of more immediate consequence was an agreement to limit slavery in the remaining Louisiana Purchase to lands south of a line drawn from the southern border of Missouri: latitude 36°30' north (see map on p. 54). The Missouri Compromise, then, resolved the question of slavery in the territories so long as no new land was added to the country (which did not occur until 1848). The 36°30' line became a nearly sacred piece of text to many Americans, who considered it almost equivalent to a constitutional amendment.

Another constitutional crisis that contained sectional undertones occurred in South Carolina between 1828 and 1833, although neither slavery nor slavery's expansion was the immediate issue. In 1828, Congress passed a new protective tariff with higher rates on many items. It was designed to boost domestic manufacturing, although it hurt American export farmers, who had difficulty selling to European buyers. Perhaps hardest pressed were South Carolina's cotton planters, struggling with depleted soil, falling yields, and competition from fresh land to the West. In response, a small faction of the state's planter-politicians decided to challenge the tariff by testing a political/constitutional theory: states' rights. This idea went back at least to 1798–1799, when Thomas Jefferson and James Madison penned (anonymously) the Kentucky and Virginia Resolutions. These statements of principle—carrying no legal authority—declared that states were ultimately superior to the federal government, and therefore the final interpreters of the Constitution. This was before the principle of judicial review was established, giving that power to the Supreme Court. If the federal government acted in a "despotic" manner, then a state had the right, indeed the duty, to intercede on behalf of its citizens and "nullify" the federal measure. It was the first time a state had ever tested the theory.

The tariff was the immediate cause of the Nullification Crisis, as it became known, but many South Carolina politicians clearly had slavery in mind. They conceived of states' rights as their "ace in the hole," a last-ditch measure that might be used to protect slavery from a federal government they saw as increasingly threatening, and in the future apt to be dominated by Yankees. Using the constitutional ratification process as a model, John C. Calhoun (the vice president at the time, who wrote anonymously) laid out the process for nullification in the "South Carolina Exposition and Protest." It called for a special election for delegates to a state convention that would consider nullification. Calhoun maintained that nullification should be an extreme measure, not undertaken lightly, and should therefore be lengthy and relatively difficult. On November 24, 1832, a special convention of South Carolina delegates voted to nullify the federal tariff rates of 1828, which they declared were "unauthorized by the Constitution of the United States, and violate the true meaning and intent thereof, and are null, void, and no law, nor binding upon this State." As a final threat, the convention delegates vowed to secede should the federal government attempt to enforce the tariff with military coercion. Secession—the voluntary withdrawal of one state from the Union—was the logical end to states' rights logic.

Nullification, of course, challenged federal authority and, in particular, President Andrew Jackson, who'd won reelection in 1832 and was a hero to Southerners—he received over three-fourths of the vote in the slave states. With Jackson a native of South Carolina, a wealthy slaveowner, and often a champion of state power, many Southerners expected he would sympathize with the nullifiers. They were wrong. The chief executive of the country is supposed to enforce federal law, and Jackson intended to do just that. On December 10, 1832, he issued his "Nullification Proclamation," in which he labeled South Carolina's action an "impractical absurdity," the "essence of anarchy," and secession itself "treason." Finally, Jackson asked for, and Congress approved, the Force Bill, granting him the authority to invade South Carolina and collect the tariff if necessary. The governor of South Carolina responded by raising a volunteer army; military conflict seemed a real possibility. Unfortunately for the South Carolinians, however, no other state nullified the tariff, even though many Southerners expressed a general sympathy for the principle of states' rights. At this point Henry Clay again stepped in and proposed compromise legislation that would gradually lower tariff rates (something Jackson had urged repeatedly). This gave the nullifiers a way out. The South Carolina convention delegates reconvened, repealed the Ordinance of Nullification, but, as if to "prove" their point, also nullified the Force Bill. Jackson chose not to respond to this last peevish action.

What lessons could be taken from the Nullification Crisis? First, many Southerners concluded that states' rights worked. South Carolinians nullified the tariff and, basically, got what they wanted: lower rates. Furthermore, others contended that threatening to secede had forced the federal government to compromise. On the other hand, a Southern, slave-owning president had called nullification "absurd" and vowed to invade South Carolina; and no other state had offered South Carolina more than sympathy. In the end, the crisis prompted many Southerners to see states' rights, nullification, and even secession as viable options in the quest to protect slavery. It also created a core of committed "nullifiers" in every state: men such as John Quitman in Mississippi and future president John Tyler in Virginia. In the following decades many of these men became leaders in the movement for secession, working to convince the majority of Southerners that states' rights would provide the last line of defense in the developing battle with Northerners over the future place of slavery in the United States.

Absent a pressing sectional crisis, Americans in the 1830s and early 1840s enjoyed prosperity and expansion. Tens of thousands of people moved west into new states and territories (in which the fate of slavery had already been decided), the population continued to grow rapidly due to natural growth and immigration, and the country's two national political parties, Whig and Democratic, became entrenched national institutions. Ever more confident, Americans articulated a new and more aggressive set of ideas about their place in the world. Taken together, they became known as "Manifest Destiny," a term coined by the Democratic editor John L. O'Sullivan in 1845. It emphasized America's Protestant heritage as God's supposedly chosen people, Anglo-Saxon racial superiority, and the blessings of capitalism and democracy. Most Americans, particularly White Anglo-Saxon Protestants (WASPs), believed they were part of the most important nation in the history of the world.

This spirit certainly infused President James K. Polk, a slaveholding Democrat from Tennessee, elected in 1844 on a platform of Manifest Destiny and territorial acquisition. Soon after Polk's victory, even before he assumed the office, Congress annexed the independent Lone Star Republic of Texas, formerly a province in northern Mexico and led by Americans who had settled there in the 1820s. In 1835, the Texans had rebelled against the Mexican government in part out of fear that it was going to move forcefully to restrict their autonomy and enforce Mexico's ban against slavery, which was broadly ignored in Texas. Most Texans expected to join the United States at once, but between 1836 and 1844, national leaders avoided the issue of annexation for fear of disrupting the country with the addition of so much slave territory. Candidate Polk sidestepped the dilemma by advocating expansion everywhere. He pledged to take the territories of Texas, California, Oregon (then jointly occupied with Great Britain), and whatever else he could get his hands on. Once in office, Polk helped engineer a war with Mexico (ostensibly over the border of Texas) in the hopes of acquiring more territory to the west and south, and particularly California.

The U.S.-Mexican War was controversial from the start, and divided the country largely along sectional lines. Southerners overwhelmingly supported the war: it started when the United States annexed a huge piece of slave territory settled by Southerners; nearly all of the volunteers who fought the war were Southerners; and the war was led by a slaveholding Southern president. Most Northerners, particularly Whigs, opposed the war. In addition to their concern over adding more slave territory, many Northerners questioned an imperialistic war that was candidly designed to add territory from a weaker nation. The Ohio senator John Sherman spoke for many Northerners when he called the war "an unjust aggression upon

a weak republic, excused by false reasons, and continued solely for the ac-
quisitions of slave territory." Furthermore, Northerners resented Polk's
1846 compromise with Great Britain over control of Oregon, something
he had pledged not to do during the campaign. It seemed as though a
Southern president had quickly abandoned what Northerners wanted,
while eagerly seeking war for the interests of slaveowners. Reports of
American troops—primarily Southern volunteers—committing gang rape
and murder of Mexican civilians fed a growing moral outrage among
Northern intellectuals, and a growing conviction that slavery bred violence, lawlessness, and cruelty.

Even before the war ended, the prospect of adding more slave territory
divided Congress and the nation. In August 1846, a Democratic congressman from Pennsylvania, David Wilmot, attached a proviso to a military
spending bill that stated there would be no slavery allowed in any territory
the United States might gain from Mexico. The Wilmot Proviso passed
numerous times in the Northern-controlled House of Representatives, but
always failed in the evenly divided Senate. Throughout the war, the issue
remained unresolved, and when the war ended, the Treaty of Guadalupe
Hidalgo transferred most of the present-day Southwest from Mexico to
the United States. All of this new land reopened the question of slavery's
expansion.

By 1848, there were three standing solutions to the question of slavery
in the territories: no slavery at all, which came to be called "Free Soil"; slavery legal everywhere and all the time, which was the Southern position
based on the Fifth Amendment; and extension of the 36°30' line (from the
Missouri Compromise) to the Pacific Ocean. To these was added a new
option: "popular sovereignty." This proposal came from the 1848 Democratic presidential candidate Lewis Cass of Michigan. Popular sovereignty
stated that the people living in each territory would decide whether or not
to allow slavery. This seemed straightforward and in line with American
democratic principles, but proved to be unworkable in practice.

In any case, most politicians believed it would be quite a long time before the new territory gained from Mexico was really settled. Much of the
land was arid and hot, and many Americans considered it uninhabitable.
All of that changed in 1849, after gold was discovered in California and
settlers flooded the region. In just a few months the residents of California
applied for statehood, without slavery. Southerners in the Senate refused

to admit California to the Union, touching off another sectional crisis. Opponents of California statehood objected partly because it would mean one more free state, ending the long tradition of equality in the Senate (there was no new slave territory poised to become a state anytime soon). They also believed California's admission would be a "back-door" means to impose the hated Wilmot Proviso, since the land was gained from Mexico. The possible addition of another free state was so threatening that it touched off a secession movement across much of the Deep South, particularly strong in Mississippi, where a majority of Democrats supported secession if California was admitted.

Into this new crisis stepped Henry Clay again. No longer the dashing "Handsome Harry," Clay was within two years of death from tuberculosis but still an imposing figure. He was joined by an even more infirm John C. Calhoun, and Daniel Webster, the great Whig senator from Massachusetts. This legendary "Great Triumvirate" joined forces, with each man speaking passionately (though in Calhoun's case, a colleague had to read his speech for him) to try to avert secession and civil war. Clay's proposal bundled together four major pieces of legislation in one big package designed to settle several outstanding sectional issues. His strategy was faulty, but his proposals were adopted one by one rather than as a piece, with a young Democratic senator from Illinois, Stephen A. Douglas, managing the compromise measures and working them through both houses of Congress.

Each part of the country, in essence, got two pieces of legislation. For the North, California was admitted as a free state and the slave trade was banned in the District of Columbia. (Selling slaves in the national capital had rankled many Northerners for years.) For Southerners there was more stringent fugitive slave legislation, and two territories in the Southwest—New Mexico and Utah—were both organized under popular sovereignty. Planters had complained for years about the difficulty of recapturing runaway slaves, and organizing the territories under popular sovereignty opened the door for them to become slave states. No one was completely happy with the Compromise of 1850, but it appealed to enough moderates in both sections who wanted to avoid secession and war, and both Whig and Democratic leaders endorsed it in hopes of preserving their national organizations.

Many Southerners still opposed the admission of California, however, and in hundreds of public meetings they laid out conditions under which they would remain in the Union. Most popular was the so-called Georgia Platform. Its supporters pledged to back secession if Congress did any of the following: abolished slavery in the District of Columbia or at federal military installations; outlawed the interstate slave trade; refused to admit a new slave state; enacted Free Soil in New Mexico and Utah territories; or in any way altered or interfered with the new Fugitive Slave Act. Any of these events, the Georgians warned, they "will and ought to resist, even (as a last resort) to a disruption of every tie which binds [us] to the Union." In short, the preservation of the Union depended on no Northern interference with the right of slaveowners to recapture runaway slaves or move into the western territories with their slave property.

At the beginning of the 1850s, then, both major parties hoped to keep slavery out of national politics by standing behind the Compromise of 1850. Strong feelings of dissatisfaction and mistrust remained among many Southerners, though, and the crisis created a core of secessionists determined not to waver from the Georgia Platform. Indeed, a sizable minority already believed that secession was inevitable. In the North, the movement for Free Soil gained momentum, and events during the 1850s prevented the parties from keeping slavery out of national politics. Attitudes in both the North and the South had also changed as Americans were less forgiving and more suspicious of one another. No two groups were more responsible for the general feelings of alienation and distrust than abolitionists in the North and proslavery spokesmen in the South.

Kentucky Resolution (1799)

*Written by Thomas Jefferson, this statement of principle
led to the theory of states' rights, the belief that states were
ultimately superior to the national government. States'
rights, in turn, was the ideological foundation for
nullification and secession.*

RESOLVED, That this commonwealth considers the federal union, upon the terms and for the purposes specified in the late compact, as conducive to the liberty and happiness of the several states:

That the principle and construction contended for by sundry of the state legislatures, that the general government is the exclusive judge of the extent of the powers delegated to it, stop nothing short of despotism; since the discretion of those who administer the government, and not the [C]onstitution, would be the measure of their powers: That the several states who formed that instrument, being sovereign and independent, have the unquestionable right to judge of its infraction; and that a nullification, by those sovereignties, of all unauthorized acts done under colour of that instrument, is the rightful remedy.

Fredrick Norcom, Vicksburg, Mississippi, to James C. Johnston, Edenton, North Carolina, January 24, 1836

*Men and women settling the Old Southwest wrote
thousands of letters like this one, describing how easily a
person could get rich with enough slaves to clear the land
and grow cotton. These sentiments help explain why
white Southerners were so intent on extending the
boundaries of slavery.*

I have met with I suppose from 50 to 100 men who (many of them are entirely destitute of a common education) five years since could not get credit for a pair of shoes, now worth 100,000 to a million of dollars— I have seen a great number who came here rich, and now immensely rich; I have not seen but one single soul, nor have I heard of 3, who have failed—and these were all merchants, who without much Capital went to speculating in Cotton—. It is in truth the only country I ever read or heard of, where a poor man could in 2 or 3 years without any aid, become wealthy—A few days of labour & lying out in the woods enabled them to find out a good body of land, & not having the money to enter it for themselves, they would sell their information to those who were too idle, or too rich to undergo the fatigue of hunting for it; by this means they would obtain money enough to enter one section, then two, & so on; soon sell that for ten or twenty times as much as they gave for it, and sometimes would absolutely make what is considered in the old States a fortune in 5 or 6 months. . . .

The demand for all species of property here is great, constant and increasing—I cannot ascertain what amount of property has been sold in any one county. More than 6,000 Negroes and 10,000 horses & mules have been sold in Yazoo County alone, and from 1st Sept. up to this time (and I am told it so continues until April) there are Negroes by the hundred in every little Log-Village for sale. . . .

I know of no point in the world with 4 times its population which sells so many goods, Negroes & provisions &c and if things go on at this rate long, we must soon have 20,000 population; goods are lying here in store in quantities, waiting for stores to be built, and all species of houses are going up as if by Magic weekly: property bought in the edge of Town twelve months since for $200 per acre sold for $4,000 per acre last week—. All species of labour here cost 3 times as much as at Edenton, and as a general rule most every thing costs about 4 times as much as in the old States, except Negroes—prime man & woman together sell for $2,000—the ordinary mode of selling here is man & wife—.

Hayes Collection, Southern Historical Collection, University of North Carolina, Chapel Hill, NC.

David Wilmot Advocates Free Soil (1847)

David Wilmot (Dem., PA) opposed the expansion of slavery, and his proviso became the basis for "Free Soil." His racial attitudes, expressed here, were typical of many white Northerners who eventually supported Free Soil and the Republican Party in the 1850s.

I make no war upon the South nor upon slavery in the South. I have no squeamish sensitiveness upon the subject of slavery, nor morbid sympathy for the slave. I plead the cause of the rights of white freemen. I would preserve for free white labor a fair country, a rich inheritance, where the sons of toil, of my own race and own color, can live without the disgrace which association with negro slavery brings upon free labor. I stand for the inviolability of free territory. It shall remain free, so far as my voice or vote can aid in the preservation of its character.

. . . The future greatness and glory of this Republic demands that the progress of domestic slavery should be arrested now and forever.

Sir, upon this subject, the North has yielded until there is no more to give up.

Men of the North—representatives of northern freedom, will you consummate such a deed of infamy and shame? I trust in God not. O, for the honor of the North—for the fair fame of our green hills and valleys, be firm in this crisis—be true to your country and your race. The white laborer of the North claims your service; he demands that you stand firm to his interests and his rights; that you preserve the future homes of his children, on the distant shores of the Pacific, from the degradation and dishonor of negro servitude. Where the negro slave labors, the free white man cannot labor by his side without sharing in his degradation and disgrace.

Congressional Globe, 29th Cong., 2nd session, 1847, Appendix, 317.

Georgia Platform (1850)

Many Southerners opposed the Compromise of 1850, particularly the admission of California as a free state. In various public meetings they passed resolutions detailing the conditions under which they were willing to stay in the Union. One of the most widely endorsed and copied was the Georgia Platform.

1st, That we hold the American Union, secondary in importance only to the rights and principles it was designed to perpetuate.

. . . [I]n this spirit, the State of Georgia has maturely considered the action of Congress embracing a series of measures for the admission of California into the Union, the organization of territorial Governments for Utah and New Mexico, the establishment of a boundary between the latter and the State of Texas, the suppression of the slave trade in the District of Columbia, and the extradition of fugitive slaves, and (connected with them) the rejection of propositions to exclude slavery from the Mexican territories and to abolish it in the District of Columbia, and whilst she does not wholly approve, will abide by it as a permanent adjustment of this sectional controversy.

Fourthly, That the State of Georgia in the judgment of this Convention, will and ought to resist even (as a last resort,) to a disruption of every tie which binds her to the Union, any action of Congress upon the subject of slavery in the District of Columbia, or in any places subject to the jurisdiction of Congress incompatible with the safety, domestic tranquility, the rights and honor of the slave-holding States, or any refusal to admit as a State any territory hereafter, applying, because of the existence of slavery therein, or any act prohibiting the introduction of slaves into the territories of New Mexico and Utah, or any act repealing or materially modifying the laws now in force for the recovery of fugitive slaves.

Fifthly, That it is the deliberate opinion of this Convention, that upon the faithful execution of the *Fugitive Slave Bill* by the proper authorities depends the preservation of our much loved Union.

The Georgia Telegraph, Dec. 17, 1850.

John Gast: *American Progress* (1872)

*Most antebellum whites generally supported the idea that
America represented a superior civilization, one that should be
spread across the continent. The most ardent supporters of
Manifest Destiny supported expansion even if that meant
military conquest. This painting, actually done after the Civil
War, is the most famous graphic representation of Manifest
Destiny.*

Library of Congress.

TWO

Abolitionists, Fugitive Slaves, and the Northern View of the South

BEFORE THE CIVIL WAR only a small minority of Northern whites ever supported immediate abolition. Even fewer believed that white and black men and women could ever be social, cultural, or intellectual equals. Yet by 1861, many Americans, particularly white Southerners, believed that abolitionists had played a central role in bringing on the Civil War. Why and how did abolitionists have such a profound impact on the sectional march toward war if their beliefs and values remained so unpopular among mainstream Americans? At the least, abolitionists forced Northerners to think about slavery and perhaps to question whether or not it was such a blessed institution—as Southern whites contended. Equal in importance were fugitive slaves. Slaves had always run away, of course, but the Fugitive Slave Act of 1850 literally brought the issue to street corners in the North for the first time. Runaway slaves and the new law's implementation prompted many Northerners to consider slaves as human beings—men and women with hopes, dreams, and feelings—for the first time. Abolitionists and fugitives combined to reshape mainstream public opinion about the nature of slavery, Southern society, and the effects of slavery on the United States.

Abolition had a long history in North America. Africans and African Americans, of course, can be considered abolitionists from the beginning of slavery on the continent. Free black men and women helped slaves escape, sheltered runaways, purchased the freedom of relatives and spouses, and undermined the institution whenever they could. Tens of thousands of slaves escaped, particularly during the Revolution and the War of 1812, and anytime the white community was divided. After 1830 many escaped slaves became spokesmen for abolition. Most famous was Frederick Douglass, a large, imposing man and gifted public speaker. Douglass escaped from Maryland, wrote his autobiography, and later published a newspaper, the *North Star*. Other fugitives worked to help more slaves escape, many via the legendary Underground Railroad.

The Quaker church was the first mainstream white church to oppose slavery. Committed to racial and gender equality, Pennsylvania Quakers formed in 1775 what is considered the first abolition society in world history. As early Baptist and Methodist preachers spoke throughout the colonies in the 1770s and 1780s, they also advocated abolition. In order to attract Southern converts, however, they had to compromise. Instead of abolition, Baptists and Methodists—eventually the two largest denominations in the South—encouraged masters to bring Christianity to slaves and to provide them better material living conditions. From the turn of the nineteenth century, discussions of abolition virtually ceased to exist in Southern churches.

The "modern" abolition movement began in 1831, a momentous year in the history of American slavery. On January 1, William Lloyd Garrison began publishing *The Liberator*, an abolition journal, in Boston. Born very poor in Massachusetts, Garrison worked in the newspaper business before turning to reform (he was also an advocate for pacifism, women's rights, and other causes). Balding and bespectacled, Garrison was a tenacious and provocative public speaker who often incited crowds by burning a copy of the Constitution, which he called "an agreement with hell" for its acceptance of slavery. He refused to vote and was mobbed repeatedly and nearly killed several times. In 1833, Garrison helped found the American Anti-slavery Society (AAS). This organization admitted men and women, black and white. Its most famous member was John Quincy Adams, a late convert to abolition. The AAS declared slavery "a heinous crime in the sight of God" and vowed to fight to the end for its "immediate abandonment." The society created a national organization with local chapters in many Northern cities and towns. Its greatest strength lay in New England, upstate New York, and northern Ohio. Abolitionists held rallies, delivered lectures, and wrote pamphlets, books, and articles. They often met with ridicule, even violence, but over time they took control of the debate and helped fix the Northern view of slavery.

As a group, abolitionists were well educated, drawn primarily from the middle and upper classes, and therefore enjoyed great access to what modern Americans would call "the media." Active support for abolition was concentrated among New England WASPs, and particularly evangelicals affected by the wave of revivals known as the Second Great Awakening, which began about 1800 and continued as a powerful force into the 1840s. A revival of American Protestantism influencing nearly all major denominations—particularly Methodists, Baptists, and Presbyterians—the Awakening focused on each person's individual relationship with God and emphasized the ability of every man and woman to be responsible for his or her own salvation. The key was to recognize one's sinfulness and reform one's behavior to be more "Godly." Awakening preachers also urged men and women to convert others and help them reform their "sinful" ways. Thus, a natural outgrowth of this religious revival was a torrent of reform societies. Temperance was certainly the most popular, but abolition drew strength from the same impulses. The great majority of abolitionists, then, were evangelical Christians, many of whom became interested in the reform after experiencing a revival and personal "rebirth."

Most abolitionists declared slavery a sin against God. That seemed simple, and obvious enough from a modern perspective. But labeling slavery a sin was a momentous step because it eliminated any sort of compromise over the institution. Slavery was likened to murder, and no one encourages murderers to "just cut back a little" this year; you also don't pay murderers to stop. If slavery was a sin, then abolition needed to be immediate and uncompensated—with no reimbursement for slaveowners. The abolitionists' message was clear: slaveowners were not good Christians, and God would punish them with eternal damnation. Many of them actually went further, arguing that slavery was a national sin that threatened the future of the United States. All people who condoned or allowed slavery to continue were equally guilty, and God's wrath would be visited on the whole country if Americans failed to act. Theodore Dwight Weld avowed that any American who did not challenge slavery was a "joint partner in the original sin, becomes its apologist and makes it the business of every moment to perpetuate it afresh."

A second line of attack was secular: slavery was contrary to the natural rights of mankind, violated the intent of the Founding Fathers, and therefore undermined the ideals of the American Revolution. It is impossible to overstate the obsession that antebellum Americans had with the revolutionary generation. Men and women who grew up after the turn of the century worshiped the Founders, who, they firmly believed, had fulfilled God's plan and created the greatest and most important nation in world history. This younger generation was entrusted with the task of continuing that legacy. Was slavery part of the Founders' plan for the United States? More and more Northerners decided no. There was evidence. First, the Declaration of Independence stated "all men are created equal," which increasingly was interpreted to mean that all men (not women), regardless of skin color, deserved basic equal rights. No one captured this belief better than Abraham Lincoln, for whom the Declaration of Independence was much more important than the Constitution. For a man born in a log cabin, self-educated, and who would eventually become a wealthy corporate lawyer, the ideal of equality of opportunity lay at the heart of the American enterprise. Second, in the Northern states, the Revolutionary War generation had voluntarily eliminated slavery, apparently the first ruling elite in the history of the world to do so. Third, the Northwest Ordinance, passed by the Confederation Congress dominated by Revolutionary War heroes, limited slavery's expansion to land south of the Ohio River (and Jefferson himself had tried to prohibit any expansion of slavery in his 1784 Ordinance). Fourth, the Founders had ended the international slave trade, albeit after a twenty-year waiting period. Finally, many of the individual Revolutionary War leaders seemed to embrace abolition as they got older: most famously, Washington freed his slaves in his will, and Franklin became president of the Philadelphia Society for Promoting the Abolition of Slavery. All of these acts, more and more Northerners believed, signaled that the true intent of the Founding Fathers was to end slavery. Slaveowners, this argument concluded, were insulting the legacy and intent of the greatest generation of men and women in the history of the world.

Abolitionists also declared slavery to be a backward economic system, contrary to the laws of capitalism: slaves were not paid wages; they had no positive incentive to work as hard as they could—only the threat of physical abuse and torture got slaves to work at all—there was no flexibility in hiring or firing; slavery limited Southerners' ability to invest capital in other improvements since its constraints as a labor system drained away most of the region's capital; it created no incentive to increase productivity and education among workers; and so forth. The logical conclusion was that Southerners were dragging down the American economy and threatening the country's destiny to lead the world by example and material success. This argument became more prominent in the 1850s, when the new Republican Party praised Northern capitalism and the "Free Labor Ideology" as economically superior to slavery. Finally, abolitionists also contended that slavery destroyed the character of Southern whites because it gave them, white men in particular, too much power over other human beings. Absolute power corrupted, creating a society of men likely to be violent, lazy, drunken, and sexually predatory—in a word: undisciplined.

This combination of religious and secular appeals characterized all of the most important reform movements of the era. As the American Antislavery Society summarized in its 1833 Declaration of Sentiments: "With entire confidence in the overruling justice of God, we plant ourselves upon the Declaration of our Independence, and upon the truths of Divine Revelation."

Like abolitionists, runaway slaves also forced Northern whites to think about slavery. The vast majority of fugitives were young, single men; most came from the border states or upper South; and most hid in Northern cities among the free population of color. Before the 1850s, runaways were not really a national issue and rarely captured public attention. That was an important reason Southerners had insisted on a much tougher fugitive slave law as part of the Compromise of 1850. The Fugitive Slave Act empowered slave catchers to bring suspected runaways up before federal commissioners, who heard evidence as to whether or not the man or woman was a fugitive. The "accused" was not allowed to speak or present evidence in his own "defense." Commissioners were paid five dollars if they ruled against the slave catcher, ten dollars if they sent the man or woman back into slavery. Obviously, the law invited abuse. Slave catchers went North with a general description of a fugitive and often found it easier to kidnap some likely looking fellow and bring him up before a sympathetic federal commissioner. In this way, hundreds, perhaps thousands, of free men and women were kidnapped and sent to slavery in the South.

Reports of runaways captured or kidnapped on Northern streets raised the ire of Yankees, and the law's inequities offended men and women who did not care much about slavery or black people but who valued America's legal tradition. Perhaps most of all, Northerners resented the law's provision that required them to help slave catchers—it stated that slave catchers could deputize any Northerner; refusal to help was punishable with six months in prison. This seemed the height of Southern arrogance and demonstrated how the political power of planters reached into local communities and commanded ordinary citizens to help sustain the slave system.

The most famous fugitive case was that of Anthony Burns, an escaped slave from Richmond, Virginia, who was working in Boston. In May 1854, he was captured, "convicted," and held for return to slavery. Several rescue attempts failed, and the city of Boston tried to purchase his freedom for a huge price. President Franklin Pierce was forced to send in the U.S. Army, which marched Burns through the streets of Boston to a ship that took him back to slavery. Some residents estimated that more than half the city protested and jeered the troops, and public buildings were draped in black to mourn the event. Burns was the last fugitive slave returned from New England.

Beginning soon after its passage, Northerners moved quickly to frustrate the Fugitive Slave Act. Vigilance committees patrolled city streets and rescued men and women from slave catchers; sympathetic juries acquitted them. More important were the "personal liberty laws" passed by Northern states. Most of these laws were designed to discourage slave catchers by making the whole process too expensive. Such laws came close to nullifying the Fugitive Slave Act, something that Southerners noted with indignation and more than a little irony, since states' rights had become known as a "Southern" ideology.

Finally, in 1852, an unlikely event brought together the abolitionist critique of slavery and Southerners with the emotional impact of runaway slaves: the publication of *Uncle Tom's Cabin*, by Harriet Beecher Stowe. Stowe was a successful writer of romance novels, and her brother, Lyman Beecher, was a well-known preacher and abolitionist. *Uncle Tom's Cabin* contained many of the same themes as Stowe's romances but was set against the backdrop of slavery. The book presents slavery as a life of cruelty and tragedy, and emphasizes how it destroyed the character of Southern whites and undermined all families, slave and free, by allowing white men—portrayed often in the book as violent, drunk, sadistic rapists—to act with impunity.

The book was wildly popular, becoming the best-selling novel of the antebellum era. Portions of it were reprinted in Northern newspapers, and the story was performed in theaters and on the streets across the North. The novel was even used in some public schools.

Uncle Tom's Cabin presented the vast majority of Northern whites with their first view of slavery other than the one handed out by Southerners. For most white readers, the novel almost certainly brought to their consideration, for the first time, the idea that slaves were not happy being slaves. By bringing together the abolitionists' critique of the South and the images and emotions that accompanied the fugitive slave issue, *Uncle Tom's Cabin* dramatically affected Northern attitudes in the 1850s.

Certainly most Northern whites, in the 1850s, were still racists (particularly by modern standards), and many of them thought about slavery only to the extent that it kept black people in the South and away from them. But the combined actions and impact of abolitionists and fugitive slaves caused more and more Northerners to question whether slavery was, as Southerners insisted, really such a blessing for all involved. Whatever their effect on Northern public opinion, abolitionists probably had a greater impact in the South. The attack on Southerners as unchristian and un-American provoked an aggressive response in the form of a revitalized proslavery crusade.

William Lloyd Garrison: *The Liberator* (January 1, 1831)

This manifesto from the first issue of Garrison's Liberator
*conveys a sense of his combative, uncompromising style and
language. It also includes the mixture of secular and religious
arguments and imagery that characterized most abolitionist
rhetoric.*

Assenting to the "self-evident truth" maintained in the American Declaration of Independence, "that all men are created equal, and endowed by their Creator with certain inalienable rights—among which are life, liberty and the pursuit of happiness," I shall strenuously contend for the immediate enfranchisement of our slave population. In Park-street Church, on the Fourth of July, 1829, in an address on slavery, I unreflectingly assented to the popular but pernicious doctrine of gradual abolition. I seize this opportunity to make a full and unequivocal recantation, and thus publicly to ask pardon of my God, of my country, and of my brethren the poor slaves, for having uttered a sentiment so full of timidity, injustice and absurdity . . . My conscience is now satisfied.

I am aware, that many object to the severity of my language; but is there not cause for severity? I *will* be as harsh as truth, and as uncompromising as justice. On this subject, I do not wish to think, or speak, or write, with moderation. No! no! Tell a man whose house is on fire, to give a moderate alarm; tell him to moderately rescue his wife from the hand of the ravisher; tell the mother to gradually extricate her babe from the fire into which it has fallen;—but urge me not to use moderation in a cause like the present. I am in earnest—I will not equivocate—I will not excuse—I will not retreat a single inch—AND I WILL BE HEARD. The apathy of the people is enough to make every statue leap from its pedestal, and to hasten the resurrection of the dead.

Angelina Grimké Weld: Speech
at Pennsylvania Hall (1838)

*Born in South Carolina, Angelina Grimké (and her sister
Sarah) moved north and became a leading abolitionist. In this
speech she refers to her personal experience with slavery and calls
on women, in particular, to become more active in the fight
against slavery.*

Men, brethren and fathers—mothers, daughters and sisters, what
came ye out for to see? A reed shaken with the wind? Is it curiosity merely,
or a deep sympathy with the perishing slave, that has brought this large
audience together? Do you ask, "what has the North to do with slavery?"
Hear it—hear it. Those voices without [shouts from an anti-abolitionist
mob outside the building] tell us that the spirit of slavery is *here*, and has
been roused to wrath by our abolition speeches and conventions: for surely
liberty would not foam and tear herself with rage, because her friends are
multiplied daily, and meetings are held in quick succession to set forth her
virtues and extend her peaceful kingdom. This opposition shows that slavery
has done its deadliest work in the hearts of our citizens. Do you ask, then,
"what has the North to do?" I answer, cast out first the spirit of slavery
from your own hearts, and then lend your aid to convert the South. Each
one present has a work to do, be his or her situation what it may, however
limited their means, or insignificant their supposed influence. The great
men of this country will not do this work; the church will never do it. A
desire to please the world, to keep the favor of all parties and of all conditions, makes them dumb on this and every other unpopular subject. They
have become worldly-wise, and therefore God, in his wisdom, employs
them not to carry on his plans of reformation and salvation. He hath chosen the foolish things of the world to confound the wise, and the weak to
overcome the mighty.

As a Southerner I feel that it is my duty to stand up here to-night and
bear testimony against slavery. I have seen it—I have seen it. I know it has
horrors that can never be described. I was brought up under its wing: I wit-

nessed for many years its demoralizing influences, and its destructiveness to human happiness. It is admitted by some that the slave is not happy under the *worst* forms of slavery. But I have *never* seen a happy slave . . .

To work as we should in this cause, we must know what Slavery is. Let me urge you then to buy the books which have been written on this subject and read them, and then lend them to your neighbors. . . .

Women of Philadelphia! allow me as a Southern woman, with much attachment to the land of my birth, to entreat you to come up to this work. Especially let me urge you to petition. *Men* may settle this and other questions at the ballot-box, but you have no such right; it is only through petitions that you can reach the Legislature. It is therefore peculiarly *your* duty to petition. . . .

Men who hold the rod over slaves, rule in the councils of the nation: and they deny our right to petition and to remonstrate against abuses of our sex and of our kind. We have these rights, however, from our God. Only let us exercise them: and though often turned away unanswered, let us remember the influence of importunity upon the unjust judge, and act accordingly. The fact that the South look with jealousy upon our measures shows that they are effectual. There is, therefore, no cause for doubting or despair, but rather for rejoicing.

It was remarked in England that women did much to abolish Slavery in her colonies. . . . Let the zeal and love, the faith and works of our English sisters quicken ours—that while the slaves continue to suffer, and when they shout deliverance, we may feel the satisfaction of *having done what we could.*

From *History of Pennsylvania Hall which was Destroyed by a Mob on the 17th of May, 1838* (New York: Negro Universities Press, 1969).

Fugitive Slave Poster (1851)

*This poster from Boston suggests the widespread public
opposition to the Fugitive Slave Law of 1850. In most
Northern cities, African Americans and some white allies
organized committees to help protect fugitive slaves and
frustrate the work of slave catchers.*

Library of Congress.

"Young Texas in Repose" (1852)

Abolitionists and many other Northerners opposed the American acquisition of proslavery Texas. This lithograph portrays the free residents of Texas as nearly subhuman, corrupted by their power over slaves.

The Beinecke Rare Book and Manuscript Library, Yale University Library.

The Proslavery Arguments
and Sectional Conflict

FOR MOST OF WORLD HISTORY, slavery was an accepted fact of life that few people questioned. As a result, until the nineteenth century, there was no need of an elaborate "defense" of slavery. In response to Northern criticism and world events, however, Southerners became more defensive, and then more aggressive, as they argued for their institution of slavery. By the 1850s, they had developed a more complex, if sometimes contradictory, set of arguments in defense of slavery. These were as much about vindicating the Southern way of life, and Southern whites, as they were about defending slavery itself. In their strained attempts to beat back abolitionist criticism, however, proslavery leaders risked alienating Northern moderates. As Southern arguments on behalf of slavery got shriller and more convoluted, many men and women in both sections wondered if the first casualty might be calm, logical, even rational debate.

In the United States before the 1830s, most Southerners explained slavery as a "necessary evil." It was inherited from their ancestors and they had an obligation to maintain it as the best solution to what American whites considered the "race problem." The "race problem" referred to whites' widespread belief that whites and blacks could never live together peacefully. Absent slavery's restraints, whites believed that racial warfare or "amalgamation" (racial mixing) would be the inevitable result (their chief example was the bloody Haitian revolution of the 1790s). Thus, the argument ran, slavery was necessary to maintain peace and prevent racial destruction. This position also helps explain the enduring popularity of colonization—the notion that slavery could be ended gradually and ex-slaves "colonized" somewhere outside the United States. In theory, this "moderate" solution would create an "all-white" society. The American Colonization Society, founded in 1817, purchased land on the west coast of Africa and established the nation of Liberia as a destination for American slaves. Colonization was a natural complement to the "necessary evil" argument, since both were designed to solve the "race problem": one by ending slavery but getting rid of non-white people; the other by continuing slavery.

Particularly in the 1830s, the tone of these arguments for slavery changed dramatically. In 1831, two dramatic events prompted many Southern whites to change their approach to the public discussion of slavery. First, William Lloyd Garrison began publishing *The Liberator*, which truly inaugurated the modern abolition movement. Second, in August, the deadliest slave rebellion in the country's history occurred in Southampton County, Virginia. Nat Turner, a well-known slave preacher, and a small core of his followers killed about sixty whites in a thirty-six-hour spree. Turner's rebels moved from farm to farm, killing everyone they could find, including infants. Local slave patrols and militia, strengthened by vigilantes from as far away as Maryland, captured or killed the rebels—and about two hundred slaves and free people of color in retaliation. Most of these victims, of course, had had nothing to do with the rebellion.

Many, probably most, Southerners were convinced that the two events of 1831 were connected. Turner, they insisted, had to have been inspired by "meddling Yankee abolitionists." For whites to admit the truth—that Turner was miserable, slaves were miserable—would have undermined their justification of slavery as a benign, uplifting institution and their claim that slaves were happy and contented. One result of the events of 1831, then, was a pathological fear and hatred of abolitionists, which eventually became directed toward all "Yankees."

The paranoia created by the feeling that abolitionism would lead to rebellion combined with the reality that Southerners were among the dwindling number of slaveowners in the Western Hemisphere. Like the Northern states, nearly all of the Latin American republics ended slavery as they achieved independence in the 1820s, Great Britain abolished slavery throughout its empire in the early 1830s, and France followed suit in

1848. By the 1850s, the U.S. South had more slaves than every other slave society in the Western Hemisphere combined (essentially Brazil, Cuba, and Puerto Rico). Thus, it was easy for Southerners to feel as if they were under siege.

In response, from the 1830s to the advent of the Civil War, Southerners advanced a more aggressive proslavery position. In general terms, they moved from the "necessary evil" argument to a set of "positive good" arguments. Rather than be restricted, slavery was so beneficial an institution that it should be spread around the world. Perhaps the most important line of attack was religious. The accusation that slaveholding was a sin cut deeply for men and women who were overwhelmingly evangelical Christians. By the 1840s, Southern ministers often took the lead in defending slavery as ordained by God. Some argued that it was part of God's plan to spread Christianity around the world; others maintained that since the Hebrews owned slaves, and they were God's chosen people, then slavery must be sanctioned by God; another defense traced African slavery to the curse of Canaan, the son of Ham. Even more pragmatic were those who noted simply the absence of any condemnation of slavery in the Bible. After all, they concluded, it was a big book, and Christ found time to condemn the moneylenders and all sorts of sin—why not slavery? As Virginia's Reverend Thornton Stringfellow concluded, "Jesus Christ has not abolished slavery by a prohibitory command" and "has introduced no new moral principle which can work its destruction."

Southerners also challenged Northern claims that slavery harmed the national economy. Most Southern economic arguments rested on the profitability of cotton, and its importance for the national balance of trade. Cotton provided nearly two-thirds of the total value of American exports in 1860, and Southerners had weathered the Panic of 1857 (a severe recession) much better than Northern businessmen had. These facts convinced many Southerners that slavery provided a more stable, profitable base than wage labor. While their reasoning was a bit murky, Southerners believed the conclusion was obvious. From a modern perspective, of course, it was the incredible worldwide demand for cotton that drove Southern profits, not slavery per se.

Southern arguments for the racial inferiority of blacks and the need to control them also remained prominent. As the slave population grew naturally—to about four and a half million by 1860—Southern whites became even more convinced that only slavery could restrain blacks' desire to commit wholesale murder and thus stop the inevitable racial warfare. Turner's Rebellion was all the "proof" that most whites needed. The most important advantage Southerners had in making their arguments was that the vast majority of whites, in the North and South, continued to assume that all African Americans were inferior and lacked the basic self-control that distinguished "civilized" people.

In the 1850s, the proslavery arguments shifted to emphasize even more the superiority of Southern slave-based society over Northern free labor. Politicians and other public spokesmen contrasted African slavery with the "wage slavery" they saw in Northern factories and cities. Immigrants constituted the North's slaves, Southerners insisted, and factory owners left their workers to starve when they became too old or too weak to work. Though paid wages, they effectively worked as slaves with just as few options and no support system. William Grayson's 1855 poem, "The Hireling and the Slave," described factory workers "in squalid hut—a kennel for the poor, / Or noisome cellar, stretched upon the floor, / His clothing in rags, of filthy straw his bed, / With offal from the gutter daily fed." By contrast, slaves were "Guarded from want, from beggary secure, / He never feels what hireling crowds endure." Proslavery writers also claimed that only with slaves to perform much of the work could a society achieve an advanced level of "civilization." "He who has obtained the command of another's labour, first begins to accumulate and provide for the future," wrote South Carolina's William Harper in 1838, "and the foundations of civilization are laid." Even more strident was planter-politician James Henry Hammond: "In all social systems there must be a class to do the menial duties, to perform the drudgery of life." Without it, he argued, "you would not have that other class which leads progress, civilization, and refinement."

By the last antebellum decade, many Southerners also believed that slavery provided the true foundation for white male democracy. Northern politics, they argued, made a mockery of the unique brilliant purity of American government. The Founding Fathers, Southerners insisted, never intended illiterate foreigners straight off the boat from Ireland to vote, much less to hold office. In the South, by contrast, all white men were truly equal because no matter how poor or uneducated, they still were not slaves.

As the sectional competition grew more intense, Southern spokesmen became more strident and outlandish in their defense of slavery and of their proslavery version of Manifest Destiny. The most extreme proslavery theorists took their arguments to the logical conclusion: the natural condition of mankind was inequality, not equality, and slavery was founded on an elaborate social, racial, and even intellectual hierarchy. Radical George Fitzhugh concluded that the premise that "all men are created equal" amounted to a "self-evident lie." Fitzhugh eventually argued that slavery was so beneficial to all, particularly society's "weaker" sort of people, that it should be extended to poor whites. His brand of "logic" incensed moderates North and South, but while most Southerners distanced themselves from Fitzhugh's extremism, Northerners often failed to distinguish such eccentric proslavery arguments from the mainstream. And increasingly they questioned the place of slavery within the American ideology of freedom, equality of opportunity, and popular Christianity. "'Give to him that is needy' is the Christian rule of charity," wrote Abraham Lincoln in his debate notebook, "but 'Take from him that is needy' is the rule of slavery." Northerners also cringed when Southerners such as Mississippi senator Albert Gallatin Brown declared, "Slavery is a good thing, per se; I believe it to be a great moral, social, and political blessing—a blessing to the master and a blessing to the slave . . . [and] it is of Divine origin. . . . What God has ordained, cannot be wrong." Leaving slavery where it existed was one thing; making it a national institution was another.

Southern whites finally concluded that slavery *must* expand not only to fulfill God's mission, but also in order for it to survive. This important new emphasis in proslavery thinking further intensified the battle for control over America's western territory as more Southern whites concluded that Free Soil—the complete nonextension of slavery—was unacceptable. Their reasons for why slavery needed to expand can be grouped into four broad categories: racial control, political power, economic viability, and honor.

First, as the slave population continued to increase, it would need to be spread out over more territory. More and more slaves in the same geographic confines—like the proverbial boiling kettle with the lid on tight—would lead to an explosion, a Haitian-style rebellion and racial warfare.

Second, for Southerners to maintain a reasonable share of national political power they needed more slave states, which would translate into votes in the Senate and the Electoral College. Because the Northern free population was expanding so fast due to immigration, Southerners could hope to preserve their national influence only with more slave states. The most threatening possible consequence of the South's dwindling political power was a constitutional amendment abolishing slavery, something that would become possible as further branches of government slipped beyond their control.

A third factor that made expansion so crucial was the economic reality that slaves represented a huge portion of Southern wealth, and nothing could be allowed to threaten their current and future value. The 1850s was a decade of fantastic increase in slave prices, driven by the continued profitability of Southern cotton. But that might not last forever: cotton exhausted the soil, and Southerners had nearly reached the limits of productive new land in 1860; worldwide demand might fall, or the British could find other sources of raw cotton. If either of those things happened, Southerners would need to find something else for slaves to do, since they were valuable only when they produced something valuable. Northerners often claimed that "nature" decreed that slavery would not expand beyond its 1850s borders, because by then the limits of cotton production had been reached. Southerners responded that slaves might be used for other work—to grow something else or dig gold out of the ground, for instance. In the 1850s, planters in Maryland and Virginia, in particular, were already struggling to find profitable ways to use their slaves; many rented them out, but some of the most successful "raised" slaves and sold them south and west. How long would it be, residents in the deep South states wondered, before slavery was so unimportant in the upper South that whites there thought they could live without it?

Finally, Southern whites simply found the notion of Free Soil insulting to their personal and collective honor. Prohibiting the expansion of slavery implied that the South's citizens and its culture were inferior to Northerners' way of life. Free Soil, as much as abolition, declared to the world that Southern culture was unworthy of expansion and America's destiny. "To deny us the right and privilege [of slavery in the territories] would be to deny our equality in the Union," declared one group of Mississippians, "and would be a wrong and degradation to which a high spirited people should not submit." Slavery, in other words, had to expand in order for Southerners to feel they were being treated equally as Americans and Christians: it was a stark acknowledgment that slavery was the basis of Southern life and inextricably tied to Southerners' sense of identity as Americans.

Thus, by the late 1850s, Southern whites had constructed a proslavery ideology that held that slavery was sanctioned by God and was an integral part of America's Manifest Destiny—that it should expand wherever possible. More than that, however, most Southern whites believed that slavery had to expand in order to ensure its long-term survival and profitability. Simply protecting what they had, in other words, was not enough. By the time of Lincoln's election, in 1860, a significant majority of Southerners failed to see much difference between abolition and Free Soil; both threatened slavery, their way of life, and their equality within the Union. The proslavery spokesmen therefore heightened sectional conflict in much the same way that the abolitionists did, by making the rhetoric even more malicious and by raising the stakes for control of America's future. Northern moderates such as Abraham Lincoln concluded that slavery forced ordinarily rational men and women to take indefensible, un-American positions.

Reverend Thornton Stringfellow Defends Slavery (1841)

*Thornton Stringfellow was a leading Southern minister who
defended slavery as a divine institution in harmony with the
Bible and Christianity. Like many Southerners, Stringfellow
was outraged by the abolitionist critique of slavery as
unchristian and sinful.*

Circumstances exist among the inhabitants of these United States,
which make it proper that the Scriptures should be carefully examined by
Christians in reference to the institution of Slavery . . .

It is branded by one portion of people, who take their rules of moral
rectitude from the Scriptures, as a great sin; nay, the greatest of sins that
exist in the nation. And they hold the obligation to exterminate it, to be
paramount to all others. . . .

It is to be hoped, that on a question of such vital importance as this to
the peace and safety of our common country, as well as to the welfare of the
church, we shall be seen cleaving to the Bible and taking all our decisions
about this matter from its inspired pages. With men from the North, I
have observed for many years a palpable ignorance of the divine will, in
reference to the institution of slavery. I have seen but a few, who made the
Bible their study, that had obtained a knowledge of what it did reveal on
this subject. Of late, their denunciation of slavery as a sin, is loud and long.

I propose, therefore, to examine the sacred volume briefly, and if I am
not greatly mistaken, I shall be able to make it appear that the institution
of slavery has received, in the first place,

1st. The sanction of the Almighty in the Patriarchal age.

2d. That it was incorporated into the only National Constitution
which ever emanated from God.

3d. That its legality was recognized, and its relative duties regulated, by
Jesus Christ in his kingdom; and

4th. That it is full of mercy.

Thornton Stringfellow, *A Brief Examination of Scripture Testimony on the Institution of Slavery* (Washington, DC: Congressional Globe Office, 1850).

Jefferson Davis Defends Slavery (1851)

Like other Southern politicians, Jefferson Davis often argued that African slavery provided the best foundation for white equality and political democracy because slavery made all white men truly equal. Proslavery arguments such as this one appealed to poor white non-slaveowners who were critical in maintaining social and cultural support for slavery and in preventing rebellion.

Col. Davis said that he had heard it said that the poor men, who own no negroes themselves, would all be against the institution, and would, consequently, array themselves on the side of the so called Union men—that the submissionists claimed them. But that he could not believe, that the poor men of the country, were so blind to their own interests, as to be thus cheated out of their privileges, which they now enjoy. That *now they stand upon the broad level of equality with the rich man.* Equal to him in every thing, save that they did not own so much property; and that, even in this particular, the road to wealth was open to them, and the poor man might attain it; and, even if he did not succeed, the failure did not degrade him. That no white man, in a slaveholding community, was the menial servant of any one. That whenever the poor white man labored for the rich, he did so upon terms of distinction between him and the negro. It was to the interest of the master to keep up a distinction between the white man in his employment, and his negroes. And that this very distinction elevated, and kept the white laborer on a level with the employer; because the distinction between the classes throughout the slaveholding states, is a distinction of color. Between the classes there is no such thing, here, as a distinction of property; and he who thinks there is, and prides himself upon it, is grossly mistaken. Free the negroes, however, and it would soon be here, as it is in the countries of Europe, and in the North, and everywhere else, where negro slavery does not exist. The poor white man would become a menial for the rich, and be, by him, reduced to an equality with the free blacks, into a degraded position . . .

In Dunbar Rowland, ed., *Jefferson Davis: Constitutionalist*, Vol. II (Jackson, MS: Mississippi Department of Archives and History, 1929), 70–75.

James Henry Hammond Defends Slavery (March 4, 1858)

James Henry Hammond, a planter and senator from South Carolina, argued (in this speech before the U.S. Senate) that slavery created a superior civilization, when compared to the North's free labor system. This argument for slavery, and its expansion, became increasingly prominent in the 1850s as Northern and Southern whites vied for national power and leadership of the country's future.

In all social systems there must be a class to do the menial duties, to perform the drudgery of life. That is, a class requiring but a low order of intellect and but little skill. Its requisites are vigor, docility, fidelity. Such a class you must have, or you would not have that other class which leads progress, civilization, and refinement. It constitutes the very mud-sill of society and of political government; and you might as well attempt to build a house in the air, as to build either the one or the other, except on this mud-sill. Fortunately for the South, she found a race adapted to that purpose to her hand. A race inferior to her own, but eminently qualified in temper, in vigor, in docility, in capacity to stand the climate, to answer all her purposes. We use them for our purpose, and call them slaves. . . .

The Senator from New York said yesterday that the whole world had abolished slavery. . . .

Your whole hireling class of manual laborers and "operatives," as you call them, are essentially slaves. The difference between us is, that our slaves are hired for life and well compensated; there is no starvation, no begging, no want of employment among our people, and not too much employment either. Yours are hired by the day, not cared for, and scantily compensated, which may be proved in the most painful manner, at any hour in any street in any of your large towns. Why, you meet more beggars in one day, in any single street of the city of New York, than you would meet in a lifetime in the whole South. We do not think that whites should be slaves either by law or necessity. Our slaves are black, of another and inferior race. The status in which we have placed them is an elevation. They are elevated from the condition in which God first created them, by being made our slaves. None of that race on the whole face of the globe can be compared with the slaves of the South. They are happy, content, unaspiring, and utterly incapable, from intellectual weakness, ever to give us any trouble by their aspirations. Yours are white, of your own race; you are brothers of one blood. They are your equals in natural endowment of intellect, and they feel galled by their degradation. Our slaves do not vote. We give them no political power. Yours do vote, and, being the majority, they are the depositories of all your political power.

Congressional Globe, 35th Cong., 1st session, 1858, Appendix, 961–62.

FOUR

The 1850s: Free Soil and the Creation of a Republican Majority

THE CRITICAL DECADE OF THE 1850S has been intensely studied to determine how the political system failed to produce another compromise. Was it inevitable that the issues surrounding slavery's expansion would end with secession and Civil War? Had Northerners and Southerners reached such an impasse, such cultural incompatibility, that they could not continue in the same country? Or was it a case of blundering, shortsighted, or inept politicians? Whatever the answers to these questions, certainly the most important event of the 1850s—in a decade filled with momentous events—was the formation and rapid success of the sectional Republican Party. As the old parties fractured in the North at mid-decade, Republicans captured and broadened the appeal of free soil. Just five years after its formation, the Republican Party stood poised to elect a free soil president in 1860; Southerners vowed secession.

As the 1850s began, both Whigs and Democrats pledged to abide by the Compromise of 1850, even though many Americans in the North and South were dissatisfied with it. Most of all, party leaders hoped to delay another conflict over slavery extension for as long as possible. Democrats had settled on popular sovereignty—the belief that people in a territory should decide whether or not to allow slavery—as their solution to the all-consuming issue. This position was popular with Southerners, since it held out the possibility that slavery would expand. The Democrats' national leader was Senator Stephen Douglas, from Illinois, although the party's greatest concentration of power still lay in the Southern states. This was significant because the Democrats operated under a peculiar rule in their national convention: to receive the nomination for president, a candidate had to get two-thirds of the delegates instead of a simple majority—that is, he needed to be acceptable to Southerners. As much as anything, Stephen Douglas wanted to be president, so he and most Northern Democrats courted Southern votes. The Whigs had no firm position on slavery in the territories, although their president, Millard Fillmore, had signed the Compromise measures into law, including the organization of Utah and New Mexico territories under popular sovereignty. The party's strength was in the Northeast, particularly among native-born WASPs, the growing middle class, and Christians energized by the Second Great Awakening. Both parties avoided slavery extension in the 1852 presidential election, offering lackluster endorsements of the Compromise of 1850. Democrat Franklin Pierce of New Hampshire won a dull campaign with unusually low turnout at the polls.

Although slavery extension ultimately brought on the Civil War, the Second Party System of Whig and Democrat foundered initially over another potent issue of the 1850s: Nativism. Between 1830 and 1860, almost two million Irish and nearly one and a half million German-speaking immigrants came to the United States. By 1860, about 20 percent of residents in New England and the Middle Atlantic states were foreign-born. Many native-born WASPs—who began calling themselves "Native Americans"—felt overwhelmed by the sheer number of non-Protestant, non–English-speaking immigrants who wore different clothes, celebrated different holidays, and often chose to live in separate ethnic neighborhoods. A majority of the immigrants were Catholic and intensely loyal to the Church; in fact, Catholicism became America's single largest denomination before 1850. Immigrants formed their own clubs, fire companies, and gangs, such as the Irish "Dead Rabbits." Urging a systematic program of assimilation, Nativists tried to force immigrants to adopt "American culture," which, as they defined it, included temperance, frugality, no business on Sunday, and Protestantism. They despaired of reforming the adults, but vowed that the immigrants' "children must be gathered up and forced into school, and those who resist or impede this plan, whether parents or priests, must be held accountable and punished."

While they had hundreds of specific complaints, Nativists generally feared and hated immigrant culture, particularly Catholicism. They also resented immigrants' growing political power. By the mid-1840s, Irish Catholics—the vast majority of whom voted Democratic—nearly controlled politics in many Northeastern cities. Nativists' most important organization was the Order of the Star-Spangled Banner, an underground club that began in New York City in 1850. Its members first entered politics secretly, electing fellow members who were not publicly known to be members or even candidates. The group went public as the American Party in 1855, though they were more commonly known by their nickname, an echo of their secret society roots: the "Know Nothings." Nativism was such a powerful force among evangelical Protestants that the Know Nothings quickly attracted a national following and, by late 1855, replaced the Whigs in many parts of the country. Thus, by mid-decade the old Second Party System was in shambles. In the North, the Whigs disintegrated; in the Deep South, they drifted away from politics or eventually shifted to the Democratic side.

Although Nativism destroyed the Whigs, it proved insufficient to sustain a national party against the powerfully divisive issue of slavery extension. In the early 1850s, fugitive slaves and abolitionists strove to keep sectional issues before the public eye. The relative calm before the coming storm was broken for the last time in 1854. In January, Senator Douglas introduced a bill to "organize" the remaining land from the Louisiana Purchase into two new territories: Kansas and Nebraska, both to be governed by popular sovereignty. This meant repealing the Missouri Compromise line, which Southerners insisted be explicit in the new legislation. Northerners were outraged at the possibility of slavery in territory from which it had been barred for the previous thirty years (see map on p. 54). Even some Northern Democrats protested the measure, labeling it a "criminal betrayal of precious rights" and part of an "atrocious plot" to turn the West "into a dreary region of despotism, inhabited by masters and slaves." Despite widespread, but not universal, opposition in the North, Douglas managed to get the bill through both houses of Congress. During debate in the House, several members drew loaded weapons. Afterward, Douglas joked that he could read on the train back to Chicago "by the light of my own effigy" burning along the tracks. For most other Northern Democrats, however, the Kansas-Nebraska Act was no laughing matter: two-thirds of them were defeated for reelection.

Kansas-Nebraska also sparked new political organizations across the free states, all of them committed to stopping the expansion of slavery. The Free Soil Party already existed, of course, and was joined by the People's, Independent, Anti-Nebraska, and Republican parties, all founded primarily on the basis of free soil. In late 1854 and 1855, these parties competed with Know Nothings and Democrats for Northern votes. National events in 1855 and early 1856 advantaged these free soil parties because they focused attention on slavery and slavery's expansion. Most important in that regard was the unfolding debacle in Kansas Territory.

Southerners decided that Nebraska was too far north for them to contest its future as a free state, but Kansas was next to Missouri, a slave state, and cotton technically could be grown in a tiny portion of the extreme southeast corner of the state. Determined to make Kansas a slave territory and then a slave state, advocates of slavery's expansion raised money and encouraged Southerners to bring slaves to settle there. Antislavery supporters in the North responded in kind, with the New England Emigrant Aid Company running money and guns to the "free staters," as they became known. Armed settlers from both sections poured into Kansas. Violence ensued.

Popular sovereignty, seemingly simple in theory, was difficult in practice. The first obvious question was who lived in the territory? "Residency" was not a firmly established concept, and of course nothing like modern identification existed, so men from Missouri and elsewhere could rush in and vote without actually living in Kansas. *When* to put the question to a vote was an even bigger problem. An organized territory could remain so for many years, during which the settlers would have local government, an elected legislature, and a governor appointed by the president. In the first territorial election, held in March 1855, pro-Southern "border ruffians" packed the polls along the Kansas-Missouri line and rigged the outcome. This illegally elected legislature moved quickly and stridently to protect slavery—even questioning slavery in public was made a felony. In response, the free-state settlers, known as "Jayhawkers," formed their own legislature.

By spring 1856, there were two legislatures claiming to govern the territory, thousands of armed men on both sides, and little hope for a peaceful resolution. Serious violence began on May 21. A proslavery mob sacked the free-state town of Lawrence, burning the governor's house and blowing up the "Free State Hotel." Partly in response to this attack, the abolitionist John Brown and some followers (including four of his sons) killed five Southern settlers in the "Pottawatomie Massacre." This grisly episode— Brown's men used broadswords to hack the victims into pieces, and left their remains as a public "warning" to other Southerners—led to widespread guerilla violence. By the end of 1856, more than two hundred people had died in "Bleeding Kansas."

The most sensational incident of sectional violence occurred on the floor of the United States Senate. On May 20, Senator Charles Sumner, an abolitionist from Massachusetts, delivered a vitriolic speech against the proslavery settlers in Kansas that included insults directed at a senior senator from South Carolina, Andrew Pickens Butler. Two days later, Butler's nephew Preston Brooks, a South Carolina representative, strode onto the Senate floor armed with a heavy-headed cane of gutta-percha and proceeded to rain blows down on Sumner's head. A report in the *Richmond Enquirer* was typical of Southern reaction to the event: "These vulgar abolitionists in the Senate . . . are a low, mean, scurvy set. . . . If need be, let us have a caning or cowhiding every day." Northerners, spying in "Bully Brooks" the arrogance and violence that abolitionists said came from slavery, responded in kind. The *New York Evening Post* asked, "Are we to be chastised as they chastise their slaves? Are we, too, slaves, slaves for life, a target for their brutal blows, when we do not comport ourselves to please them?" The incident polarized the nation. Censured by the House, Brooks resigned in a huff and went home to South Carolina, where the voters reelected him without opposition (and he received hundreds of canes from admiring supporters). The Southern adulation heaped on Brooks, combined with extreme proslavery arguments, turned thousands of moderate Northerners into abolitionists.

The mounting violence hung over the 1856 presidential election, the first for the new Republican Party, which had brought together the various free soil parties under one name. They nominated John C. Frémont, a romantic adventurer who fought briefly in California during the Mexican War and liked to ride around in a buckskin leather jacket. He was young and handsome, probably his most evident qualifications for office. Democrats wanted a candidate removed from the disaster in Kansas, which ruled out both Senator Douglas and President Pierce; they nominated James Buchanan, Minister to England. The Know Nothings, still influential early in 1856, chose Millard Fillmore, the former president who had signed the Compromise of 1850 into law. Fillmore remained popular with moderate Southerners, which proved reason enough for most Northern Know Nothings to bolt the party and join the Republicans. That the Republicans had included a Nativist plank in their platform rendered that move even easier. Buchanan won a fairly close election. Most surprising of all was the Republican power across the North. They won eleven states, sweeping New England and the upper North. Surveying the electoral map, Republicans realized that winning every Northern state would mean winning the presidency. Thus, for the next four years, they broadened the appeal of free soil to attract more moderate voters, particularly in the lower North: New Jersey, Pennsylvania, Ohio, Illinois, Indiana, and Iowa.

Free soil ultimately appealed to the Northern majority because Republicans shaped it so effectively, linking it to four mainstream values among white voters: racism, greed, the desire for political power, and Nativism. No slavery in the West, Republicans argued, meant, first, that whites would not have to live among black people. (When Oregon entered the Union in 1858, for instance, it prohibited slavery but also barred any black people from living there. An "all-white" society was the state's goal.) Second, "hard-working, white, family farmers" would not have to compete with wealthy slaveowners for good land. No slavery also appealed to white skilled workers, who feared competition from slaves, which would drive down wages. Third, stopping slavery's expansion would cut off the political power of Southern planters. "Anti-Southernism," as Republicans developed it, focused on the idea of a "Slave Power Conspiracy"—a conspiracy of wealthy planters—to control the national government in order to protect slavery. Republicans cited the string of Southern slaveowning presidents, the three-fifths compromise that gave Southerners additional representation in the House, Southerners' ability to block legislation due to their longtime insistence on parity in the Senate, and their ability to manipulate Northern Democrats eager to win Southern votes into supporting slavery. Examples of the Slave Power Conspiracy in action included the Mexican War, the Fugitive Slave Act, and the Kansas-Nebraska Act. "The question is," one Iowa editor wrote, "shall we have a free government, or a slave empire? . . . It is not a *black* question at all but emphatically a *white* question." Fourth, immigrants, particularly Catholics, voted consistently for the Democratic Party, which in turn sustained Slave Power. Thus, one could vote Republican and be anti-Southern, Nativist, and racist, all at the same time.

Finally, more and more Northerners also supported free soil in the genuine hope that it would lead to the end of slavery. Slavery was immoral, they thought, but it was a local institution that could not be abolished directly under the Constitution. Limiting its expansion, however, would ultimately destroy it. Abraham Lincoln, as always, went back to the Declaration of Independence. All men, black and white, were entitled to life, liberty, and the pursuit of happiness: "There is no reason in the world why the negro is not entitled to all the natural rights enumerated in the Declaration of Independence. . . . I hold that he is as much entitled to these as the white man." This sentiment grew within the Republican Party, particularly in New England, where the abolition movement was most powerful. By the late 1850s, in fact, abolitionists controlled the Republican Party in several states.

Between 1856 and 1860, the Republicans hammered at these themes, and increasingly featured anti-Southernism and the Slave Power Conspiracy. The Supreme Court decision in *Dred Scott v. Sandford*, in 1857, afforded Republicans another chance to exploit growing Northern resentment of Southern power. The Court ruled against Scott—a slave who was suing for his freedom after the death of his master—declaring that black men were "so far inferior, that they had no rights which the white man was bound to respect." Chief Justice Roger B. Taney's decision, and the language he used to express it, was the most extreme pro-Southern position the Court could take. Five of the nine justices were Southerners. Here was proof, Republicans proclaimed, that the last branch of the federal government was now taken over by the Slave Power. The next year, after a bewildering round of confused elections, a proslavery constitution was submitted by the Kansas legislature, even though over 90 percent of the settlers were opposed to slavery. Southerners supported this Lecompton Constitution, as did President Buchanan—further proof, Republicans charged, of the Slave Power, which apparently had Buchanan in its employ. Despite his desire to court Southern votes, Senator Douglas broke with the administration and opposed the evidently undemocratic, unrepresentative constitution. This split the party and crippled Douglas's standing among Southerners.

No one articulated the central themes of Republicanism better than Abraham Lincoln. In his famous debates with Stephen Douglas in 1858, Lincoln grabbed national attention and laid the groundwork for his presidential nomination in 1860. He also drew a sharp contrast with the Democrats and their leader with regards to American equality and the place of slavery and race in the United States. The Lincoln-Douglas debates were a part of the Senate contest in Illinois, with seven held across the state. Lincoln's speeches collectively made up a nearly perfect summary of the Republican Free Soil ideology (the exception was Nativism, which Lincoln always hated). There was racism: Lincoln argued that whites could prevent "the mixture of races" in the West only by prohibiting slavery, and he vowed repeatedly that he did not believe in racial equality. He also reminded voters of the Slave Power Conspiracy, which he saw at work most evidently in the Kansas-Nebraska Act.

Finally, Lincoln underscored the key differences between Republicans and Democrats. The former believed in equality of opportunity, that slavery should be limited and put on the path to extinction, and that black men and women deserved "all the natural rights enumerated in the Declaration of Independence." Black Americans would never be considered wholly equal, Lincoln admitted, "but in the right to eat the bread, . . . which his own hand earns, he is my equal and the equal of Judge Douglas, and the equal of every living man." In a preview of Civil War partisan tactics, Douglas attacked Lincoln and the Republicans as abolitionists and advocates of equal rights and racial "amalgamation." Douglas won reelection to the Senate, but Lincoln set the stage for the Republican presidential victory in 1860. In a masterstroke of oratory, he had appealed to the voters' racism and asserted his own belief in white superiority, but simultaneously distinguished his positions on slavery and equality from those of Douglas. Republicans claimed the moral high ground while still appealing to racism, and simultaneously painted Democrats as defenders of inequality and privilege.

During the 1850s, the crucial development was the birth of the Republican Party and its rapid ascendancy across the North. This coalition included ex-Whigs, ex–Know Nothings, and ex-Democrats, many of whom came to the new party for very different reasons. But it was held together by a steadfast support for Free Soil, albeit for sometimes wildly different reasons. By the late 1850s, the Republican Party included abolitionists such as Charles Sumner of Massachusetts, ex-Whigs such as Lincoln, and slaveowners such as Francis Blair of Missouri. Republican leaders had broadened the appeal of free soil to make it a comprehensive ideology that the majority of Northerners could support. Now all they had to do was win the presidency and see how Southerners reacted.

New York Evening Post
(May 23, 1856)

Northerners were outraged by the attack on Senator Charles Sumner (Rep., MA), and used his assailant, Representative Preston Brooks (Dem., SC), as an example of how slavery affected Southern whites, making them arrogant and violent.

The excuse for this base assault is, that Mr. Sumner, on the Senate floor, in the course of debate had spoken disrespectfully of Mr. Butler, a relative of Preston S. Brooks, one of the authors of this outrage.

Has it come to this, that we must speak with bated breath in the presence of our Southern masters; that even their follies are too sacred a subject of ridicule; that we must not deny the consistency of their principles or the accuracy of their statements? If we venture to laugh at them, or question their logic, or dispute their facts, are we to be chastised as they chastise their slaves? Are we, too, slaves, slaves for life, a target for their brutal blows, when we do not comport ourselves to please them?

The truth is, that the pro-slavery party, which rules in the Senate looks upon violence as the proper instrument of its designs. . . . violence has now found its way into the Senate chamber. Violence lies in wait on all navigable rivers and all the railways of Missouri, to obstruct those who pass from the free states to Kansas.

Richmond Enquirer
(June 2, 1856)

Most Southern newspapers supported Representative Brooks when he attacked Senator Sumner, expressing indignation and outrage at Northern criticism of slavery. Editorials

*such as this one provided tremendous propaganda for
Republicans, who maintained that Southern planter-
politicians were controlling the national government
in a "Slave Power Conspiracy."*

In the main, the press of the South applaud the conduct of Mr.
Brooks, without condition or limitation. Our approbation at least is entire
and unreserved.

These vulgar abolitionists in the Senate are getting above themselves.
They have been humored until they forget their position. They have grown
saucy, and dare to be impudent to gentlemen! Now, they are a low, mean,
scurvy set, with some little book learning, but as utterly devoid of spirit or
honor as a peck of curs. Intrenched behind "privilege," they fancy they can
slander the South and insult its Representatives, with impunity. The truth
is they have been suffered to run too long without collars. They must be
lashed into submission.

It is equally useless to attempt to disgrace them. They are insensible to
shame; and can be brought to reason only by an application of cowhide or
gutta percha. Let them once understand that for every vile word spoken
against the South, they will suffer so many stripes, and they will soon learn
to behave themselves, like decent dogs—they can never be gentlemen.

We trust other gentlemen will follow the example of Mr. Brooks, that
so a curb may be imposed upon the truculence and audacity of abolition
speakers.—If need be, let us have a caning or cowhiding every day. If the
worse come to the worse, so much the sooner so much the better.

Abraham Lincoln on Equality (ca. 1857–1858)

*Abraham Lincoln used simple language and logic to appeal
to voters, as evidenced in this passage. No one articulated
Americans' belief in equality of opportunity better than
Lincoln, for whom it held special meaning.*

The ant, who has toiled and dragged a crumb to his nest, will furiously defend the fruit of his labor, against whatever robber assails him. So plain, that the most dumb and stupid slave that ever toiled for a master, does constantly *know* that he is wronged. So plain that no one, high or low, ever does mistake it, except in a plainly *selfish* way; for although volume upon volume is written to prove slavery a very good thing, we never hear of the man who wishes to take the good of it, by being a slave himself.

Most governments have been based, practically, on the denial of equal rights of men, as I have, in part, stated them; *ours* began, by *affirming* those rights. *They* said, some men are too *ignorant*, and *vicious*, to share in government. Possibly so, said we; and, by your system, you would always keep them ignorant and vicious. We propose to give *all* a chance; and we expect the weak to grow stronger, the ignorant, wiser; and all better, and happier together.

We made the experiment; and the fruit is before us. Look at it. Think of it. Look at it, in all its aggregate grandeur, of extent of country, and numbers of population . . .

The Gilder Lehrman Collection, 3251, the Pierpont Morgan Library, New York, NY.

Abraham Lincoln on Race, Speech in Springfield, IL (July 17, 1858)

*Lincoln addressed racial equality in this portion of a speech
to the people of his adopted hometown. Characteristically,
he waffled on the general question of race; although he asserted
that he did not believe in complete equality, he defended the
right of African Americans to be rewarded for their hard work.*

My declarations upon this subject of Negro slavery may be misrepresented, but cannot be misunderstood. I have said that I do not understand the Declaration to mean that all men were created equal in all respects. They are not our equal in color; but I suppose that it does mean that all men are equal in some respects; they are equal in their right to "life, liberty, and the pursuit of happiness." Certainly the Negro is not our equal in color—perhaps not in many other respects; still, in the right to put into his mouth the bread that his own hands have earned, he is the equal of every other man, white or black. In pointing out that more has been given you, you cannot be justified in taking away the little which has been given him. All I ask for the Negro is that if you do not like him, let him alone. If God gave him but little, that little let him enjoy.

The Gilder Lehrman Collection, 2955, the Pierpont Morgan Library, New York, NY.

Robert Goodenow: "Astounding Disclosures!" (August 18, 1858)

This broadside expressed the deepening conviction that
Southern planters were controlling the national government
through their power in the Democratic Party. After 1856,
anti-Southernism became a central tenet of the Republican
Party's widening appeal among Northern voters.

What will the Pirate Democracy do next?

The Democratic Party has become so startlingly wicked, and its crimes and outrages so frequent and enormous, that active efforts are now being made . . . to turn the attention from the *corrupt* and *putrid* carcass, to the imaginary faults of the Republican Party. . . .

A party which has more capital invested in human flesh than in any other twenty articles of Commerce in our whole country;—a party which makes *men for the market* and *women for the harem*, as we raise sheep for the shambles. A party which would render the piracies of . . . [Captain] Kidd respectable by re-opening the Slave Trade, with all the soul-sickening horrors of the "middle passage!" A party which would *rob* weak and powerless Spain of the Island of Cuba, for the purpose of bringing a million of Slaves into the confederacy, and giving it the control of the vast National Councils! A party which would open our vast territories to this vile and withering curse. . . . A party that tried to make Kansas the burial place of liberty, that Slavery might flourish upon its gravel. A party which cheered on the assassin, who, with wood from dishonored soil, struck down, in the Senate House, Charles Sumner, "Liberty's chosen Senator," WHICH FOUL AND MURDEROUS ACT WAS DEFENDED UPON THE HILL-TOPS. . . . A party which openly defends ballot-box stuffing. . . . A party which stigmatizes the yeomanry and laboring men of the North as "mudsills and greasy mechanics!" . . .

The Gilder Lehrman Collection, 2955, the Pierpont Morgan Library, New York, NY.

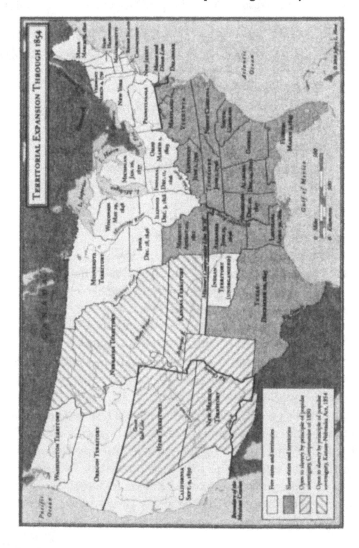

FIVE

The Election of 1860, Secession, and the Confederate States of America

THE 1860 ELECTION WAS the most anticipated contest that Americans could remember, and many voters believed that the fate of the Union hung in the balance. If Republicans won, a significant portion of Southern whites had vowed to secede. Would they actually do it? No one was sure, of course, but prevailing Northern opinion held that Southerners were bluffing. At least since the Nullification Crisis in 1832, Northerners had become accustomed to Southern threats of disunion; most believed that the great mass of Southern whites would never support such a drastic step to protect slavery, in which most of them had no direct investment. No one, however, doubted the stakes; bluff or not, secession suggested civil war.

The presidential election of 1860 really began almost immediately after Buchanan's narrow victory in 1856. Republicans targeted mainstream Northern voters, particularly those in the lower Northern states that were most evenly divided between them and the Democrats. Republicans exploited the sectional incidents of the late 1850s to broaden the appeal of their free soil ideology, accentuating anti-Southernism, racism, and the economic benefits of wage labor. Meanwhile, in the party's New England stronghold, abolitionists gained strength, nearly controlling several state political organizations by 1860. Recognizing that they had a good chance to win the presidential election, party leaders realized that much would depend on choosing a popular, middle-of-the-road candidate who could unite the party's various factions: New Englanders and Midwesterners; abolitionists and racists, ex-Whigs, ex-Democrats, and ex–Know Nothings.

Well before they had the opportunity to nominate a candidate, however, a single event brought forth from Southerners a flood of pent-up emotion and hostility. In October 1859, abolitionists led by John Brown (already famed for killing Southerners in Kansas; see chapter 4), and financed by wealthy Boston sympathizers, sneaked into the South and seized the federal arsenal at Harpers Ferry, Virginia. They intended to distribute weapons to the local slaves and spark a rebellion that would, somehow, force whites to end slavery. After taking the arsenal, Brown's somewhat murky plans fell apart when no Virginia slaves rallied to the cause, and his men were either killed or captured by U.S. Marines led by Robert E. Lee. Virginia quickly tried and convicted Brown for treason, murder, and inciting slave rebellion; he was hanged on December 2.

Throughout his captivity and trial, Brown maintained a dignified presence, never denying his intention to end slavery but vowing he did not seek wanton violence. A tall, imposing figure, Brown won grudging sympathy, even from some Southerners, with his behavior in court. Many Northerners who were appalled by his violent plans admired his steadfastness and moral convictions, his willingness to "forfeit my life for the furtherance of the ends of justice." In the end, he became a martyr for the cause of freedom and his body a metaphor for Southern arrogance and violence. Following the Harpers Ferry incident, the room within which politicians could maneuver narrowed.

The vast majority of Southerners, of course, were incensed at the Northern reaction and Brown's posthumous elevation in status. Here was, after all, the ultimate Southern nightmare: a Yankee agent slipping into the South to incite "rebellion, rapine, and murder," as hundreds of editorials phrased it. Southerners identified Brown with abolitionists, and in turn with the Republican Party. That the new party simply was hostile to slavery was enough "proof" for many Southerners that Republican leaders tacitly blessed Brown's actions. More directly, when Brown invoked a "higher law" to justify his invasion, it recalled the infamous speech of Senator William H. Seward, perhaps the country's leading Republican, who once avowed that a "higher law" than the Constitution labeled slavery as wrong. For most Southerners the evidence and conclusions were obvious: abolitionists controlled the Republican Party; the Republicans now constituted a majority in the free states; Brown was emboldened to act because of the Republican majority and its raving anti-Southern orators. Even in

Congress, violence seemed imminent. "The only members who do not carry a gun and a knife," claimed one representative, "are those who have two guns."

Brown's raid, then, only heightened the drama that was about to unfold in 1860. In April the Democrats held their convention in Charleston, South Carolina. They could not have chosen a worse location. The city's most influential politician was Robert Barnwell Rhett, editor of the *Charleston Mercury*, and perhaps the leading voice for secession in the entire South. Every day the convention met, Rhett helped fill the galleries with supporters who shouted anti-Northern insults at the free-state delegates. The leading candidate was Stephen Douglas, but many Southerners no longer trusted him after the debacle of popular sovereignty in Kansas and his lukewarm defense of slavery's expansion during the Lincoln-Douglas debates. Deep South leaders now demanded a federal "slave code" to protect their property in the western territories, an idea introduced in Congress earlier in 1860 by Senator Jefferson Davis of Mississippi. Davis essentially called on the federal government to guarantee protection for slavery in all territories. This was a significant step, one that nearly eliminated any compromise. Not incidentally, it also demonstrated that slavery—not some abstract devotion to "states' rights"—was the bottom line for Southerners: an activist, interventionist federal government or states' rights and secession—anything that protected slavery. Douglas and Northern Democrats refused to abandon popular sovereignty, and the convention split over the issues of slavery in the territories and a presidential nominee. The party tried another reconciliation, but with no success. Northern Democrats and a few Southerners nominated Douglas; most Southerners chose John C. Breckinridge of Kentucky (at the time he was Buchanan's vice president). The last national party had split in two.

The Democratic meltdown gave Republicans even more confidence. Meeting in Chicago in May, they had several leading candidates. Most prominent was William Seward of New York. He was a national figure and a gifted speaker, and was backed by an efficient political machine headed by a shrewd tactician, Thurlow Weed. But Seward was considered too "radical," an identification that eventually ruined his chances with moderates. Salmon Chase of Ohio also wanted the nomination, but was thought to be secretly an abolitionist. Intent on a united party, and with Brown's polarizing raid in mind, Republicans felt that even a hint of abolitionist leanings would be too much. Simon Cameron was the party leader in Pennsylvania, a state that Republicans had to win, but he was widely regarded as a crook. Lincoln was a new face, and so had few enemies. He seemed moderate on slavery but firmly committed to free soil, and came from Illinois, another state critical to Republican success. Furthermore, his own personal history would appeal to voters raised in the American tradition of Jacksonian democracy: born in a log cabin, self-educated, and now a successful corporate lawyer, he had a peerless reputation for honesty. On the third ballot, Lincoln received the nomination.

Meanwhile, fearing both the Republicans and Southern secessionists, a new organization formed just for this election: the Constitutional Union Party. It was led mainly by old Whigs and appealed to moderates in the upper South. Deliberately vague as to a platform, the party advocated "the Constitution of the Country, the Union of the States, and the enforcement of the laws." They chose John Bell, a moderate slaveowner from Tennessee, for president.

The campaign was really two contests: Lincoln versus Douglas in the North; Breckinridge versus Bell in the South. Lincoln was not even on the ballot in ten slave states. Douglas alone tried to run a national campaign. It was, in fact, his primary appeal to voters: he was the compromise candidate, his supporters argued, and only he could keep the nation from tearing apart. He also appealed to Democrats' party loyalty, emphasizing traditional themes: expansive nationalism, low tariffs, and a small government that did not make moral judgments about personal behavior. Breaking with all tradition, Douglas became the first presidential candidate to campaign in person, delivering hundreds of speeches around the country. The diminutive, whiskey-drinking "Little Giant" even took his fiery oratory into the deep South, where he denounced secession and risked assassination nearly every day. Republicans repeated the now-familiar free soil ideology: nonexpansion of slavery would "preserve the West for white, family farmers" and prevent "racial amalgamation"; undermine planters' political power and break the Slave Power Conspiracy; and fulfill the Founding Fathers' intention to limit slavery's growth. The party also advocated a higher, protective tariff and government policies to make western settlement easier, which appealed to Midwesterners in particular. In response, Southern Democrats pursued votes by railing against "Black Republicans" and their supposed plans for abolition, racial equality, and "amalgamation," and pledged secession if Lincoln was elected. They insisted that while disunion was a last, dreaded resort, it would be the only hope to protect slavery and white supremacy in a nation led by Republicans. John Bell's Constitutional Unionists vaguely promised to uphold the Constitution and, above all, opposed secession. They appealed to upper South voters who feared a possible war that would be fought primarily in their backyards.

The outcome was largely decided by early voting in Indiana, Ohio, and Pennsylvania, all of which held polls in October, a month before most states. When Lincoln carried all three of these crucial states it was clear to most Americans that he would win the election. In the end he won just under 40 percent of the popular vote, but nearly two-thirds of the electoral votes (see map on p. 68). Notably, Lincoln ran last in each of the five slave states in which he appeared on the ballot. In the wake of his victory, a wave of outrage engulfed much of the South.

Many secessionists had dreamed of the moment when they could lead their states out of the Union. Although it had never been tried, most Southerners believed secession was legal, yet the mechanism for achieving it was not clear. Some favored a "cooperative" approach in which several states would secede together. The majority, however, held that logic dictated separate state secession: if each state was truly sovereign, then it should act alone. Nearly everyone who favored secession assumed that the individual states would unite to form a new slave-based nation.

Following the Republican victory, legislatures in nearly all slave states called for elections to choose delegates for special conventions that would decide secession. In each of the seven deep South states a majority of pro-secession delegates was elected. Some Unionists tried to stall the momentum by pushing for a cooperative movement that would take more time, during which post-election passions might calm. Others urged convention delegates to submit secession to the voters for a straight "yes" or "no" referendum. These delaying tactics, however, were defeated in the conventions (only in Texas did delegates submit their Ordinance of Secession to the voters, who approved it overwhelmingly). By February 1, 1861, seven states had declared themselves sovereign nations; lame-duck President Buchanan did nothing to stop disunion.

Deep South secessionists explained their action by recounting a long list of Northern "aggressions." Central to all Southern complaints, of course, was the Republican Party and its free soil ideology. Thereafter, prominent justifications for secession were the Republicans' entirely sectional appeal and support (including votes from black men in several New England states); Northern state laws that effectively nullified the Fugitive Slave Act; Northerners' refusal to admit Kansas as a slave state in 1858; and Northerners' supposed support for John Brown and slave insurrection. Most of all, secessionists labeled Republicans and Lincoln as abolitionists. By electing a president with no Southern votes, Northerners "have denounced as sinful the institution of Slavery," read the South Carolina Declaration of Causes of Secession, and they "have united in the election of a man to the high office of President of the United States whose opinions and purposes are hostile to Slavery." Finally, most Southern voters declared Lincoln's election—and all it symbolized—as an insult to the South and their claim to equality within the Union. Over and over, Southerners used the same words to describe the Republican triumph: humiliating, insulting, degrading. Secession was "one firm resolve, one bold and manly move," declared one editor, that would rescue and defend their honor. The alternative was "to be whipped into submission—aye, whipped and cowed like *slaves*, by . . . a hireling army lead and directed by abolitionists."

With seven states gone, congressional leaders worked to effect a compromise before Lincoln took office. Most promising were the efforts of the Kentucky senator John Crittenden. He had good reason to avoid war, since his state would be bitterly divided in any conflict; indeed, he had sons who eventually served in both the Union and Confederate armies. The centerpieces of Crittenden's proposal were a revival, and extension to the Pacific Ocean, of the Missouri Compromise line, and a constitutional amendment that would guarantee slavery in those states where it already existed. Lincoln and most Republicans had no problem with the latter; in fact, the president-elect also vowed that he would enforce the Fugitive Slave Act and not interfere with the interstate slave trade or slavery in the District of Columbia. But on no account would Lincoln and nearly all Republicans compromise on free soil, the founding principle of their party and the basis of its popularity. "You think slavery is *right* and ought to be extended," Lincoln wrote to Alexander Stephens of Georgia, an old ally from the House of Representatives, "while we think it is *wrong* and ought to be restricted. That I suppose is the rub." Crittenden's proposal failed in the Senate, thanks to the Republican votes united against it.

In February 1861, representatives from the seceded states met in

Montgomery, Alabama, and created the Confederate States of America. The provisional Confederate Constitution, written in four days by a small group led by Alexander Stephens, was a virtual copy of the United States Constitution. It limited the president to one six-year term, gave him a line-item veto, specifically prohibited the international slave trade (largely in hopes of gaining diplomatic recognition from Great Britain), and provided for slavery in territories that the would-be nation might acquire. The choice of president was perhaps the crucial decision to be made. Robert Toombs of Georgia was the heavy favorite. Long considered a moderate, and a late convert to secession, Toombs had been both a Whig and a Democrat. A tall, imposing orator and renowned lawyer, he was popular with colleagues and voters. In Montgomery, however, he raised doubts when he drank considerably too much at several functions. In his place, the delegates chose Jefferson Davis of Mississippi. The last of ten children, Davis had been raised by his older brother Joseph, a millionaire planter in the Mississippi Delta. He had graduated from West Point, fought and been wounded in the Mexican War, served as secretary of war for President Franklin Pierce, and in 1861 was a United States senator. He was almost universally respected as a clear constitutional thinker, someone who put together logical arguments and delivered them well. For all that, few people liked him. Most described him as cold, aloof, haughty, selfish, and obsessively ambitious. Davis had never been a popular politician, and had been defeated in his most high-profile campaign, for governor of Mississippi in 1851. Perhaps most ominous was his intense dislike of political give-and-take; one colleague summarized that Davis always assumed he was the smartest man in the room, and once he made up his mind he expected everyone else simply to agree. These qualities helped lead to his wartime style of individual leadership, sometimes brilliant but other times ineffective. On February 9, 1861, he became provisional president of the Confederate States of America.

Finally, on March 4, Abraham Lincoln took the oath of office and delivered the most anticipated inaugural address in national history. He appealed to anxious Southerners, hoping to keep as many states from the upper South in the Union as possible. Like most Northerners, he believed that Southern Unionists were the true silent majority, and that if he appeared as moderate and conciliatory as possible they would overwhelm the radical secessionists. Quoting directly from Andrew Jackson's Nullification

Proclamation of 1832, Lincoln declared secession to be the "essence of anarchy" and vowed that the Union was inviolable. He said the government would "hold, occupy, and possess" federal property within the seceded states; exactly what that meant he left open to interpretation. Then he closed with some of the most memorable words ever spoken by any president:

> In *your* hands, my dissatisfied fellow countrymen, and not in *mine*, is the momentous issue of civil war. . . . We must not be enemies. Though passion may have strained, it must not break our bonds of affection. The mystic chords of memory, stretching from every battlefield, and patriot grave, to every living heart and hearthstone, all over this broad land, will yet swell the chorus of the Union, when again touched, as surely they will be, by the better angels of our nature.

Moderates everywhere hoped his words would appease Southern Unionists, embolden them to act, and prevent a war.

Mississippi Secession Convention: Declaration of Causes (January 1861)

Typical of those from other Southern states, the Mississippi declaration of causes summarized why so many whites feared and resented the Republican Party and its new national power. Throughout the document, the future security and stability of slavery is a central theme.

In the momentous step which our State has taken of dissolving its connection with the government of which we so long formed a part, it is but just that we should declare the prominent reasons which have induced our course.

Our position is thoroughly identified with the institution of slavery—the greatest material interest of the world. Its labor supplies the product which constitutes by far the largest and most important portions of commerce of the earth. These products are peculiar to the climate verging on the tropical regions, and by an imperious law of nature, none but the black race can bear exposure to the tropical sun. These products have become necessities of the world, and a blow at slavery is a blow at commerce and civilization. That blow has been long aimed at the institution, and was at the point of reaching its consummation. There was no choice left us but submission to the mandates of abolition, or a dissolution of the Union, whose principles had been subverted to work out our ruin. . . .

The hostility to this institution . . . refuses the admission of new slave States into the Union, and seeks to extinguish it by confining it within its present limits, denying the power of expansion.

It tramples the original equality of the South under foot.

It has nullified the Fugitive Slave Law in almost every free State in the Union, and has utterly broken the compact which our fathers pledged their faith to maintain.

It advocates negro equality, socially and politically, and promotes insurrection and incendiarism in our midst. . . .

It has invaded a State, and invested with the honors of martyrdom the wretch whose purpose was to apply flames to our dwellings, and the weapons of destruction to our lives.

Journal of the State Convention (Jackson, MS: E. Barksdale, State Printer, 1861).

Abraham Lincoln: First Inaugural Address (March 4, 1861)

In the most anticipated presidential address in American history, Lincoln appealed to Southern moderates and what he believed to be their deep commitment to the Union. He also acknowledged that slavery and its expansion had caused the crisis, but pledged not to interfere with slavery where it existed.

Plainly the central idea of secession is the essence of anarchy. A majority held in restraint by constitutional checks and limitations, and always changing easily with deliberate changes of popular opinions and sentiments, is the only true sovereign of a free people. Whoever rejects it does of necessity fly to anarchy or to despotism. Unanimity is impossible. The rule of a minority, as a permanent arrangement, is wholly inadmissible; so that, rejecting the majority principle, anarchy or despotism in some form is all that is left. . . .

One section of our country believes slavery is *right* and ought to be extended, while the other believes it is *wrong* and ought not to be extended. This is the only substantial dispute. . . .

Physically speaking, we can not separate. We can not remove our respective sections from each other nor build an impassable wall between them. A husband and wife may be divorced and go out of the presence and beyond the reach of each other, but the different parts of our country can not do this. They can not but remain face to face, and intercourse, either amicable or hostile, must continue between them. . . .

I understand a proposed amendment to the Constitution—which amendment, however, I have not seen—has passed Congress, to the effect that the Federal Government shall never interfere with the domestic institutions of the States, including that of persons held to service. To avoid misconstruction of what I have said, I depart from my purpose not to speak of particular amendments so far as to say that, holding such a provision to now be implied constitutional law, I have no objection to its being made express and irrevocable. . . .

By the frame of the Government under which we live this same people have wisely given their public servants but little power for mischief, and have with equal wisdom provided for the return of that little to their own hands at very short intervals. While the people retain their virtue and vigilance no Administration by any extreme of wickedness or folly can very seriously injure the Government in the short space of four years. . . .

Intelligence, patriotism, Christianity, and a firm reliance on Him who has never yet forsaken this favored land are still competent to adjust in the best way all our present difficulty.

In *your* hands, my dissatisfied fellow-countrymen, and not in *mine*, is the momentous issue of civil war. The Government will not assail *you*. You can have no conflict without being yourselves the aggressors. *You* have no oath registered in heaven to destroy the Government, while I shall have the most solemn one to "preserve, protect, and defend it."

I am loath to close. We are not enemies, but friends. We must not be enemies. Though passion may have strained it must not break our bonds of affection. The mystic chords of memory, stretching from every battlefield and patriot grave to every living heart and hearthstone all over this broad land, will yet swell the chorus of the Union, when again touched, as surely they will be, by the better angels of our nature.

Alexander Stephens: the "Cornerstone Speech" (March 21, 1861)

Confederate vice president Stephens, a successful Georgia politician and friend of Lincoln, famously declared slavery the "corner-stone" of the new Southern nation, contending that Jefferson's notion of equality expressed in the Declaration of Independence was a mistake.

* * * *

The prevailing ideas entertained by him [Thomas Jefferson] and most of the leading statesmen at the time of the formation of the old constitution, were that the enslavement of the African was in violation of the laws of nature; that it was wrong in *principle*, socially, morally, and politically. . . .

Those ideas, however, were fundamentally wrong. They rested upon the assumption of the equality of races. This was an error. . . .

Our new government is founded upon exactly the opposite idea; its foundations are laid, its corner-stone rests upon the great truth, that the negro is not equal to the white man; that slavery—subordination to the superior race—is his natural and normal condition. This, our new government, is the first, in the history of the world, based upon this great physical, philosophical, and moral truth.

Fred Spooner, Providence, RI, to Henry Joshua Spooner, Albany, NY (April 30, 1861)

Many Northerners—such as the author of this letter—welcomed the war. He considered it a chance to confront all of the Southern bluster and bluff, as he saw it, that Northerners had endured over the previous decades. The writer expressed clearly the feelings of many Northerners who were outraged at secession, which they saw as the result of Southern arrogance and, indirectly, slavery.

Dear Henry,

Your letter was received, and I now sit down in my shirt sleeves (as it is warm) to write in return.

For the last few weeks there has been great excitement here, and nothing has been thought of scarcely except that one subject which now received the undivided attention of the whole loyal North,—war.

And well may war, so hideous and disgusting in itself receive such attention when carried on for such noble and just principles as in the present case.

Traitors have begun the conflict, let us continue and end it. Let us settle it now, once and for all.

Let us settle it, even if the whole South has to be made one common graveyard and their cotton soaked in blood. let us do it *now* while the whole North is aroused from the inactivity and apparent laziness in which it has been so long.

There are plenty of men, an abundance of money, and a military enthusiasm never before known in the annals of history, all of which combined will do the work nice and clean, and if need be will wipe out that palmetto, pelican, rattlesnake region entirely. The holy cause in which our volunteers are enlisted will urge them on to almost superhuman exertions. The South *may* be courageous but I doubt it, they can *gas* and *hag* first rate; they can lie and steal to perfection, but I really do believe that they cannot fight—"Barking dogs never bite." Southern senators can bluster, bully and blackguard, but I believe them to be cowards at heart.

Besides the very nature of their country and their manner of living, have a tendency, I think to make them otherwise than brave.

They have prospered in dealing with human flesh,—let them now take the results of it.

They have had what *they* consider the *blessings* of slavery,—let them now receive the *curses* of it.

They must be put down, conquered and thoroughly subdued if need be. They have no earthly hope of overcoming this government. The fifteen weak states of the South can stand no chance against the nineteen powerful states of the North.

Affcnly Fred

Letters of Fred Spooner and Henry Joshua Spooner, Henry J. Spooner Papers, Rhode Island Historical Society, Providence, RI. Quoted in Nina Silber and Mary Beth Sievens, eds., *Yankee Correspondence: Civil War Letters Between New England Soldiers and the Home Front* (Charlottesville: University Press of Virginia, 1996), 55–58.

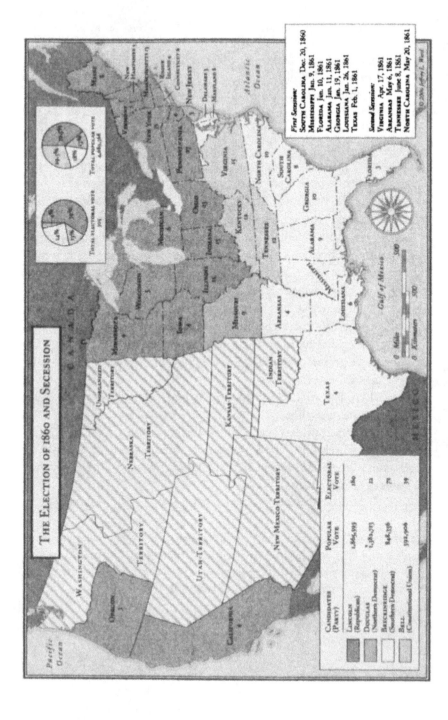

SIX

Fort Sumter and the Beginning of the War

W HEN LINCOLN TOOK OFFICE he faced not only a divided country, but a Northern public that ranged from openly hostile to unsure of his ability to lead the nation. Few Americans knew much about him, and many feared he was simply too inexperienced. Many Republican leaders, particularly from the Northeast, privately considered Lincoln an uneducated, uncultured buffoon. Certainly Lincoln faced a greater crisis than any previous president. He knew his every statement was being scrutinized, and on every decision might hang the future of the country. His first goal was to avoid any war, if possible, and related to that, he needed to keep as many states in the Union as possible. In his first days in office, as in the inaugural address, Lincoln courted Southern moderates—the great Unionist majority he and most Northerners believed existed. He wanted to avoid "provoking" Southerners and, if it came to a shooting war, avoid firing the first shot. Despite his great efforts to appear conciliatory, however, Lincoln steadfastly insisted that the Union was sacred and absolute, and that secession could not be tolerated. Thus, although Confederates had seized nearly all federal property in the seven seceded states, Lincoln vowed to defend what was left.

Before Lincoln could confront the nascent Confederacy, however, he had to put together his administration. The Cabinet had seven members, and Lincoln followed tradition by balancing constituencies within his party. He chose ex-Whigs and ex-Democrats, New Englanders and Midwesterners (he tried to include a Southerner but his choice from North Carolina declined). William Seward (New York), secretary of state, became the most important member, and ultimately a close advisor and even friend of the president. Seward initially hoped to lead a malleable Lincoln, but when Lincoln proved otherwise, Seward adjusted and came to appreciate Lincoln's abilities. Secretary of the Treasury Salmon Chase (Ohio), a pre-convention rival for the Republican nomination, was a famed lawyer and ex-Democrat respected by abolitionists. Secretary of the Navy Gideon Welles (Connecticut), a former Democrat, proved to be an efficient administrator. Simon Cameron (Pennsylvania), secretary of war (soon replaced by the superior Edwin Stanton); Edward Bates (Missouri), the attorney general; Caleb Smith (Indiana), the secretary of the interior; and Montgomery Blair (Maryland) as postmaster general, filled out the Cabinet. Unlike Jefferson Davis, Lincoln ultimately relied on his Cabinet and benefited from their skills and advice; the range of talent available to Lincoln simply dwarfed that of his Southern counterpart.

The Republican administration's first real crisis concerned two federal forts: Fort Pickens in Pensacola and Fort Sumter in Charleston. These installations presented an immediate dilemma because, low on food and water, they needed to be resupplied, reinforced, or abandoned within a few weeks. Northern opinion was divided between those who urged a conciliatory approach, and a growing majority who favored demonstrating the North's determination to preserve the integrity of the Union. Initially, Lincoln's Cabinet (and General-in-Chief Winfield Scott) solidly opposed any "provocative" moves to reinforce or resupply the forts; by the end of March, however, the Northern public and most of the Cabinet stiffened. Lincoln opted to resupply both Pickens and Sumter, although he acknowledged that doing so would probably lead to violence. For his part, Davis faced mounting public pressure to take action. Many Southern leaders considered Union occupation of Fort Sumter, in particular, an insult to their honor and a direct challenge to Confederate independence. Many Confederates also worried about the effect of inaction on voters in the upper South. Would Unionists be strengthened by the delay, as secessionists lost the momentum for disunion and independence?

Lincoln dispatched the relief fleet on April 6, informing the governor of South Carolina that the ships were instructed not to open fire unless fired upon first. The impassioned civilians in Charleston virtually ensured that the Union fleet would come under some kind of attack; an earlier relief ship, the *Star of the West,* had already been fired at by some South Carolinians in January 1861. Jefferson Davis risked losing his credibility if he ceded the initiative to an individual state, allowing its private citizens to start a civil war. Deciding that inaction or allowing the fort's resupply would be more harmful than a conflict, Confederate leaders chose to force the action. They demanded the fort's surrender. Major Robert Anderson, the Union commander inside Sumter, refused. At 4:30 a.m. on April 12, 1861, the Confederate general P.G.T. Beauregard's men—many of them young cadets from The Citadel—opened fire. On April 13, after nearly two days of bombardment, Anderson surrendered Fort Sumter. Lincoln's relief ships arrived in time to evacuate the Union troops. No one was killed. Both Lincoln and Davis had professed a desire for a peaceful resolution, although each also had reasons to welcome a confrontation. Neither side wanted to fire the first shot, although it was more important for Lincoln to avoid doing so for he faced greater dissent and needed to convince wavering Northerners that the Confederates had chosen war over diplomacy.

Two days after Sumter's surrender, Lincoln called for seventy-five thousand volunteers to suppress "an insurrection" in the seceded states. The Sumter battle and Lincoln's call for troops galvanized both sides as men and women chose Union or Confederacy. One of the most important spokesmen for the Union became Lincoln's old nemesis Stephen Douglas. He visited the president, offering to do whatever he could to raise troops and rally Northern public opinion, particularly among Democrats. Many editors followed his lead, commonly referring to Southern sympathizers as "traitors." It was a commendable, worthy effort by Douglas, although sadly his last great campaign. Weakened from his presidential effort and years of too much whiskey, Douglas died in June 1861. Perhaps most famously, Virginia's Robert E. Lee resigned his commission in the United States Army and followed his beloved state into the Confederacy. First offered command of all Union armies, Lee declined and instead began his Civil War career as head of Virginia's militia.

Like Lee's Virginia, the rest of the upper South—Tennessee, Arkansas, and North Carolina—quickly seceded and joined the Confederacy. Although they had rejected secession in the months following Lincoln's election, large majorities in each state now favored disunion. The immediate prospect of a war between Yankees and fellow Southerners made the choice clear for most voters. Public spokesmen called on men to defend their homes against invasion, to prevent the humiliation of fellow Southerners at the hands of a "Black Republican infidel" such as Lincoln, and to preserve the "proper" relationship between the races. The Confederate commissioner to Kentucky summarized that Republican rule would inaugurate "servile insurrection, consigning [Southern] citizens to assassinations and . . . wives and daughters to pollution and violation to gratify the lust of half-civilized Africans." The thought of Northern invasion sent some Southerners nearly into a frenzy. "Heaven forbid that they ever attempt to set foot upon this land of sunshine, of high-souled honor, and of liberty," Savannah's Charles Jones wrote to his father. "It puzzles the imagination to conceive the stupidity, the fanaticism, and the unmitigated rascality which impel them to the course which they are now pursuing." Reinforced by the upper South, Confederates such as Jones looked confidently toward a quick victory that would teach "insolent Yankees" a thing or two.

Having lost four more slave states, Lincoln concentrated on those that remained: Delaware, Maryland, Kentucky, and Missouri. Taken together they had several hundred thousand men of military age, successful agricultural economies with impressive resources of livestock, horses, and draft animals, rich mining areas, and urban manufacturing and shipping centers such as Baltimore, St. Louis, and Louisville. No one understood the gravity of keeping these states loyal more than Lincoln. When one of his advisors tried to reassure him that God would be with the Union, Lincoln supposedly responded that he would rather have Kentucky. Across the border states, Unionists enjoyed the advantage of geographic, demographic, and economic ties to the free states. Perhaps most important, slavery was declining in importance there, and most residents simply felt less threatened by the Republican administration. Families were often divided as a balance of Unionists, Conditional Unionists, and secessionists vied for power in each state.

Unionists controlled Delaware. Led by the wealthy DuPont family, they easily beat back all attempts to encourage secession. There were only about 1,800 slaves in the whole state, and its economy was oriented toward New Jersey and Pennsylvania. Maryland was more divided. Secessionists held sway in Baltimore, on the Eastern Shore, and in many areas that bordered Virginia; elsewhere, Unionists dominated. Soon after his inauguration, Lincoln ordered the U.S. Army to occupy Baltimore, and Northern troops moving through the state became easy targets. On April 19 (the eighty-sixth anniversary of the battles at Lexington and Concord), Confederate sympathizers attacked the Sixth Massachusetts Infantry; four soldiers and twenty-two civilians died. Overall, though, the state was Unionist, including Governor Thomas Hicks and the legislature. When combined with Lincoln's actions to fortify Baltimore and suppress pro-Confederate activities, the Unionist majority held Maryland and ensured that Washington, D.C., would not be surrounded by rebel territory.

Popular sentiment in Kentucky and Missouri split more evenly among Unionists, Conditional Unionists, and secessionists. Both governors favored secession and refused to help Lincoln raise troops for the Union. Kentucky's Beriah Magoffin was balanced by popular senator John Crittenden, a steadfast Unionist. After Sumter, Magoffin declared "neutrality" for his state, vowing that if either side "invaded" his "sovereign" state, Kentucky would support the other side. This fanciful idea appealed to many residents who hoped to avoid widespread bloodshed and families torn apart. Publicly both Lincoln and Davis said they would respect Kentucky's "neutrality"; privately, both sides raised troops in the state. Finally, in September 1861, a Confederate force occupied Columbus, Kentucky, on the Mississippi River, prompting the state's legislature officially to recognize its constitutional loyalty to the Union. Although many Kentuckians held sympathy for fellow Southerners, and slaves constituted nearly one-fifth of the state's population, secession never had significant popular support there.

Missouri's governor, Claiborne Jackson, was a former "border ruffian" who had helped rig elections in 1855–1856 in the Kansas Territory. His response to Lincoln's request for troops became legendary: "Your requisition is illegal, unconstitutional, revolutionary, inhuman, diabolical, and cannot and will not be complied with." Fighting within the state started early and continued throughout the war, becoming a war within the war and an extension of the violence from antebellum Kansas. Only in Missouri were large numbers of civilians deliberately targeted, by both sides, as part of a guerilla campaign to terrorize the population. Confederate "irregulars" such as Cole Younger, William Quantrill, and Jesse James were matched by Kansas Jayhawkers looking for revenge. In May 1861, Republican Frank Blair, Jr., and Union general Nathaniel Lyon suppressed the secessionists by occupying St. Louis, which forced Governor Jackson into exile. This secured Missouri for the Union.

The Union also gained a new border state in West Virginia. When Virginia seceded from the Union, many residents in the northwestern counties opted to separate from Virginia. This mountainous region contained few slaves and had close ties to western Pennsylvania and southeastern Ohio, including shared access to the Ohio River. Residents also had long-standing grievances with the eastern-dominated state government over tax policies and representation. On June 19, 1861, delegates from thirty-four counties declared themselves a separate government, eventually joining the Union in 1863. West Virginia entered as a free state, however, after Congress required emancipation, and the state remained bitterly divided throughout the war, with nearly as many men fighting for the Confederacy as for the Union.

Across the border states, the population remained split. Overall, perhaps three-fourths of the enrolled troops from these states fought for the Union and one-fourth for the Confederacy. Lincoln's war effort also benefited immeasurably from their industrial and material wealth. This support came with a price, however. By remaining in the Union, these slave states blurred the nature of the war and greatly complicated any government policy that dealt with slaves or potential emancipation.

As Americans chose Union or secession in the spring and summer of 1861, it was evident that the Union enjoyed substantial material advantages over the Confederacy. The most obvious was population. Union states contained more than twenty-two million people; the Confederacy had about nine million, but nearly half were slaves. This meant that the disparity between free men of military age was more than four to one in the North's favor. The Union produced over 90 percent of the nation's manufactured goods, including virtually all of the shoes, textiles, iron products, firearms, and railroad equipment. In all of the Confederacy there was one iron foundry (the Tredegar Works, in Richmond). In hindsight, of course, these comparative advantages make the Union appear invincible. The obvious question seems to be not "why did the Union win," but "how did the Confederacy last four years?"

Southerners had many reasons to believe they would win, however, and numerous contemporary observers, particularly Europeans, predicted a Confederate victory. A common comparison was to the American Revolution, in which the more powerful British Army simply could not be everywhere at once. Confederates, in other words, had a huge expanse of territory, and it would be virtually impossible for the Union to occupy all of it. The London *Times* opined in July 1861, "It is one thing to drive the 'rebels' from the south bank of the Potomac or even to occupy Richmond, but another to reduce and hold in permanent subjugation a tract of country nearly as large as Russia . . . and inhabited by Anglo-Saxons." Southerners also did not need to win the war, just not lose it. Fighting mainly on the defensive and on familiar terrain, Southerners could expect friendly civilians to provide local knowledge. Topography also helped Confederates trying to resist a Union invasion. In Virginia, where many of the largest battles were fought, the terrain was hilly, heavily forested, and crisscrossed with rivers and streams that became impassable in the rainy season (roughly November to April). The Appalachian Mountains resisted Union troops for nearly three years, keeping them at bay in western Virginia, eastern Tennessee and Kentucky, and northern Georgia. Confederates also benefited from a strong military tradition, including graduates not only from West Point but also from numerous private military schools. The Virginia Military Institute and The Citadel were perhaps the most famous, but hardly the only ones. This critical mass of professionally trained men, many of whom became Confederate officers, was something the Union initially could not match. Finally, the South had slaves. With slaves to perform agricultural and industrial labor, the Confederacy could mobilize a much higher percentage of its white men of military age. By the end of the war nearly 85 percent of Southern white men between ages seventeen and fifty had served in the armed forces. This massive mobilization eventually led to the internal collapse of slavery, but the Confederacy could not have survived four years without so many slaves to perform the physical labor normally done by white men.

So in the spring and summer of 1861 the fighting began, Americans chose sides, and the country descended into the bloodiest war in national history. Both Lincoln and Davis took office hoping to avoid armed hostilities, but compromise eluded politicians just as it had for the previous decade. Dozens of individual decisions shaped the eventual start of the war, and thousands of men and women made personal, sometimes agonizing, choices to support the Union or the Confederacy. Lincoln and a majority of Northerners stood firm that the Union was perpetual and that slavery should not expand; Confederates insisted on independence and believed that slavery was ultimately doomed under a Republican administration. White Northerners and Southerners hoped for, and expected, a short war that would settle quickly the question of Confederate independence without significant social change. It didn't work out that way.

Richmond Dispatch (April 15, 1861)

The surrender of Fort Sumter brought forth celebrations across the Confederacy, such as the one in Richmond described here. This passage also conveys many Southerners' sense of Lincoln's presidential ability.

THE SURRENDER OF FORT SUMTER
GREAT REJOICING AMONG THE PEOPLE
UNPARALLELED EXCITEMENT

The interest of our citizens in the exciting events lately occurring in the neighborhood of Charleston, South Carolina, always intense, as manifested by the crowds that have thronged around the bulletin boards of the different newspapers during the past week, culminated on Saturday evening on the reception of the news of the surrender of Fort Sumter, in one of the wildest, most enthusiastic and irrepressible expressions of heartfelt and exuberant joy on the part of the people generally, that we have ever known to be the case before in Richmond. Nothing else was talked of, or thought of, save the great triumph achieved by the heroic troops of the glorious Southern Confederacy in obliterating one of the Illinois ape's standing menaces against the assertion of Southern rights and equality.—So far as the opinion of the people is concerned, it would have been more to the old rail-splitter's credit had he ordered Anderson to leave Fort Sumter, as an untenable and undesirable place, than to attempt, as he and his coadjutors did, to make the undoubtably gallant Major the scapegoat of his insidious and damnable views. We repeat, that had wise counsels prevailed, the old ape would have had all the credit between a graceful leave taking and an ignominious expulsion at the cannon's mouth.

As soon as the news was ascertained to be undoubtedly true, crowds of citizens assembled on the different street corners, and by sundown the advocates of Southern rights had resolved to celebrate the momentous

event by an appropriate salute of cannon. The services of the Fayette
Artillery were procured, and amid the shouts of several thousand people,
ladies and gentlemen included, one hundred rounds were fired with a
will, judging from the regularity of the discharges and their loudness.
Afterwards, the cannon were discharged in battery of the whole, producing
a grand climax to the noise of the single guns.

About twenty-five hundred persons were congregated on the Square,
and patriotic and soul-stirring addresses were delivered by Messrs. J. B.
Sheffey, W. M. Ambler, C. Irving, Jno. M. Patton, Jr., G. L. Gordon, and
B. R. Wellford, Jr. The reception accorded to the speakers was but the
echo of that sentiment of loyalty to section, which is the distinguishing
characteristic of the true Southron everywhere, under all circumstances,
in evil as well as good report. . . .

During Saturday evening the raising of a Southern Confederacy flag
at the Tredegar Iron Works was made the occasion of a pleasant re-union
of many friends of the Southern cause. The flag was saluted with seven
guns, and one big one was fired in honor of Virginia, in hopes that her
representatives will soon do their duty. Speeches, sparkling with talent
and wit, and all aglow with the instincts of true patriotism, were delivered
by John Randolph Tucker, Attorney General, and L. S. Hall, Esq., the
able delegate of Wetzel county in the State Convention. These gentlemen
urged immediate secession, and they had in their hearers an appreciative
audience. . . .

Hardly less than ten thousand persons were on Main street, between
8th and 14th, at one time. . . . Bonfires were lighted at nearly every
corner of every principal street in the city, and the light of beacon fires
could be seen burning on Union and Church Hills. The effect of the
illumination was grand and imposing. The triumph of truth and justice
over wrong and attempted insult was never more heartily appreciated by
a spontaneous uprising of the people. Soon the Southern wind will sweep
away with the resistless force of a tornado, all vestige of sympathy or
desire of co-operation with a tyrant who, under false pretenses, in the
name of a once glorious, but now broken and destroyed Union, attempts
to rivet on us the chains of a despicable and ignoble vassalage. Virginia is
moving.

The Markesan Journal (Wisconsin, April–May 1861)

*These articles trace the evolution of sentiment in one Northern
community in the weeks after the Fort Sumter surrender.
Evident are the initial feelings of unity and enthusiasm, efforts
to inspire men to volunteer, and, later, worries about "traitors"
who did not fully support the Union war effort.*

✳ ✳ ✳ ✳

Friday, April 19, 1861 (vol. 2, no. 22)

1. THE CRISIS IS UPON US

The event that has so long been fearfully anticipated has at last
arrived.—Our country, that has so long been the pride of every American,
and the envy and dread of other nations of the earth is to-day deluged
in civil war. The seat of our national government trembles under its
destructive influence. The menaces that have long been hurled at the
people of the Northern States by a portion of the slaveholding States
have been put in execution. Fort Sumter has been bombarded by the
rebels, and the gallant Anderson has been made to surrender the Fort.
Such intelligence is sickening in the extreme. Every honest lover of his
country must feel an unlimited degree of humiliation at the thought, that
our own United States of America has become so embecile and feeble as
to be compelled to surrender to the hands of a few rebels and traitors.

That Fort Sumter will again be retaken, and that within a short time
there can be no doubt. The rebels have commenced a game that two can
play at, and from present appearances, they will soon have all the business
they can attend to. There is one united voice throughout the North for the
Union, and the cup of patriotism seems to be overflowing in every town
and hamlet in the Northern States.

Friday, April 19, 1861 (vol. 2, no. 22)

THE REBELLION!!

Fort Sumter Surrendered to the Rebels!
The Entire North Ablaze

LATEST NEWS!

The latest news we have received up to the time of going to press is that of the 17th, and as our space is limited, we simply give a brief synopsis of the news to the above date. Every paper that reaches us is filled with dispatches from all parts of the country, giving evident signs that the Northern people are aroused to a man, fully determined to put down treason and mete out a just punishment to the traitors. Political parties have all crumbled into ashes, and Union is the cry from every lip, throughout the free States. An opportunity is now presented to all those who manifested so much enthusiasm in the canvass, and who did seem to care "whether slavery was voted up or down," to show to the world that theirs was no idle profession—that they meant all they professed. Who in Markesan will be first to enroll his name? Don't have it said that our town is lacking heroic blood.

Friday, April 26, 1861 (vol. 2, no. 23)

TRAITORS IN MARKESAN

Strange as it may seem, there are at this time, when our country is involved in a desperate struggle for the maintenance of political and religious freedom, men in our midst who are daily in the habit of expressing sympathy for the rebels, who have rebelled against the purest and most magnanimous government on earth, and who are determined to rob us here at the North, of our dearly bought liberties, and trample our free institutions in the dust. Should the rebels succeed in this struggle, slavery will be planted on every inch of ground that is now occupied as homes of the *free*.

Notwithstanding the awful condition that we are placed in, there are

men—no not men! there are traitors in Markesan! Thank God, there
are but a few, and they are marked. The traitors of 1861 will be long
remembered—their names will go down to posterity, recorded upon
the pages of history, with the word disgrace written opposite each of
them. It is indeed humiliating to us to be obliged to make this public
acknowledgement, but such is the case. But our traitors do not possess
enough of intelligence to do us or the cause we are called upon to defend,
any harm. Our advice to them is, to join the Southern army at once,
where they can enjoy privileges so much more congenial to their tastes.

Friday, May 17, 1861 (vol. 2, no. 26)

THE WAR

It is in vain for any one to attempt to attend to the common duties of
life, at this present time, as man's whole mile and energies are completely
absorbed in the one great subject now before the country, viz., the war.
The rebellion against our government only excited in *embryo* six months
ago, and a[t] that time had the government manifested a disposition to
suppress it, it might have been done at an expense of a few thousand
dollars, and without the loss of a single life. But if it has been allowed to
go on unmolested, traitors have formed themselves into combinations, in
open resistance to the laws, taken possession of our Forts and Arsenals,
and what was a short time since "a mere drop in the bucket," has grown
in magnitude, and become more formidable than any rebellion that has
ever existed since the foundation of the earth. Nothing short of a united
solid phalanx of the people of the whole North, will be able to redeem
our insulted and demoralized flag. Thank God we have this same Union
sentiment through[ou]t the length and breadth of the land, which is all
powerful in itself, and it will never falter. The people are determined, and
rivers of blood shall flow from patriot's veins, but that our flag shall be
redeemed. The blood of the patriots that was spilled at Baltimore on the
19th of April calls to us from the ground. Let the cry be from every hill
top and valley, that our brother's blood shall be avenged. That for every
drop of blood that flowed on that occasion, there shall be barrels flow
from the camp of the traitors. Every intelligent person can have but one
opinion as to the result of this struggle, and there is but one course to

pursue, that is to press on the warfare, carry it into Africa, let sleep be a stranger to our eyelids, until every one of the rebels are made to offer up their lives as a penalty for the greatest of crimes known to God or man. Nothing short of a total annihilation of every leading rebel, will ever appease the wrath and just indignation of the whole northern people. We have no fears as in the result. Our abiding faith, in the firmness and wisdom of our great leader and captain, assures us that the grand result will be the redemption of the Stars and Stripes, which are destined to float over thirty millions or more of free and happy people, to time *ad fin item.*

This will be a good opportunity for military men to reap fame, and honor of distinction by their courage and loyalty. . . .

Samuel Storrow, Boston, MA, to His Father (October 12, 1862)

Like many men whose parents did not want them to enlist, Samuel Storrow tried to explain his reasons in this letter to his father. It is typical of the idealism expressed by many Northerners when they first joined the army, particularly in 1861 or 1862.

The excitement and intensity of feeling, the daily agony of doubt and suspense, is a thing scarcely to be appreciated in full by one who was not here at the time, and who did not pass through it. I assure you, my dear father, I know nothing in the course of my life which has caused me such deep and serious thought as this trying crisis in the history of our nation. What is the worth of this man's life or of that man's education, if this great and glorious fabric of our Union, raised with such toil and labor by our forefathers, and transmitted to us in value increased tenfold, is to be shattered to pieces by traitorous hands, and allowed to fall crumbling into the dust? If our country and our nationality is to perish, better that we should all perish with it, and not survive to see it a laughingstock for all posterity to be pointed at as the unsuccessful trial of republicanism. It seems to me the part of a coward to stay at home and allow others to fight my battles and incur dangers for me. What shame, what mortification would it cause me years hence to be obliged to confess that, in the great struggle for our national existence, I stood aloof, an idle spectator, without any peculiar ties to retain me at home, and yet not caring or not daring to do anything in the defense of my country.

Letters of Samuel Storrow, Samuel Storrow Papers, Massachusetts Historical Society, Boston, MA. Quoted in Silber and Sievens, eds., 70–73.

SEVEN

Organization, Strategy,
and the First Battle of Bull Run

I N A P R I L 1861, P R E S I D E N T S Lincoln and Davis wrestled with the same set of problems: formulating war strategy, raising and supplying troops, and uniting and inspiring their citizens. How best to accomplish these fundamental tasks occupied most of their time and energy. Both men made decisions based on their own assumptions, the pressure of anxious public opinion expressed in newspapers, and whatever real information they had. These first few months of war were both chaotic and tense. The politicians, most military commanders, and nearly all the fighting men were inexperienced in wartime decision-making or actual combat; both sides stumbled around trying to organize mass armies while planning strategy and avoiding embarrassment on the battlefield. After several months of small skirmishes and a few larger engagements, a major battle took place in northern Virginia—the first of many in that lush, wooded countryside—and it helped set the tone for the war's first year and a half. Americans also began to adjust to life amid war, although its initial limited nature ensured that many families were not directly touched by the conflict. No one, however, failed to notice that Americans had started killing other Americans.

Most Americans thought the war would be a short conflict. This perspective was shaped largely by the recent U.S.-Mexican War of 1846–1848. In Mexico, Americans won several "traditional" battles in which the forces met on open ground; the war concluded when the United States captured

Mexico City, the enemy's capital. This conception of warfare was hard for Civil War Americans to escape, and it helps explain the obsession—among some high-ranking officers and politicians, and much of the general public—with the tantalizing proximity of Richmond, Virginia, and Washington, D.C. Most Americans envisioned a war that went something like this: win a few battles fought somewhere out in the open, away from civilians or towns, and invade the enemy's country to capture his capital. Among Northerners, this scenario was reinforced by the belief that Southern resolve would crumble when it came to actually fighting the war and suffering the consequences of a federal invasion. After one or two defeats, the prevailing Northern opinion went, the great Southern Unionist majority would rise up and oust the radical secessionists. Many Southerners were equally convinced that Yankees would never fight—they were "cowardly shopkeepers" and "dirty immigrants," and no match for "aristocratic," noble Southerners.

The real war, of course, proved to be long, and costly in human lives and money, and for Southerners in particular, it involved civilians directly as victims or refugees. In other words, most Americans, North and South, were completely surprised by and unprepared for the actual nature of the conflict. This basic fact is critical for understanding wartime public opinion in both sections; when early assumptions were upended, many ordinary folks blamed their leaders for "misleading" them or bungling the war effort. There was misleading and bungling, to be sure, but mostly it was a case of unrealistic expectations. Not everyone predicted a short war, and notably some more experienced military men accurately foresaw what was coming. William Tecumseh Sherman famously derided Lincoln's call for just seventy-five thousand three-month volunteers: "You might as well attempt to put out the flames of a burning house with a squirt-gun." In April 1861, however, that was a minority opinion, and both presidents faced high expectations for a quick victory.

President Lincoln still believed that the best general approach was to court Southern Unionists, and particularly he hoped to limit the destruction of Southern property and the loss of lives. To these ends, General-in-Chief Winfield Scott devised an overall strategy that became known as the "Anaconda Plan," after the giant snake that squeezes its opponent to death. Scott's plan relied on Union naval superiority and greater manpower, calling for a blockade of Confederate commerce and control of major rivers, especially the Mississippi, while troops moved to take Richmond. The plan would be slow and expensive (especially the construction of naval vessels), but it could limit human costs and protect Southern property. In essence, it was to be a giant siege of the Confederacy. It was sound strategy, relied on the Union's long-term advantages, and in many ways was how the Union eventually won the war—although it took much longer and consumed more lives than anyone imagined in 1861. The strategy was unpopular with the public, who wanted more "action," and in 1861, editors everywhere called on Lincoln to force General Scott to launch an aggressive Union invasion of Virginia. In understated fashion, the general called it "the impatience of our patriotic and loyal Union friends."

The limited war strategy also coincided with Lincoln's insistence that the war's only goal was national reunion and not to weaken, much less destroy, the institution of slavery. This caution was necessary, he thought, to maintain majority support for the war effort—managing public opinion was one of Lincoln's two great tasks during the next four years. He refused, for instance, to allow free black men to enlist in the army. The sight of armed black men marching through the streets of Northern cities, Lincoln feared, would be too inflammatory for most whites.

In contrast, the Confederate president, Davis, enjoyed a more unified population but faced a more critical strategic dilemma. When Lincoln called for troops to invade their region, Southerners rallied to the fledgling Confederacy. But while the goal of independence galvanized support, Davis had tough decisions to make regarding his overall military strategy. A number of the most important Confederate advantages were short term, particularly the initial edge in military discipline and leadership, their ability to mobilize so many white men because slaves shouldered so much physical labor at home, local knowledge of the terrain and topography, and a unified populace. The problem, however, was that the most effective strategy seemed to be the "Revolution model" of dragging out the war until Northerners grew tired of the costs and gave up. This approach called on Confederates to conserve and spread out resources, defend as many points along the border as possible, and seek European intervention (again, as the Patriots had done). In short, Confederate strategy was at odds with the South's comparative advantages. The longer the war lasted, the more Union troops would gain experience, slavery would become fragile, Confederate civilian morale would decline, and so forth. Confederates could have gambled on winning a quick victory by invading the Union and trying to capture Washington, D.C., but that risked wasting resources of men and materiel. Balancing all of these considerations was Jefferson Davis's chief task. The Confederacy began the war with some important advantages, but it could not gamble too often with such a small margin for error. Considering the Union's lopsided manpower and economic advantages, Confederates needed to conserve their precious resources, meaning every strategic decision they made had potentially far greater consequences than those made in the Union.

The Confederate and Union armies had similar organizations, and both were composed primarily of amateur volunteers. The Union Army also included its regular, professional troops from 1860, the vast majority of whom remained loyal when the war began. General Scott decided to keep these regiments intact, hoping to rely on them as elite units he could trust to perform under fire. This decision proved costly during the first year of the war. Instead of using his West Point graduates and experienced officers to instill discipline among the amateurs, Scott left volunteers at the mercy of equally untrained officers. Starting from scratch, the Confederate Army, in this case, advantageously sprinkled its professional officers throughout the volunteer regiments. As a result, many Southern troops benefited from professional officers' experience and, according to most observers and historians, were better trained and more disciplined during the first months of the war. In 1861 and 1862, Southern troops tended to march farther in a day than Union men, for instance. This advantage lasted only so long, and the Union was catching up in 1862, and certainly matched Confederate training and discipline by 1863.

Both sides enrolled volunteers according to their place of origin. Local politicians and other community leaders normally organized rallies; when one hundred men signed up they formed a company, and ten companies made a regiment (commanded by a colonel), the two basic units in each army. Regiments were designated by a number and state of origin: the 11th Wisconsin Infantry, for instance (made up of men from around Madison). As the war progressed, most new troops enrolled into new units rather than joining old ones that had suffered attrition from death or desertion. This offered local and state politicians more chances to reward friends with appointment as officers. Also, officers believed that morale and unit pride would suffer if new men from other towns were mixed with veterans.

Thus, in theory, regiments had one thousand men, but that number quickly declined and rarely rebounded to full strength. As one example, when the legendary Twentieth Maine Infantry went into battle at Gettysburg in July 1863, it had about 350 men active for duty. Between four and six regiments made a brigade (led by a brigadier general), three or four brigades became a division (major general), and two or more divisions formed a corps. Corps-level commanders were lieutenant generals in the Confederacy and major generals in the Union. These included some of the most famous officers of the war: Confederates Thomas "Stonewall" Jackson and James Longstreet, and the Union's Winfield Scott Hancock, William Tecumseh Sherman, and Ambrose Burnside.

Troops were divided into three branches: infantry, cavalry, and artillery. The infantry was expected to do the bulk of the fighting, supported by the artillery, while the cavalry provided information on the enemy and "screened" (covered or disguised) the movement of infantry in order to confuse the other side. The cavalry offered some "romantic" attractions for many men, not least of which was riding instead of trudging through the mud. Early in the war, the cavalry also drew more men from the upper class, since this branch required a volunteer to provide his own horse. Later, that identification with class waned as men stole horses or governments provided mounts. Over time, the Union enjoyed a growing advantage in artillery as the Confederacy had greater difficulty replacing equipment. Infantry made up between 75 and 80 percent of troops on both sides (slightly higher in the Union), and absorbed nearly 90 percent of casualties. That factor, too, prompted some men to choose the cavalry or artillery when they had the chance.

In both armies, most officers were elected by their men, although higher-level choices had to be certified by the appropriate state governor. This long-standing tradition had its roots in the early American militias, and was reinforced by the rhetoric of antebellum democracy that preached equality among white men. Most elected officers held some prewar distinction, and a certain amount of deference was guaranteed when men chose their immediate superiors. Enlisted men elected the junior officers; junior officers then chose the regimental officers—major and colonel. In many units there was a degree of equality—not unlike the relationship between a politician and his voters—which certainly hurt discipline as amateur officers tried to control unruly, poorly trained citizen-soldiers.

Initially, all generals were appointed, normally by-products of political influence, and they earned a notorious reputation as inept bunglers. Some were truly awful, but it is important to distinguish between politician-generals and political appointments. The former included disasters such as Nathaniel Banks, a Know Nothing/Republican from Massachusetts, and John C. Frémont, the former Republican nominee for president in 1856. In contrast, many generals who received appointments were West Point veterans and made outstanding commanders: William Tecumseh Sherman and Ulysses Grant are obvious examples. Most generals were civilians when the war started, but nearly half (in both armies) had trained at West Point or other military schools, and West Pointers held overall command in nearly all of the war's major battles.

Battlefield leadership notably affected the course of battle. Irregular, slow, and handwritten or oral communication hindered the influence of the commanding general once the battle started, meaning that middle-grade officers often made crucial tactical decisions in the midst of combat, frequently changing the course of events with a single action.

In spring 1861, both sides worked feverishly to train and equip the new armies, but the start of major hostilities would fall to the North. Confederate leaders believed that the onus was on the Union to invade and subdue the South, and they were content to let the war come to them. The army's state of preparedness was not, however, the only factor determining when the Union attacked. Northerners were particularly restless, and newspaper editors urged Lincoln to order the troops south to "whip the Rebs" and end the folly of secession. In Washington, the commander of the Army of the Potomac—the Union force in northern Virginia—hesitated to send his raw recruits into battle. By July, though, Lincoln had heard enough from the press and insisted that his army advance toward Richmond. When General Irvin McDowell protested that his men needed more training, Lincoln responded, "[Y]ou are green, it is true, but they are green also. You are all green alike." McDowell himself was untried in battle.

This initial Northern invasion and the resulting First Battle of Bull Run typified much about the Union's efforts in the East during the first two years of the war. First, it was a good plan. McDowell intended to take his main force, about thirty-five thousand men (a huge army, at that time the largest in American history), and attack the Confederates encamped at

Manassas Junction, an important rail center just southwest of Washington. Confederate forces were divided between Manassas (twenty thousand) and the Shenandoah Valley (twelve thousand), a rich farming area about sixty miles west. General P.G.T. Beauregard commanded the main Southern force at Manassas. A skilled engineer and artilleryman, Beauregard came from an aristocratic French Creole family, had graduated from West Point, served in Mexico, and before secession ended his U.S. Army career, was named superintendent of West Point in 1861.

To keep the Confederates divided, the Union plan called for General Robert Patterson to make a feint with his smaller force in the Shenandoah Valley, holding the Southern troops there. The Union plan required timing and coordination; veteran soldiers might have pulled it off, but not the Northern army at this point. Instead, the timing was off—a second general characteristic of Union attacks—as troops got lost in the unfamiliar and heavily forested terrain, and their march was slower than expected. (Some men stopped to pick blackberries.) Patterson was fooled by a cavalry screen in the valley, allowing General Joseph E. Johnston to move his Confederate infantry (by rail) toward the main battle; consequently, when the two forces came together their strength was roughly even. Emblematic of the prevailing optimistic assumptions, dozens of Northern civilians traveled after the army with opera glasses and picnic lunches of oysters and champagne, hoping to watch the first and last great battle of the Civil War.

On July 21, 1861, the Army of the Potomac met the Confederates in an open field just north of Manassas Junction and along the small creek of Bull Run. The day-long battle revealed the inexperience of men on both sides, and the Union lost the battle, in part because it failed to coordinate its attacks or exploit its numerical advantage—the third characteristic of Northern attacks. In the morning and early afternoon, McDowell's men pushed the Confederates back toward Manassas, and seemed close to victory. But late in the afternoon, Beauregard and General Thomas J. Jackson rallied the Confederates and made a stand. According to legend, Southern general Bernard Bee, trying to inspire his own men, pointed to Jackson's troops holding firm "like a stone wall" and told them to "rally behind the Virginians." (The alternative story claims that Bee was actually criticizing Jackson for standing stupidly like a "stone wall" instead of retreating as he should have.) As the Union advance was slowed by Jackson's men, Johnston's troops arrived in the nick of time and pushed straight into the battle. For the first time, the Confederates screamed wildly as they launched a furious counterattack: the "rebel yell" was born. The tide of the battle turned as thousands of Union troops retreated in total confusion. The soldiers became entangled with civilians trying to escape the Confederates (two Northern congressmen were captured). The Southern press called it the "great skedaddle," and the Union was humiliated. Senator Lyman Trumbull of Illinois termed it "the most shameful rout you can conceive of."

The human cost of the battle staggered the nation. It was the deadliest in American history to that point, but only a small taste of the carnage yet to come. Nearly nine hundred men were killed at First Bull Run (almost as many as died in battle during the entire Mexican War), another 2,600 were wounded. The Union defeat and miserable retreat to Washington gave the Confederacy a psychological edge for the next eighteen months. Among Union troops and officers in the East it created a sense of inferiority and doubt that was difficult to overcome. Southerners, of course, were jubilant; some predicted a quick negotiated peace. Instead, though, a sort of stubborn determination took hold among most Northerners. McDowell, perhaps unfairly, was relieved. In his place, Lincoln appointed a young general with a gift for making headlines: George Brinton McClellan. McClellan remains a controversial figure in Civil War history, but there is little debate that his great strengths—training men, instilling discipline, and raising morale—were just what the Army of the Potomac needed in July 1861.

Major Sullivan Ballou, Camp Clark, Washington, DC, to Sarah Ballou (July 14, 1861)

This letter expresses the feelings of many husbands and fathers—from both the Union and the Confederacy—as they faced the fear and possibility of death. Ballou, a thirty-two-year-old Republican lawyer who joined the Union Army out of patriotism and devotion to Lincoln, was killed just a few days later at the First Battle of Bull Run.

Our movement may be one of a few days duration and full of pleasure—and it may be one of severe conflict and death to me. Not my will, but thine O God, be done. If it is necessary that I should fall on the battlefield for my country, I am ready. I have no misgivings about, or lack of confidence in, the cause in which I am engaged, and my courage does not halt or falter. I know how strongly American Civilization now leans on the triumph of the Government, and how great a debt we owe to those who went before us through the blood and sufferings of the Revolution. And I am willing—perfectly willing—to lay down all my joys in this life, to help maintain this Government, and to pay that debt.

But, my dear wife, when I know that with my own joys I lay down nearly all of yours, and replace them in this life with cares and sorrows—when, after having eaten for long years the bitter fruit of orphanage myself, I must offer it as their only sustenance to my dear little children—is it weak or dishonorable, while the banner of my purpose floats calmly and proudly in the breeze, that my unbounded love for you, my darling wife and children, should struggle in fierce, though useless, contest with my love of country? . . .

Sarah, my love for you is deathless, it seems to bind me to you with mighty cables that nothing but Omnipotence could break; and yet my love of Country comes over me like a strong wind and bears me unresistibly on with all these chains to the battlefield.

The memories of the blissful moments I have spent with you come creeping over me, and I feel most gratified to God and to you that I have enjoyed them so long. And hard it is for me to give them up and burn to ashes the hopes of future years, when, God willing, we might still have lived and loved together, and seen our sons grown up to honorable manhood, around us. I have, I know, but few small claims upon Divine Providence, but something whispers to me—perhaps it is the wafted prayer of my little Edgar, that I shall return to my loved ones unharmed. If I do not, my dear Sarah, never forget how much I love you, and when my last breath escapes me on the battlefield, it will whisper your name. . . .

But, O Sarah! If the dead can come back to this earth and flit unseen around those they loved, I shall always be near you; in the garish day and in the darkest night . . . always, always; and if there be a soft breeze upon your cheek, it shall be my breath; or the cool air fans your throbbing temple, it shall be my spirit passing by.

Sarah, do not mourn me dead; think I am gone and wait for thee, for we shall meet again.

As for my little boys, they will grow as I have done, and never know a father's love and care. Little Willie is too young to remember me long, and my blue eyed Edgar will keep my frolics with him among the dimmest memories of his childhood. Sarah, I have unlimited confidence in your maternal care and your development of their characters. Tell my two mothers his and hers I call God's blessing upon them. O Sarah, I wait for you there! Come to me, and lead thither my children.

Albert Pike: "Dixie" (1861)

There were many versions of this Southern song—the first appeared in September 1859, written by Dan D. Emmett. Pike was a poet and writer born in Massachusetts, but he joined the Confederate Army when the war began, even though he opposed secession and slavery.

* * * *

Southrons, hear your country call you!
Up, lest worse than death befall you!
To arms! To arms! To arms, in Dixie!
Lo! all the beacon-fires are lighted,—
Let all hearts be now united!
To arms! To arms! To arms, in Dixie!
Advance the flag of Dixie!

Hurrah! Hurrah!
For Dixie's land we take our stand,
And live or die for Dixie!
To arms! To arms!
And conquer peace for Dixie!
To arms! To arms!
And conquer peace for Dixie!

Hear the Northern thunders mutter!
Northern flags in South winds flutter!
Send them back your fierce defiance!
Stamp upon the accursed alliance!

Fear no danger! Shun no labor!
Lift up rifle, pike, and sabre!
Shoulder pressing close to shoulder,
Let the odds make each heart bolder!

How the South's great heart rejoices
At your cannon's ringing voices!
For faith betrayed and pledges broken,
Wrongs inflicted, insults spoken.

Strong as lions, swift as eagles,
Back to their kennels hunt these beagles!
Cut the unequal bonds asunder!
Let them hence each other plunder!

Swear upon your country's altar
Never to submit or falter,
Till the spoilers are defeated,
Till the Lord's work is completed!

Halt not till our Federation
Secures among earth's powers its station!
Then at peace and crowned with glory,
Hear your children tell the story!

If the loved ones weep in sadness,
Victory soon shall bring them gladness,—
To arms!
Exultant pride soon vanish sorrow;
Smiles chase tears away to-morrow.
To arms! To arms! To arms, in Dixie!
Advance the flag of Dixie!
Hurrah! hurrah!
For Dixie's land we take our stand,
And live or die for Dixie!
To arms! To arms!
And conquer peace for Dixie!
To arms! To arms!
And conquer peace for Dixie!

Julia Ward Howe: "Battle-Hymn of the Republic" (1862)

Born in New York City, Howe was a poet, writer, pacifist,
abolitionist, and woman's rights activist. She wrote this poem
to provide more "noble" lyrics for the tune to "John Brown's
Body," which was popular in the Union early in the war. The
"Battle-Hymn of the Republic" was published in February 1862
and became the greatest Northern song of the war.

✯ ✯ ✯ ✯

Mine eyes have seen the glory of the coming of the Lord;
He is trampling out the vintage where the grapes of wrath are stored;
He hath loosed the fateful lightning of his terrible swift sword;
*   His truth is marching on.*

I have seen Him in the watch-fires of a hundred circling camps;
They have builded him an altar in the evening dews and damps;
I can read His righteous sentence by the dim and flaring lamps;
*   His day is marching on.*

I have read a fiery gospel, writ in burnished rows of steel;
"As ye deal with my contemners, so with you my grace shall deal;
Let the Hero, born of woman, crush the serpent with his heel,
*   Since God is marching on."*

He has sounded out the trumpet that shall never call retreat;
He is sifting out the hearts of men before his judgment-seat:
Oh! be swift, my soul, to answer him, be jubilant, my feet!
*   Our God is marching on.*

In the beauty of the lilies Christ was born across the sea,
With a glory in his bosom that transfigures you and me:
As he died to make men holy, let us die to make men free,
*   While God is marching on.*

He is coming like the glory of the morning on the wave,
He is wisdom to the mighty, he is honor to the brave,
So the world shall be his footstool, and the soul of wrong his slave,
*   Our God is marching on!*

A Group of Soldiers

This photograph captures the determination and close camaraderie that characterized so many Civil War units, often composed of men who had grown up together and known each other for years.

Library of Congress.

EIGHT

War on Land and at Sea in 1862

I N 1862, THE WAR TOOK ON frightening new dimensions. Thousands of men died in major battles across the nation, and both sides encountered difficulty raising new troops. The Union pressed forward in the West and at sea, beginning the daunting task of trying to blockade the Confederacy. Northern forces pioneered joint army-navy operations in Tennessee, taking advantage of their numerical advantage and naval superiority. In the East, the Union launched a massive amphibious invasion of Virginia aimed at capturing Richmond. Throughout the fighting of 1862, the critical factors of topography and tactical decision-making were also evident. Confederates took advantage of the terrain to frustrate the Union in Virginia; where the land was flat and open or where the Union Navy could operate effectively, Confederates were forced to retreat. Finally, 1862 was a critical point in the evolution of Union war aims and strategy. Lincoln abandoned the limited war policy as the much-anticipated Unionist uprising in the South failed to materialize. But how far should he go? Could the Union Army take a more vigorous approach without destroying the fragile coalition of Northerners who supported the war? A more aggressive strategy would mean greater destruction and hardship for Southern civilians. Most important, of course, and still uncertain was whether or not slavery itself would become a casualty of the war.

The fall and early winter of 1861–1862 was a depressing time for the Union. After the debacle at First Bull Run, the Army of the Potomac, now under General McClellan, stayed outside Washington to train and to re-store some confidence. In the West, the Federals had failed to clear all Confederate forces out of Missouri or Kentucky, both Union states. But Ulysses Grant was about to change Northern fortunes and begin his rise from obscure army officer and failed businessman to General-in-Chief and eventually President of the United States. Hiram Ulysses Grant was born in Ohio in 1822. As a young boy, he excelled at horsemanship, seem-ing more comfortable around animals than people. He entered West Point, and in 1843 graduated near the middle of his class. Grant earned recognition for valor in the Mexican War (which he personally opposed), but was assigned to the West Coast after the war. Poor and lonely (his new wife stayed home), he resigned in 1854 and drifted back to Missouri, where he failed at farming. He was working in his father's leather shop in Galena, Illinois, when the Civil War began. Grant had a reputation not only for honesty and bravery, but also for stubbornness and difficulty with authority. (His supposed alcoholism is now considered a myth.) Through political connections, Grant was appointed to command the Twenty-first Illinois Infantry and had a small success against Confederates in southern Missouri. In 1862, he commanded all Union forces west of the Tennessee and Cumberland rivers. He and his superior, General Henry Halleck, identified two forts—Henry and Donelson, located on the two large rivers—as keys to the entire Confederate position in the region. In January 1862, they began an invasion of Tennessee designed to take the forts, split the Confederate line of defense, and open the state for Union forces.

Opposing Grant and Halleck was Confederate General Albert Sidney Johnston, a Kentucky native, West Point graduate, and close friend of Jefferson Davis. The Confederate forces defended a line from Colum-bus, Kentucky, on the Mississippi River, to Bowling Green. Forts Henry and Donelson anchored the Confederate center and controlled access to the Tennessee and Cumberland rivers, and, in turn, to the state capital, Nashville. Grant planned a coordinated attack on Henry and Donelson with Flag Officer Andrew Foote, a New England temperance advocate who commanded the Union Navy gunboats on the Tennessee River. On February 6, Grant moved his men south of the fort to begin his attack, but Foote's gunboats were so effective that the Confederates surrendered be-fore Grant launched his assult. This defeat put Johnston in a vulnerable position: Foote's gunboats now controlled the Tennessee River all the way to northern Alabama. When the Union destroyed a railroad bridge over the river just south of Fort Henry, the Confederate supply line was cut. After a few days' rest, Grant moved on Fort Donelson. He and Foote planned a similar joint operation, but Fort Donelson was more formidable than Fort Henry. Nearly fifteen acres surrounded by trenches and heavily fortified, Donelson was commanded by General John B. Floyd, who had about sixteen thousand men in and around the fort. On February 14, Foote's gunboats failed to dislodge the Confederates, whose own guns caused extensive damage to the Union vessels and mortally wounded Foote. Still, Grant surrounded the fort by land, and the Confederates were faced with slow starvation. Instead of waiting for a prolonged death, the Southerners launched a breakout attack early the next morning. They briefly broke through the Union lines and opened an escape route to the southeast, but then they paused, allowing Grant just enough time to rally his own troops and launch a counterattack that sealed the Confederates inside Donelson again. Confederate general Floyd decided to surrender the garrison, although he personally escaped and fled south. Grant famously refused to consider any terms other than "unconditional surrender," which soon became his nickname (matching his initials, "U.S."). With the Cumberland River now in Union hands, on February 23, Albert Sidney Johnston had to abandon Nashville, the first Confederate state capital to be taken.

Grant's invasion was a great success, and it raised Northern spirits. But he wasn't finished. Continuing south, Grant intended to move into Mississippi, and by late March he assembled thirty-five thousand men at Pittsburg Landing, Tennessee, on the Tennessee River, just a few miles from the state border. In addition, an even larger Union army under General Don Carlos Buell was moving south from Nashville to join Grant's men. But before Buell arrived, Confederate general Johnston decided to attack while he still held a slight numerical advantage. Early on April 6, 1862, Johnston's forty thousand men advanced on Grant's Union lines, strung out to the west of the river, near a small church called Shiloh. The long day's fighting was a confused nightmare for most of the men. In the wooded, rolling hills, units from both sides got lost and blundered around. By the afternoon, most of the Union forces were in full retreat toward the Tennessee River, where Johnston hoped to trap them. General Benjamin Prentiss, however, held the Union middle, with his men arrayed along a country road amid a thicket of trees known as "the hornet's nest." Confederates launched nearly a dozen attacks against Prentiss's division, but it refused to give way. Johnston personally led the last attack, was shot in the leg, and bled to death. Finally, late in the day, Prentiss and his surviving troops surrendered. By that time, Grant had established a strong position, and in the middle of the night some of Buell's reinforcements arrived. The next morning the Confederates—now commanded by General Beauregard, the hero of Fort Sumter and First Bull Run—attacked again. But the Union outnumbered them, and Grant's counterattack pushed the Southerners off the field by nightfall. The battle was a tactical Union victory, but really a draw.

More than 3,500 men were killed at Shiloh and another 16,500 wounded; about 2,000 of those died of their wounds. It was the deadliest battle in American history—about five thousand men had died in the entire American Revolution. Americans expressed shock and horror. The correspondent of the *Cincinnati Times* wrote his account "with the dead and wounded . . . all around me. The knife of the Surgeon is busy at work, and amputated legs and arms lie scattered in every direction." One Union soldier appealed to God in his diary: "Can there be anything in the *future* that *compensates* for this slaughter?" He recorded men "torn all to pieces leaving nothing but their heads or their boots. Pieces of clothing and *strings of flesh* hang on the limbs of trees round them." The killing at Shiloh ended any romantic notions of war that so many men and women had held the year before; it also convinced leaders on both sides that their war efforts would require many more men than they had anticipated.

The Union Navy also enjoyed success in late 1861 and 1862. To blockade the entire Confederacy was a huge undertaking, and the Union began by taking ports along the coast to use as bases for the ocean fleet. Their first major success was capturing Port Royal, between Charleston and Savannah, in November 1861. In spring 1862, the Union took Jacksonville, Apalachicola, and Pensacola in Florida; Biloxi in Mississippi; and Norfolk in Virginia. The climax of these efforts came at New Orleans. The "Crescent City" was the Confederacy's greatest ocean port and the center of the antebellum cotton trade. Although the city itself was unfortified, it was guarded by two intimidating forts—Jackson and St. Philip—far to the south, which commanded the mouth of the Mississippi River. Admiral David G. Farragut led the Union naval forces. Born in Tennessee, Farragut lived in Virginia, but he stayed loyal to the Union in 1861, having already served more than fifty years—since age nine—in the U.S. Navy (including during the War of 1812). In April 1862, his fleet reached the Mississippi River and began a fruitless artillery duel with the two Confederate forts. Frustrated, Farragut decided to take a chance and simply sail his ships past the forts. In the middle of the night, on April 24, the Union fleet moved upriver, trading thousands of shells with the Confederate artillery. The gamble paid off as Farragut lost just one ship. New Orleans surrendered without a shot, and Farragut continued up the river, taking Baton Rouge. From the north, a separate Union flotilla captured Memphis, Tennessee, on June 6. Thus, by early summer 1862, the Union controlled most of the Mississippi. Only Vicksburg remained as a significant Confederate fort and railroad crossing that connected the Trans-Mississippi West with the rest of the South.

The Union successes of 1862 demonstrated the importance of topography and vigorous leadership. West-central Tennessee was flat and relatively open, and its large rivers allowed Union infantry and gunboats to move quickly against the outnumbered Confederates. Grant's aggressiveness underscored what the Union could accomplish with superior numbers, efficient transportation (particularly on the rivers), and open country in which to operate. At sea the Union began its blockade with several key victories. Confederate leaders, particularly President Davis, had to determine how thinly to spread their forces. Certainly they could not defend every port and piece of coastline. But to abandon some areas caused political bickering among Confederates and declining confidence in the fledgling Richmond government. Indeed, by early summer 1862, Davis and the Confederacy were desperate for some good news. They were about to get it, thanks to timid Union leadership and their own audacious generals in Virginia.

General George McClellan had spent the winter of 1861–1862 reorganizing and training the Army of the Potomac. These were his great strengths; his deficiencies on the battlefield were not yet evident. When the war began, McClellan was just thirty-four, a West Point graduate (he finished second in his class), a decorated soldier in Mexico, and a successful railroad engineer. Early in the war, he won a series of small but widely publicized victories in western Virginia. When he replaced McDowell after First Bull Run, the press hailed him as a savior, the "Young Napoleon" who would whip the Rebels and restore the Union. Dark-haired and handsome, McClellan thrived on the adoration, which fed his already advanced ego. "I almost think that were I to win some small success now," he wrote his wife just days after taking command, "I could become Dictator or anything else that might please me—but nothing of that kind would please me—*therefore* I *won't be* Dictator. Admirable self-denial!" Before long, McClellan's arrogance knew no limits. He often refused to meet with General-in-Chief Winfield Scott or with the secretary of war. And he ignored Lincoln, whom he described as "nothing more than a well meaning baboon." Still, McClellan's Army of the Potomac stayed put, and though the president grew impatient with McClellan's stalling, at this point in the war Lincoln still deferred to professional soldiers.

In late March 1862, McClellan finally launched an invasion of Virginia. After months of planning (much of it done in secret; he wouldn't even tell Lincoln his plans), McClellan moved the bulk of his army—seventy thousand men plus horses, wagons, artillery, and all the rest of its supplies—on three hundred ships to Fortress Monroe, at the tip of the peninsula in southeast Virginia. His plan was to move up the narrow peninsula toward Richmond and join forces with the rest of the Army of the Potomac—about thirty-five thousand men under Irvin McDowell, who would start from Washington. These two forces would crush the Confederates between them, take Richmond, and end the war. It was a good plan, and Lincoln seemed to like it. Once in the field, however, McClellan refused to move, paralyzed by fear of failure or of risking his beautiful army. He also employed his own private intelligence agency, which reported enemy troop strengths to him. McClellan was forever convinced that he was outnumbered, so his agents fed him the information they knew he wanted, which only heightened his paranoia. Lincoln demonstrated more insight into Civil War tactics than his commander when he warned McClellan that "by delay the enemy will relatively gain upon you—that is, he will gain faster, by *fortifications* and *re-inforcements*, than you can by re-inforcements alone." Lincoln also angered McClellan by detaching a larger portion of the army in order to protect Washington.

In April, with glacierlike speed, McClellan's great army inched up the peninsula. He was stopped at Yorktown for a month by seventeen thousand Confederates under General John Bankhead Magruder, who tricked McClellan with fake artillery (made out of pine trees) and nonexistent troops. Still believing he was outnumbered, McClellan laid siege to the town instead of blowing through its defenses in a day. It then took until late May for the Union forces—still holding a three-to-one advantage—to reach a position just a few miles east of Richmond. This delay allowed the Confederates to move forty thousand men to the peninsula, giving them a total of about sixty thousand. Their commander was General Joseph E. Johnston, a Virginian and a West Point classmate and close friend of Robert E. Lee. Distinguished in features with a pointed goatee, Johnston served with distinction in the war with Mexico and against the Seminole in Florida. His Civil War career was marked by considerable successes (such as at the First Battle of Bull Run) but also by a bitter feud with Jefferson Davis, who never liked or trusted him. As the Confederates waited for an all-out Union attack on the capital, Davis and Lee, who was serving as Davis's chief military advisor, devised a plan to disrupt Union strategy and relieve the pressure on Richmond.

In the Shenandoah Valley, "Stonewall" Jackson commanded a small force that in April was raised to about seventeen thousand men. Opposing him were more than thirty thousand Federals divided between Generals Nathaniel Banks and John Frémont. The Valley is an open swath of lush farmland between the imposing Blue Ridge and Appalachian mountains. It runs southwest to northeast and generally toward Washington. Lee's idea was that Jackson would move toward the capital and compel Lincoln to prevent McClellan's reinforcements (nearly forty thousand more men) from marching on Richmond from the North.

Jackson remains a legendary figure in American military history. Born to a poor family in western Virginia, he read and studied in every free moment, graduated from West Point in 1846, and was decorated for bravery in Mexico. He became a professor at the Virginia Military Institute, in Lexington, where he was known as the worst teacher anyone could remember. Jackson had numerous eccentric behaviors that made him a notoriously odd character—for instance, he ate only foods he did not like, as a punishment for his sins. A fanatical Presbyterian, he considered the Confederate cause to be part of his service to God, and he pursued (and killed) the enemy with Old Testament zeal. Piercing blue eyes and a bushy beard dominated his appearance; his shabby clothes, high-pitched voice, and physical clumsiness belied his battlefield skill. From early May to early June, Professor Jackson conducted a lesson on military tactics in the Shenandoah Valley. He confounded the Union by marching farther than they had imagined possible and controlling the mountain passes in and out of the Valley, using the topography to prevent the Federals from maximizing their two-to-one numerical advantage; his actions forced Lincoln three times to withdraw troops from McClellan's planned operation. Ultimately, the "Valley Campaign" probably saved Richmond and the Confederacy in 1862.

Outside the Confederate capital, McClellan waited, complaining that Lincoln had sabotaged his plan and believing he faced superior numbers—he actually had a nearly two-to-one edge. His forces were arrayed on either side of the Chickahominy River, only a few miles east of the city. When heavy rains made the river seem impassable, General Johnston decided to attack the Union Army's south flank. On May 31, the Southerners advanced, but in this instance it was the Confederates who got lost and confused in the wooded, swampy terrain. Fortunately for the Union, one corps under General Edwin Sumner managed to make it south of the river—even as flood waters topped the bridges—and stabilize the south flank. Johnston tried again the next day, with even less success. In two days of chaotic fighting (known as the Battle of Seven Pines or Fair Oaks) the Confederates suffered six thousand casualties; the Union five thousand.

Of lasting importance was that Johnston himself was severely wounded, and Davis replaced him with Robert E. Lee. McClellan dismissed Lee as "timid and irresolute," but Lee turned out to be the ultimate risk-taker. Descended from a distinguished Virginia family (his father was Revolutionary War hero "Light Horse Harry" Lee), Lee graduated from West Point second in his class and embarked on a distinguished career in the United States Army. Known for his handsome features and flirtatious personality (and sometimes bawdy humor), but also for honor, piety, and hospitality, Lee seemed the very embodiment of the "Southern gentleman." Conflicted about secession, he stayed loyal to his state despite his love of the Union and an offer from Lincoln to take field command of all Union armies.

Having replaced Johnston, Lee planned another attack against McClellan's superior forces. In late June, with the two armies in virtually the same positions as the month before, Lee decided to attack the Union Army's north flank. Jackson had returned from the Valley to give Lee nearly ninety thousand men; McClellan had about one hundred thousand troops (his intelligence claimed Lee had more than two hundred thousand against him). As unobtrusively as possible, Lee moved Jackson and the bulk of his army north of the Chickahominy River, gambling that McClellan would fail to exploit the precarious Confederate position to the south, where fewer than twenty-five thousand Rebels defended Richmond against seventy thousand Yankees. On June 25, Lee's attack began, but almost nothing went right. Jackson performed especially poorly and drew stinging criticism from another fiery Confederate, General A. P. Hill. Lee pressed the attack several more days, with ever-greater losses. Still, the Union retreated slowly south and east, away from Richmond and toward its supply base at Harrison's Landing on the James River. The last day of heavy fighting was July 1, when Confederates launched nearly a dozen charges against a heavily fortified Union position. Losses were staggering. In the Seven Days Battles, as they are known, Confederates reported twenty thousand casualties, the Union "only" sixteen thousand.

McClellan had an even greater edge now than before the fighting began, but still he refused to attack. Instead, he wrote to Secretary of War Edwin Stanton and blamed his defeat on lack of support from Washington: "If I save this Army now, I tell you plainly that I owe no thanks to you or any other persons in Washington. You have done your best to sacrifice this army," McClellan told Stanton. Unnerved by the level of killing, he concluded that "I have seen too many dead and wounded comrades," a sentiment that apparently forestalled any more attacks. McClellan's failure underscored how important were both a commanding general's ability to sense the opponent's strengths and weaknesses, and his willingness to take advantage of them. These were qualities McClellan lacked, but that Lee had in abundance.

Bitterly disappointed, Lincoln ordered McClellan to return his army to Washington. Before McClellan and his men made it to the capital, a separate new force took the field, commanded by General John Pope. A tall, combative, and supremely confident man, Pope quickly charged into northern Virginia, pledging to take the whole Confederate army. In mid-August, Lee rushed his army north to meet this new threat, leaving Richmond guarded by a skeleton force. McClellan's army was still encamped on the James River, just south of the city, but he refused to support Pope's invasion by moving on Richmond. Instead, McClellan's inactive forces slowly died from disease during the height of summer in Virginia. Jackson first stopped the Union advance at the Battle of Cedar Mountain, and then he and Lee joined forces in northern Virginia. They outmaneuvered the Union and took a defensive position north of Manassas Junction, actually on the same ground where the First Battle of Bull Run was fought the previous year. There, on August 29–30, Lee won the Second Battle of Bull Run, which he considered his greatest victory. Outnumbered again, the Confederates suffered nine thousand casualties against Pope's sixteen thousand, making it one of the more lopsided defeats of the entire war. Lincoln fired Pope, exiled him to Minnesota, and unhappily reinstated McClellan. While his advisors complained (Salmon Chase said McClellan deserved to be shot), Lincoln felt he had no choice; the army needed confidence, and the troops still loved "little Mac."

The rift between McClellan and Pope was about more than professional jealousy. It also reflected two growing divisions within the Union war effort: Republicans versus Democrats, and "limited war" versus "total war" advocates. McClellan was a high-profile proslavery Democrat who believed the war needed to be fought "upon the highest principles of Christian civilization." In a July 1862 letter to Lincoln he summarized this attitude about the war, which was supported by most Democrats. "It should not be at all a war upon population; but against armed forces and political organizations. Neither confiscation of property . . . [n]or forcible abolition of slavery should be contemplated," and "all private property and unarmed persons should be strictly protected." Finally, "a declaration of radical views, especially upon slavery, will rapidly disintegrate our present armies." The war effort, in short, must not damage Southern property or target civilians. Of course Lincoln himself had once supported basically the same policy, but much had happened since April 1861.

A growing number of antislavery Republicans—increasingly known as "Radical Republicans"—favored a more aggressive strategy. Among them was Pope. When he invaded Virginia in July 1862, he put Southern civilians on notice that their property was subject to confiscation and that he would tolerate no interference with his army. "If a soldier or legitimate follower of the army be fired upon from any house the house shall be razed to the ground," he announced. And even more draconian: "If any person, having taken the oath of allegiance [to the Union] be found to have violated it, he shall be shot." Finally, Pope declared that he would detail no men to guard civilian property, which critics charged was a virtual authorization for Union troops to pillage the country. In separate orders from

Washington in July and August, Lincoln essentially approved Pope's field orders, allowing commanders "in an orderly manner [to] seize and use any property, real or personal, which may be necessary or convenient . . . for supplies." Tales of Yankee aggression were soon common among Southern civilians and troops in northern Virginia. Lee's men were shocked when they returned to the counties south of Manassas, where Pope's men had been encamped, to find destroyed fields and homes. Union war strategy was changing.

From spring 1861 to fall 1862, there was no decisive military turning point. The Confederacy beat back two Union invasions of Virginia, while the North made significant progress in its western offensive, particularly along the Mississippi River. Both sides suffered shocking human losses, forcing Lincoln and Davis to reassess strategy and what victory required. Among Republicans, growing sentiment favored a more aggressive war strategy as no real Unionist movement emerged in the Confederacy. Most important, Lincoln himself seemed convinced that a limited war could not succeed. This led him to confront the question of how far he could go without shattering the Union war effort. The ultimate task of balancing the needs and desires of his military commanders with public opinion, of course, fell to Lincoln. Southerners' determined resistance made it seem that a quick victory was no longer possible. Finally, the battles at Shiloh, Seven Pines, and the Seven Days changed the war for civilians as well as soldiers. By late 1862, the war had affected nearly every family in some way, and the conflict reached into small communities across the Confederacy and the Union.

John D. Billings on His Decision to Enlist in the Union Army (1862)

This passage, written long after the war, describes the decision, made early in the war, of one Union man to volunteer. It is part of a much larger work that discusses camp life in the Union Army and the evolving conditions and sentiments among the men as the war continued and grew more deadly.

After I had obtained the reluctant consent of my father to enlist—my mother never gave hers—the next step necessary was to make selection of the organization with which to identify my fortunes. I well remember the to me eventful August evening when that decision to enlist was arrived at. The Union army, then under McClellan, had been driven from before Richmond in the disastrous Peninsular Campaign, and now the Rebel army under General Lee was marching on Washington. President Lincoln had issued a call for three hundred thousand three-years' volunteers. One evening, shortly after this call was made, I met three of my former school mates and neighbors in the chief village of the town I then called home, and after a brief discussion of the outlook, one of the quartette challenged, or "stumped," the others to enlist. The challenge was promptly accepted all around, and hands were shaken to bind the agreement. I will add in passing that three of the four stood by that agreement; the fourth was induced by increased wages to remain with his employer, although he entered the service later in the war and bears a shell scar on his face to attest his honorable service.

After the decision had been reached . . . I returned to my home and either that night or the next morning informed my father of the resolution I had taken. Instead of interposing an emphatic objection as he had done the previous year, he said, "Well, you know I do not want you to go, but it is very evident that a great many more must go, and if you have fully determined upon it I shall not object."

John D. Billings, *Hard Tack and Coffee: Soldier's Life in the Civil War* (Boston, 1888).

Ulysses S. Grant at the Battle of Shiloh (1862)

Grant finished his long memoirs just before his death in 1885. This description of the Battle of Shiloh captures the on-field conditions and its fierce nature, which made it a famously brutal encounter.

Shiloh was the severest battle fought at the West during the war, and but few in the East equalled it for hard, determined fighting. I saw an open field, in our possession on the second day, over which the Confederates had made repeated charges the day before, so covered with dead that it would have been possible to walk across the clearing, in any direction, stepping on dead bodies, without a foot touching the ground. On our side National and Confederate troops were mingled together in about equal proportions; but on the remainder of the field nearly all were Confederates. On one part, which had evidently not been ploughed for several years, probably because the land was poor, bushes had grown up, some to the height of eight or ten feet. There was not one of these left standing unpierced by bullets. The smaller ones were all cut down.

Contrary to all my experience up to that time, and to the experience of the army I was then commanding, we were on the defensive. We were without intrenchments or defensive advantages of any sort, and more than half the army engaged the first day was without experience or even drill as soldiers. The officers with them, except the division commanders and possibly two or three of the brigade commanders, were equally inexperienced in war. The result was a Union victory that gave the men who achieved it great confidence in themselves ever after.

The enemy fought bravely, but they had started out to defeat and destroy an army and capture a position. They failed in both, with very heavy loss in killed and wounded, and must have gone back discouraged and convinced that the "Yankee" was not an enemy to be despised.

Ulysses S. Grant, *Personal Memoirs of U. S. Grant, Volume I* (New York: The Library of America, 1990; orig. 1885), 238–39.

Henry Morton Stanley: The Battle of Shiloh (1862)

Henry Morton Stanley details his unit's assault at the Battle of Shiloh. It is a particularly vivid account of battlefield action, and captures the important role that emotion played in getting men to keep going under fire. Stanley was born in Wales, served in the Confederate and later Union armies, and famously "found" the missionary and explorer David Livingstone in Africa in 1871.

* * * *

We loaded our muskets, and arranged our cartridge pouches ready for use. Our weapons were the obsolete flintlocks and the ammunition was rolled in cartridge-paper, which contained powder, a round ball, and three buckshot. When we loaded we had to tear the paper with our teeth, empty a little powder into the pan, lock it, empty the rest of the powder into the barrel, press paper and ball into the muzzle, and ram home. Then the Orderly-sergeant called the roll, and we knew that the Dixie Greys were present to a man. Soon after, there was a commotion, and we dressed up smartly. . . .

After a steady exchange of musketry, which lasted some time, we heard the order: "Fix Bayonets! On the double-quick!" in tones that thrilled us. There was a simultaneous bound forward, each soul doing his best for the emergency. The Federals appeared inclined to await us; but, at this juncture, our men raised a yell, thousands responded to it, and burst out into the wildest yelling it has ever been my lot to hear. It drove all sanity and order from among us. It served the double purpose of relieving pent-up feelings, and transmitting encouragement along the attacking line. I rejoiced in the shouting like the rest. It reminded me that there were about four hundred companies like the Dixie Greys, who shared our feelings. Most of us, engrossed with the musket-work, had forgotten the fact; but the wave after wave of human voices, louder than all other battle-sounds together, penetrated to every sense, and stimulated our energies to the utmost. . . .

Those savage yells, and the sight of thousands of racing figures coming towards them, discomfited the blue-coats; and when we arrived upon the place where they had stood, they had vanished. Then we caught sight of their beautiful array of tents, before which they had made their stand, after being roused from their Sunday-morning sleep, and huddled into line, at hearing their pickets challenge our skirmishers. The half-dressed dead and wounded showed what a surprise our attack had been. . . .

After being exposed for a few seconds to this fearful downpour, we heard the order to "Lie down, men, and continue your firing!" . . .

How the cannon bellowed, and their shells plunged and bounded, and flew with screeching hisses over us! Their sharp rending explosions and hurtling fragments made us shrink and cower, despite our utmost efforts to be cool and collected. I marveled, as I heard the unintermitting patter, snip, thud, and hum of the bullets, how anyone could live under this raining death. I could hear the balls beating a merciless tattoo on the outer surface of the log, pinging vivaciously as they flew off at a tangent from it, and thudding into something or other, at the rate of a hundred a second. One, here and there, found its way under the log, and buried itself in a comrade's body. One man raised his chest, as if to yawn, and jostled me. I turned to him, and saw that a bullet had gored his whole face, and penetrated into his chest. Another ball struck a man a deadly rap on the head, and he turned on his back and showed his ghastly white face to the sky.

"It is getting too warm, boys!" cried a soldier, and he uttered a vehement curse upon keeping soldiers hugging the ground until every ounce of courage was chilled. He lifted his head a little too high, and a bullet skimmed over the top of the log and hit him fairly in the centre of his forehead, and he fell heavily on his face. But his thought had been instantaneously general; and the officers, with one voice, ordered the charge; and cries of "Forward, forward!" raised us, as with a spring, to our feet, and changed the complexion of our feelings. . . .

Our progress was not so continuously rapid as we desired, for the blues were obdurate . . .

"Forward, forward; don't give them breathing time!" was cried. We instinctively obeyed, and soon came in clear view of the blue-coats, who were scornfully unconcerned at first; but, seeing the leaping tide of men coming on at a tremendous pace, their front dissolved, and they fled in double-quick retreat. Again we felt the "glorious joy of heroes." It carried us on exultantly, rejoicing in the spirit which recognises nothing but the prey. We were no longer an army of soldiers, but so many school-boys racing; in which length of legs, wind, and condition tell.

Henry Morton Stanley, *The Autobiography of Henry Morton Stanley* (Boston: Houghton Mifflin, 1909).

Soldiers from Company G., 71st N.Y. Volunteer Infantry

Library of Congress.

NINE

Families at War in 1861–1862

W HEN THE WAR STARTED, most Americans expected it would be short, and therefore a minor disruption to their lives. As the war continued, however, leaders on both sides had to mobilize more manpower and resources, all the while balancing these military needs with what civilians were willing, or able, to give and endure. Many families found it difficult to function when husbands, fathers, and sons left for the battlefield. Societal expectations pressed particularly hard on women, who were supposed to suffer without complaint the absence—or the permanent loss—of their men for the good of "the cause." Politicians and military leaders in both sections also counted on women to inspire men to volunteer and to stay in service no matter how miserable the war became. In turn, to Lincoln and Davis primarily fell the tasks of energizing and sustaining a greater sense of patriotism among all their citizens. The dynamics of these relationships and considerations proved difficult to gauge and balance. What goals and war aims would reach and inspire the greatest number of men and women? How far could civilians be pushed before they questioned whether or not the war was worth all of the sacrifices, all of the death and destruction? As the war affected more and more families, these questions became more imperative and harder to answer. Lincoln and Davis wrestled with the big questions—war aims, strategy, allocating resources—but tens of thousands of ordinary folks, in cities and small towns and on farms across the country, felt the war's effects and had to decide how, or even if, they would lend their support.

Early in the war, both sides had too many volunteers; men wanted to get into battle "before it was too late" and they "missed all the fun." In May 1861, Lincoln authorized forty-two thousand three-year volunteers; in July, Congress raised that to one million. As a result, more than seven hundred thousand men joined the Union Army, and they became its veteran core for much of the fighting. Across the Union and Confederacy, local community leaders organized the recruiting efforts, often relying on women to play a central role. Many towns or counties held competitions to determine which could raise the most men, with a flag or banner sewn by local women as the prize. Naturally the prize would be presented "by a representative of the fair, gentle sex," as hundreds of announcements stated, a public moment "that no gentleman would want to miss." Rallies included food, drink, music, and dancing, and appealed to young, single men—those expected to answer the call first. Union imagery featured "Lady Liberty," the feminine embodiment of the nation and heritage of the Revolution. American mothers and wives were also asked to emulate the ideals of "Spartan motherhood"—a self-sacrificing philosophy named for the legendary Greek city-state that existed on a culture of warfare.

Certainly for the first six months of the war—from April 1861 through the end of that year's campaign season—the vast majority of Union and Confederate families felt the war only in a limited way. The armies had not reached massive proportions, casualties were relatively limited, and both sides sustained their efforts largely with existing money and materiel. Of course there was death and destruction, even in these first few months. Significant fighting in northern and western Virginia, Kentucky, and Missouri involved some civilians, but most families and communities remained untouched. For Confederates, there was really no occupation by Union forces anywhere until very late in 1861, and their armies could be sustained with food and military supplies the Southern states already had when the war started. Most recruits simply brought clothes and a gun with them; the Confederacy never achieved a standard uniform. The most common color of Southern clothes was "butternut," a soft brown dye (made from the shells of walnuts) that farm families often applied to homespun cloth.

For most Union families the war's first months were similarly undemanding. The humiliating rout at First Bull Run was shocking, and forced many Northerners to admit that the Southern rebellion would not collapse when simply confronted by Union forces. But that realization did not materially affect the vast majority of men and women in the North. Instead, the Northern economy benefited from increased orders for Union ships and supplies, something particularly profitable to skilled and unskilled workers in cities. The U.S. Navy, for instance, had about 40 ships in service in April 1861, but nearly 250 by the end of the year. Many were converted merchant vessels, which required some modifications by skilled metalworkers in New York and other Atlantic Coast cities. As in the Confederacy, there was no shortage of volunteers in 1861. Men flocked to join Union forces, determined to demonstrate that First Bull Run did not characterize Northern manliness or fighting spirit. These first troops often brought uniforms—a wild mixture of colors and designs—and arms purchased by their home communities. The War Department did not function efficiently or effectively until Edwin Stanton replaced Simon Cameron in January 1862. Curtailing corruption and general bungling, Stanton became a trusted advisor for Lincoln, and coordinated purchasing and distribution so that Union forces had everything they needed (often more than they needed) by mid-1862.

The war's first winter—neither army normally campaigned between November and late March—brought only slightly greater uncertainty to most people's lives. Of critical importance was that the harvest cycle was not significantly disrupted by the first months of fighting. Particularly in the Southern states, most crops were planted before the war started, and certainly before heavy enrollments began in midsummer. Also, many white men and most slaves were still on their farms when harvest time arrived, ensuring that the Confederacy had nearly a full season of production. It would be the last one. Compared with the South, in 1861 there was even less trouble for Union farms, very few of which lost more than one adult male to the army, and therefore suffered no real measurable drop in production. In short, through the winter and early spring of 1862, civilians' lives were different, but though several hundred thousand men were in military service and away from home for the first time, there was not widespread material hardship or even great inconvenience.

In the spring and summer of 1862, however, the war suddenly produced massive dislocation and death—epitomized by the horrific results at Shiloh and the battles in Virginia—and the lives of many families changed forever. The nature of the war was transformed in 1862, which brought the conflict "home" to communities across the country, but particularly in the Confederacy. Both Union and Confederate leaders had difficulty adjusting their economies and finding ways to pay for growing military demands, and war weariness became a significant factor, severely limiting volunteers. The Confederacy turned to conscription early in 1862, a decision that bitterly divided Southerners. By the end of 1862, in other words, what began as an "insurrection" (as Lincoln called it), which was supposed to be short and quick, had become a war unlike anything Americans had ever experienced or even imagined.

The single most important transforming development in 1862 was the unprecedented level of killing and dying. At Shiloh in April, more than five thousand men died in the battle or of wounds suffered there; the battles around Richmond and in northern Virginia claimed more than twice that number. The incompatibility of tactics and technology led to such high rates of battlefield casualties. Officers generally followed the Napoleonic formula: move troops quickly and mass your forces to take advantage of the enemy's weak points, then attack, even if outnumbered. Using these tactics, well-led, disciplined, determined troops could defeat a numerically superior opponent. These tactics had made Napoleon a legend and worked well for Americans in Mexico, where they faced an enemy with inferior equipment and training. But in the Civil War, both sides possessed roughly equal discipline and armaments. Perhaps most important, the vast majority of men had rifles instead of smooth-bore muskets. Muskets fired a round shell that came out with no spin (think of a knuckleball pitch in baseball) and were accurate to about 60 yards; rifles, with grooves inside the barrel, fired conical-shaped shells that spun in a spiral (imagine a football pass) and were accurate to about 350 yards. In the hands of trained men, muzzle-loading rifles could be shot twice about every minute or so. This made infantry charges over open ground nearly suicidal, and meant that a small number of men, well-positioned and supplied, often could hold off vastly superior forces. Most generals continued to attack, however, and defenders continued to mow them down.

Diseases killed even more men than battle did. With no clear understanding of germs or sanitation, troops came down with infectious diseases such as influenza, typhoid, and yellow fever, all of which spread through camps like wildfire. Through 1862, both sides suffered more than two hundred thousand casualties and forty thousand deaths. As these figures and long casualty lists appeared in newspapers, by early summer both sides had difficulty refilling their ranks. In the Union, Lincoln's government called for another three hundred thousand men in June, but received few volunteers. The following month, Congress passed the Militia Act, which authorized Lincoln to use some state troops in federal service for a limited time. This provision was designed primarily to prompt state and local leaders to intensify recruiting efforts. Volunteers also received a federal bounty (essentially a "signing bonus") of one hundred dollars, which had started in July 1861. Thus, just one year into the war, Union leaders encountered difficulties enrolling enough volunteers to meet demands. They began to consider other means of raising troops, and they had to weigh the impact that such massive mobilization would have on civilian life and morale.

The Confederacy's manpower shortage required more drastic action. Jefferson Davis had only 1.1 million white men of military age available (compared with the Union's 4.6 million). Many Southerners volunteered in the first few months, but as in the Union, that enthusiasm quickly waned. Most of the first Confederate troops had signed on for twelve months, and their terms were due to expire in April/May 1862, just as that year's campaign season began. By late April, in fact, General McClellan's huge Union army was just outside Richmond. On April 16, the Confederate Congress (pushed by Davis and Lee) enacted the first conscription law in American history. The law held all white men between ages eighteen and thirty-five liable for military service for the duration of the war; in September, the upper age rose to forty-five. Men currently in the army, in effect, reenlisted for life. Finally, conscription was implemented by the central government in Richmond, bypassing states and local communities, which violated the supposed Confederate ideology of states' rights.

Conscription alienated Southerners more than any other single action of the Richmond government. Publicly, men declared it unnecessary and insulting; "real men," they asserted, did not need to be forced to do their duty. In reality, the Confederacy could not have survived long without conscription: mandatory reenlistment kept veterans in the army; and the threat of being labeled a conscript prompted tens of thousands more to volunteer. But it also divided Confederate communities and even families. Men and women across the South petitioned for exemptions, citing as grounds the security of women and children or the needs of rural farming communities. Conscription exposed wide cracks in the supposedly united white Confederacy, making people wonder about the "loyalty" and devotion of their neighbors. As the year progressed, the combination of heavy losses and conscription caused men and women to question Confederate leadership, and even the whole cause of independence.

Beyond general opposition to the idea of centralized conscription, specific provisions of the laws alienated poor, non-slaveowning farmers. Numerous exemptions allowed men—particularly wealthy, educated, and middle-class men—to avoid conscription. Teachers, professors, ministers, and a variety of skilled artisans could apply for exemptions. Most unpopular, however, were two provisions that obviously favored wealthy planters. First, the September 1862 act included a provision that men who owned twenty or more slaves could be exempted from mandatory service. The logic was sound: slavery depended on white men to maintain authority through violence, and so a certain number needed to stay at home. Furthermore, only a few hundred men ever avoided conscription because of the rule. But it was a public relations disaster, and non-slaveowners complained about "a rich man's war but a poor man's fight." Second, the law also allowed men to hire substitutes from among those not otherwise eligible. Substitutes served for three years or until they were eligible themselves. Lawyers in Southern cities became "substitute brokers" and took out regular advertisements in local newspapers. These two provisions raised furious protests from poor Confederates, and in whole sections of the South—particularly mountainous areas, where families owned few slaves—there was an immediate, and measurable, decline in support for Davis and the war effort.

In the summer of 1862, some Confederates also faced a new type of threat from Union invasion, reflected in the policies of General John Pope in northern Virginia. Pope notified Southern civilians that he would confiscate property needed by his army, seize that of anyone who aided the Confederates, including their slaves, and execute men who shot at Union troops. As many feared, Pope's orders encouraged some Union officers and men to steal or simply destroy civilian property at will. Confederates reacted angrily. Jefferson Davis announced that for every civilian killed under Pope's command he would order one of Pope's captured officers hanged. With each new Yankee "outrage" reported, men absent from northern Virginia were driven nearly to tears by the thought of their wives and children exposed to such dangers. For thousands of Southerners, Union invasion marked the true commencement of war and the moment their lives changed forever. Many Confederate soldiers, as General Joseph E. Johnston phrased it, "were compelled to choose between their military service and the strongest obligations men know—their duties to their wives and children." How long would the Southern war effort continue in the face of that choice?

Resentment and anger over Union occupation superficially worked to unite white Confederates, but in the long term it divided communities and bred suspicion. The Union Army offered occupied Southerners the chance to make money by selling them food and other supplies. It also meant that men were beyond the reach of Confederate conscription officers, something many men and their families welcomed. Those opportunities and changed conditions appealed to some Southerners, especially those who questioned secession in the first place. Men and women who came slowly to "the cause" could now register their Unionism openly, although they faced reprisal when Northern troops left. Who was really loyal? Who might be friendly with the Yankees? Those questions were increasingly difficult to answer. These dissentious issues threatened to become more intense and cause greater problems for Confederate leaders as the Union Army advanced into more and more Southern territory.

Union invasion also increased Southern anxieties about the slave population. At the least, slaves found it easier to escape when Union troops were nearby. Many Southern whites, however, feared much more than runaways. Stories circulated of slaves murdering women, refusing to work, running away, and plotting rebellion. In Alabama, Addie Harris wrote, "I lay down at night, and do not know what hour . . . my house may be broken open and myself and children murdered. . . . My negroes very often get to fighting." White women everywhere assumed new responsibilities, adding to their already long list of duties. Many wives of non-slaveowners, for instance, had often helped in the fields during harvest time, but with husbands in service, they had to work daily at weeding and other physically demanding farm chores previously left to men. Many slaveowning women faced the additional challenge of trying to motivate and discipline slaves. This was work that women normally did not perform and for which they were physically unprepared or incapable; many slaves simply did not respect white women's ability to force them to work through the threat of violence. "The negroes just won't work, no matter how I threaten," one Georgia woman wrote to her husband.

Also in 1862 the Union blockade began to affect Southern civilians.

Although far from perfect, the blockade limited what Confederates could import and export, causing shortages of some luxury goods and necessities. The yearly agricultural production in 1861 was mostly undisturbed by the war, but unfortunately for the Confederacy, few planters changed their habits and stuck with cotton instead of growing more food. That decision meant that Southern armies and civilians began experiencing shortfalls by early 1862, after which the fighting disrupted normal production in many areas and exacerbated the problem. Davis and other Confederate leaders tried to balance production of cotton and food in a way that most benefited their overall strategic goals. In particular, they anticipated paying for the war with cotton exports, not an unreasonable assumption given antebellum trends. In 1860, cotton amounted to nearly two-thirds of all American exports (by value). Confederates expected a Union blockade, of course, but for that they had a confident answer: King Cotton.

"Would any sane nation make war on cotton?" South Carolina senator James Henry Hammond asked in 1858. Without Southern cotton, "England would topple headlong and carry the whole civilized world with her, save the South. No, you dare not make war on cotton. No power on earth dares to make war upon it. Cotton *is* king." Upon this widely accepted set of beliefs rested Confederate diplomacy. The scenario that Southerners outlined went like this: after one lost cotton season, British textile manufacturing would slow to a crawl; workers would lose jobs and riot in the streets; mill owners would pressure Parliament to reopen trade with the South; and therefore the British navy would intervene and break the Union blockade. After decades of phenomenal growth in cotton exports, and accompanying profits, nearly all Southern planters and politicians accepted this as truth. The King Cotton strategy, of course, depended on continued production of the great Southern staple so it would be on hand when Britain came calling. But the Confederacy's growing armies needed food, niter (or saltpeter) for gunpowder, artillery pieces, leather, and dozens of other necessities. With labor already growing scarce in 1862, how best to balance these competing needs became a matter for the leaders in Richmond. Beyond that, Davis had to persuade or compel Southerners to adhere to the policies he thought necessary. These strategic decisions were difficult, and became more troublesome as the war progressed. Also uncertain was just how much influence Davis's government could exercise in, for instance, rural Arkansas or Alabama.

In 1862, after nine months of probing and desultory inaction, Union and Confederate forces slaughtered one another in unprecedented numbers. Through 1862, Americans lost about five times more husbands, sons, and brothers than in all of the country's previous wars combined. Southerners experienced invasion, occupation, conscription into national military service, and the beginning of slavery's disintegration as thousands of men and women ran away. By the end of the year, nearly one-half of all Southern white men between ages eighteen and forty-five were in military service or already dead. Thousands of women and children became refugees. Union families experienced less trauma, but there was less unanimity about the war itself. Democrats, border-state slaveowners, and disillusioned men and women across the Union questioned Lincoln's leadership and military strategy, and the entire direction of the war. Both presidents faced difficulties filling out their armies and paying for the rapidly widening war efforts. How to meet these spiraling military needs and still maintain civilian morale and support became increasingly complicated. And the longer the war continued, and the more men killed, the more likely it became that revolutionary change would result.

Ada W. Bacot: Diary of a Confederate Nurse
(October 27, 1861)

*Ada Bacot, a South Carolina widow without children, describes
her reasons for volunteering as a nurse and the emotions
surrounding that decision. Many women, Northern and
Southern, experienced the same conflicting sentiments and
advice as they considered how to contribute to the war effort.*

I am at last almost sure of my trip to Virginia, I had a letter from Mr.
Barnwell this morning asking me to go on at once, also one from Mr. Kirk-
patrick saying he is quite willing to alow me the proceeds of the cotton I
sent down last week. I can't discribe my feelings I am so thankful I can go,
God has heard my prayer. Oh! that I may be able to perform my duty. Pa
is going on with me, tis too delightful to be true. Everyone at church today
seemed to be glad for me, they seemed to think I was going to do something very noble. I only feel I am about to do my duty—I can't see that I
am going to do anything so wonderful. Most people wonder I am willing
to under take it they say to me, just think of the hardships you will be
obliged to endure. If I were not willing to endure them I can see no virtue
in my going. I am not going for my own pleasure.

Jean V. Berlin, ed., *A Confederate Nurse: The Diary of Ada W. Bacot, 1860–1863*
(Columbia, SC: University of South Carolina Press, 1994), 50.

Margaret Junkin Preston Describes Inflation
in the Confederacy (April–September 1862)

*Inflation was a problem for civilians, particularly in the
Confederacy, throughout the war. In this diary entry,*

Southerner Margaret Preston describes the growing problem of inflation, and her own personal loss. It suggests the war's widening impact on civilians throughout 1862.

✯ ✯ ✯ ✯

April 3d

... Calico is not to be had; a few pieces had been offered at 40 cents per yard. Coarse, unbleached cottons are very occasionally to be met with, and are caught up eagerly at 40 cents per yard. Such material as we used to give ninepence for (common blue twill) is a bargain now at 40 cents, and then of a very inferior quality. Soda, if to be had at all, is 75 cents per lb. Coffee is not to be bought. We have some on hand, and for eight months have drunk a poor mixture, half wheat, half coffee. Many persons have nothing but wheat or rye.

These are some of the *very trifling* effects of this horrid and senseless war. Just now I am bound under the apprehension of having my husband again enter the service; and if he goes, he says he will not return until the war closes, if indeed he come back alive. May God's providence interpose to prevent his going! His presence is surely needed at home; his hands are taken away by the militia draught, and he has almost despaired of having his farms cultivated this year. His overseer is draughted, and will have to go, unless the plea of sickness will avail to release him, as he has been seriously unwell. ...

Sept 3d

... Yesterday asked the price of a calico dress; "Fifteen dollars and sixty cents!" Tea is $20. per lb. A merchant told me he gave $50. for a pound of sewing silk! The other day our sister, Mrs. Cocke, purchased 5 gallons of whiskey, for which, by way of favor, she only paid $50.! It is selling for $15. per gallon. Very coarse unbleached cotton (ten cent cotton) I was asked 75 cts. for yesterday. Eight dollars a pair for servants' coarse shoes. Mr. P. paid $11. for a pair for Willy. These prices will do to wonder over after a while.

Sept. 4th

The worst has happened—our fearful suspense is over: Willy, the gentle, tender-hearted, brave boy, lies in a soldier's grave on the Plains of Manassas! This has been a day of weeping and of woe to this household. I did not know how I loved the dear boy. My heart is wrung with grief to think that his sweet face, his genial smile, his sympathetic heart are gone. My eyes ache with weeping.

Elizabeth Preston Allan, *The Life and Letters of Margaret Junkin Preston* (Boston: Houghton, Mifflin, and Co., 1903), 134–47.

Sarah Fales, Middletown, RI, to Edmund Fales (May 13, 1862)

As the war became more brutal and deadly in 1862, many Northerners worried about a general draft. This letter recounts the feelings in one community, and the efforts of men there to avoid being forced into Union service.

✳ ✳ ✳ ✳

. . . you ask how the Middletown boys feel about the draft I do not know much about the boys but some of the men have ben terribly frightend they met at the townhouse again last week not to raise recruits but to raise money to hire men to go for thim they voted $5.00 bounty some proposed raising enough to make a bargain with the railroad contractor to furnish Irishmen long enough to fill out their quota Father says there will be no drafting as long as there is a dollar left in the town, what do you think of that for patriotism and love of country in such times of danger as these we have reason to be thankfull it is not so everywhere

Father says he understands that those in the Service when the draft is made up are not subject to it in less than six months or a year the draft for the last three hundred thousand men has been postpond until the first of september these are to be nine months militia men. . . .

Letters of Sarah E. Fales, Edmund W. Fales Family Papers, Rhode Island Historical Society, Providence, RI. Quoted in Silber and Sievens, eds., 110–11.

Governor Joseph Brown (Canton, GA) to President Jefferson Davis (October 18, 1862)

Georgia governor Joseph Brown opposed Confederate conscription as a violation of states' rights and individual liberty. He also believed that it weakened the defense of Southern states and lowered morale among the fighting men. In this letter—one of many that he wrote to Davis—he outlines some of his constitutional and practical objections to conscription.

At this critical period in our public affairs, when it is absolutely necessary that each State keep an *organization* for home protection, Congress, with your sanction, has extended the Conscription Act to embrace all between 35 and 45 subject to military duty, giving you the power to suspend the Act as above stated. If you refuse to exercise this power and are permitted to take all between 35 and 45 as conscripts, you *disband* and *destroy* all military organization in this State, and leave her people utterly powerless to protect their own families even against their own slaves. . . .

The late act of Congress . . . utterly destroys all State military organizations, and encroaches upon the reserved rights of the State, but strikes down her sovereignty at a single blow, and tears from her the right arm of strength, by which she alone can maintain her existence, and protect those most dear to her and most dependent upon her. . . .

The volunteer enters the service of his own free will. . . . He may be as ready as any citizen of the State to volunteer, if permitted to enjoy the constitutional rights which have been allowed to others, in the choice of his officers and associates. But if these are denied him, and he is seized like a serf and hurried into an association repulsive to his feelings, and placed under officers in whom he has no confidence, he then feels that this is the Government's war, not his; that he is the mere instrument of arbitrary power, and that he is no longer laboring to establish constitutional liberty, but to build up a military despotism for its ultimate but certain overthrow.

Allen D. Chandler, ed., *The Confederate Records of the State of Georgia*, Vol. II (Atlanta: Charles P. Byrd, State Printer, 1910), 294–302.

Richmond Enquirer: Advertisements for Substitutes (1862)

Confederate men who were liable for conscription could avoid service by providing a substitute. Substitute "brokering" became a major business in many Southern cities in the summer of 1862 (and in the Union when its draft went into effect the next year).

WANTED—A SUBSTITUTE for a conscript to serve during the war. Any good man over the age of 35 years, not a resident of Virginia, or a foreigner, may hear of a good situation by calling at Mr. GEORGE BAGBY'S office, Shockoe Slip, to-day, between the hours of 9 and 11 A.M.

A COUNTRYMAN

WANTED—Immediately, a SUBSTITUTE. A man over 35 years old, or under 18, can get a good price by making immediate application to Room No. 50, Monument Hotel, or by addressing "J.W.," through Richmond P.O.

WANTED—A SUBSTITUTE, to go in a first-rate Georgia company of infantry, under the heroic Jackson. A gentleman whose health is impaired, will give a fair price for a substitute. Apply immediately at ROOM, No. 13, Post-Office Department, third story, between the hours of 10 and 3 o'clock.

A Soldier's Farewell

This image—from a pictorial envelope, popular in the Union during the war—portrays an idealized scene of a wife and her small children bidding a tearful good-bye to their husband and father. Women were supposed to support the war effort by encouraging men to enlist.

Collection of the New-York Historical Society, #AJ88016.

Our Hearts Are with Our Brothers in the Field

This is another image from a Northern envelope, depicting a woman sacrificing for the cause and supporting "her men" in the field by sewing shirts.

Collection of the New-York
Historical Society, #AJ88007.

TEN

Military Strategy and the War in 1862: Runaway Slaves, the Battle of Antietam, and the Emancipation Proclamation

FROM THE BEGINNING OF THE WAR, white men and women on both sides insisted that they were not fighting about slavery. President Lincoln tried to keep slavery out of any discussion of the war, repeating that he was fighting only to restore the Union and uphold the principles of popular government and majority rule. Others, however, acknowledged that the war was likely to engulf slavery. Ulysses Grant noted in the war's first weeks that "In all this I can but see the doom of slavery." A student of war, Grant knew that all wars are progressive, tending to promote greater and faster social change than ever occurred in peacetime. The great abolitionist speaker and ex-slave Frederick Douglass conceded that in 1861 most white Americans were not ready to discuss slavery. But "in the end," he predicted, all would have to admit that "the war now being waged in this land is a war for and against slavery."

No one knew better what the war was about than the slaves themselves. Most enslaved men and women exhibited little interest in debating the nature of freedom or the meaning of American democracy. But they recognized a good chance to escape when they saw one. Slaves had always taken advantage of confusion or division within the white community—tens of thousands ran away during the American Revolution and the War of 1812. As the Union Army invaded the Confederacy, slaves ran away by the hundreds, then by the thousands; runaways who did not make it to Northern cities gravitated to the closest elements of the Union Army.

These refugees presented Northern generals with a dilemma. Technically, under the Fugitive Slave Act of 1850, they were obligated to return runaway slaves to their masters, and initially many Northern officers tried to do so. Union general Benjamin Butler, of Massachusetts, decided that returning slaves to help the Confederate war effort made no sense (other Northerners expressed the same sentiment). Balding, overweight, and sporting a disheveled, drooping moustache, Butler was a shrewd politician who sensed the growing popularity of abolition in his native state. In May 1861, while commanding Union forces in eastern Virginia, Butler refused to return three runaways who came to his camp, labeling them "contraband of war"—a term applied to property that aided the enemy. His phrase entered the public vocabulary, and Lincoln, after some consideration, approved Butler's decision. On August 6, 1861, the Republican-controlled Congress passed the Confiscation Act, authorizing seizure of slaves who escaped from "rebel" masters on grounds they had been "employed" in the Confederate cause.

As news of these Northern decisions spread among slaves, they flocked to Union lines across the Confederacy, often announcing, "I'm contraband," as they came into camp. Many Union commanders honestly tried to distinguish between those slaves who ran away from "rebel" masters or those who had fled "loyal" masters, and then returned slaves to pro-Union owners. Over time, however, the distinction became nearly impossible to maintain; slaves from the border states, of course, were shrewd enough never to admit that they had escaped from Union masters. Furthermore, as the number of contrabands swelled, Union generals came to appreciate their contributions to the war effort. Runaways worked as teamsters, cooks, laundresses, grave diggers, and in dozens of other manual jobs—according to one estimate nearly two hundred thousand African American men and women worked for the Union Army during the war.

Susie King, for instance, was only fourteen when she and her uncle escaped from Savannah, Georgia. She worked as a laundress and a teacher, and eventually married a Union soldier. John Boston's experience probably was not unusual. He ran away from his Maryland master early in 1862, finding refuge and work as a personal servant to a Union soldier (likely an officer) with a New York regiment. Writing to his wife, he proclaimed himself "free from al the Slavers Lash." He went on to say, "I am With a very nice man and have All that hart Can Wish." Thousands of slaves also worked as spies, giving information to the Union Army and helping Northern men to escape from behind enemy lines.

Even with all this work on behalf of the Northern war effort, the most important contribution that runaway slaves made was to force Union leaders, especially President Lincoln, to confront the fact that the war was, somehow, about slavery. Many abolitionists, of course, had argued from the beginning that the war presented a chance to strike at slavery. Massachusetts senator Charles Sumner, mostly recovered from his 1856 caning at the hand of South Carolina representative Preston Brooks, and Frederick Douglass, whom Lincoln came to respect, were among the most persistent antislavery leaders who lobbied the president. Despite the president's basic agreement that slavery was the most important underlying cause of the war, abolitionists struggled to overcome his conviction that widespread racism among Northern whites would doom any move toward emancipation. In short, Lincoln feared it would divide the North and wreck the Union war effort.

Eventually, however, slaves and abolitionists convinced the president that there was one way that he could "sell" emancipation to Northern voters. The pitch was simple: freeing slaves would weaken the Confederate war effort, hastening a Union victory. The war would end sooner and the lives of Northern boys would be saved. The argument was straightforward, logical, and accurate. It had the great advantage of skirting a debate about civil rights or equality because it did not rest on the assertions that slavery was morally wrong or that African Americans deserved basic human rights. In short, it was an argument that accommodated Northern racism and made emancipation simply part of the war effort, not the goal of the war. Perhaps most important, it appealed to the army itself. This was critical for President Lincoln, who feared a wave of desertion if he made the war a contest for emancipation. Similarly fearful, Charles Sumner wrote in November 1861 that emancipation should "be presented strictly as a measure of military necessity." This great advocate of ending slavery pragmatically conceded, "Abolition is not to be the object of the war, but simply one of its agencies." Following this same logic, Republicans in Congress passed a second Confiscation Act on July 12, 1862. It allowed for seizure of all property owned by anyone supporting the rebellion and promised that slaves already liberated or escaped would be "forever free." Again the course of the war and its unexpected brutality proved critical. By mid-

1862, Union casualties were great enough that Lincoln and many other Republicans began to believe that enough Northerners would embrace emancipation—probably gradual and partial—in order to shorten the war.

Weakening the Southern war effort was one practical consideration. Another was European diplomacy. If the Union made emancipation part of the war, then Great Britain—the world's foremost antislavery government—would not intervene to help the Confederacy. Finally, Lincoln came to believe that all the sacrifices had to be made worthwhile. Simply restoring the old Union seemed insufficient—not after Shiloh, Fair Oaks, the Seven Days, and Second Bull Run. Emancipation would bring a higher purpose to the Union cause, and to fight and win such a brutal conflict without addressing its primary cause seemed increasingly foolish. What if the Union prevailed after years of struggle and hundreds of thousands of deaths, only to have to fight another war in twenty years? Thus, on July 21, 1862, President Lincoln announced to his shocked Cabinet members that he had decided to issue a presidential proclamation that would emancipate slaves in the unoccupied Confederacy. His Cabinet was divided on the idea, and Lincoln followed the advice of Secretary of State William Seward, who believed that any proclamation should wait for a Union victory, or the measure might seem desperate. President Lincoln would have to wait two months for the victory he needed, and first suffered the jarring defeat at Second Bull Run, where Pope was humiliated by Lee. In its aftermath, McClellan, still dedicated to a limited war, reassumed command of the Army of the Potomac.

Buoyed by his victories in Virginia, Lee decided to invade the Union for the first time. Targeting the railroad center of Harrisburg, Pennsylvania, he crossed the Potomac in early September with nearly forty-five thousand men. He had several goals in mind. First, it was nearing harvest time in Virginia, and Lee knew that both Union and Confederate armies had already stripped much of the state bare during the first year of the war. Giving his native state a much needed rest, Lee hoped his men could live off the fertile fields of Maryland and Pennsylvania for a while. Second, Southern leaders hoped that one more big victory—especially on Northern soil—might convince Great Britain that the Confederacy was there to stay. If the British recognized the Confederacy, it could lead to England's financial or even military intervention. Finally, if Lee and his men could win a dramatic victory in the Union, they might even force Lincoln to consider a negotiated peace settlement. At the least, a Confederate victory would hurt Republicans in the upcoming fall elections. Democrats, Southerners knew, would be more inclined to consider peace.

The invasion began poorly for Lee. In what remains one of the most famous incidents of the war, on September 13, a Union soldier discovered a copy of Lee's battle plan (wrapped around three cigars), which was accidentally left by a Confederate officer in a field near Frederick, Maryland. The plan showed Lee's army dangerously divided into five pieces. McClellan vowed, "Here is a paper with which if I cannot whip 'Bobbie Lee,' I will be willing to go home." Still, McClellan failed to move for nearly twenty-four hours. Given an extra day to recover, Lee hastily reunited much of his scattered army. By the night of September 16, 1862, the two great armies came together outside the small town of Sharpsburg, Maryland. The Confederates took up a defensive position east of the town and in front of a small river known as Antietam Creek.

The Battle of Antietam Creek, which turned out to be the deadliest day in American history (still), unfolded as three nearly separate engagements (see map on p. 134). McClellan still had not learned to coordinate his attacks or take advantage of his numerical superiority, and the day was a series of tantalizing but missed opportunities for the Union. Lincoln, growing more confident in his own grasp of military strategy, had urged a more coordinated approach for months, and had McClellan thrown all his troops into the battle—at any one of several points—he would have won an overwhelming victory and possibly ended the war.

At dawn on September 17, the Federals opened the attack by moving forward on their right flank, led by the First Corps under General Joseph "Fighting Joe" Hooker. Hooker was famous for drinking whiskey and playing poker, and he reveled in his colorful nickname. Advancing through a large cornfield, grown high and ready for harvest, Hooker's men moved toward a plain white church on top of a small plateau. As they emerged from the tall stalks of corn, they ran into the Confederate corps led by "Stonewall" Jackson. The Southerners drove back the Federal assault, only to run into another Union corps that surged back through the flattening cornfield. Union troops again seemed ready to break through and "roll up" the Confederate left flank, but Lee advanced some of his last reserves and stopped the second Union attack. A third Union assault broke through the Confederate line at about noon, but they, too, were stopped by Southern reinforcements drawn from elsewhere on the field. After five hours of continuous fighting more than twelve thousand men lay dead or wounded, and no ground had changed hands.

The last Union attack on the Confederate left helped shift the battle toward the center of both lines, where Confederates occupied a small sunken road that formed a crucial link in their position. Two regiments led by General John B. Gordon held off a series of Union attacks, using the sunken road as a trench from which to cut down the attackers. Gordon was shot five times, but limped along behind his men until the last bullet ripped through one of his cheeks; amazingly, he survived the battle and the war. Finally, some Northerners overwhelmed the stubborn defenders of "Bloody Lane," as it became known, and the Confederate center split open. Again McClellan faltered. He refused to send in his unused reserves, eight thousand men in the Union Sixth Corps, whose commander begged McClellan to let him attack. One Confederate officer wrote later that "the end of the Confederacy was in sight." But saved by McClellan's hesitancy, the Confederates cobbled together another makeshift line and held against the Union breakthrough.

About the same time, the third part of the battle reached its climax. At the southern end of the line—the Confederate right—Union troops had tried most of the day to fight their way across a stone bridge that crossed Antietam Creek. The Union left was commanded by General Ambrose Burnside, an old friend of McClellan, whose muttonchop whiskers (now called sideburns) were his most distinctive feature. The land on the Confederate side of "Burnside's Bridge" rose sharply to a small flat-topped hill that gave the Southerners a commanding view of the creek and a perfect defensive position from which to fire on the attacking Yankees. The Confederates on the bluff were led by Georgia lawyer-politician Robert Toombs, who had been the favorite to be named president of the Confederacy in 1861. Famous for his dramatic, sometimes blustering speeches, the red-faced Toombs lost the presidency in part because of a drinking problem. Toombs apparently was sober, however, for what proved to be his finest military moment as his four hundred men held off nearly thirteen thousand Federals for more than three hours. Once again, though, the Union men finally overwhelmed the outnumbered defenders and threatened to engulf the Confederate right flank. Lee's army was saved when his last reserves arrived from Harpers Ferry. Led by General Ambrose Powell Hill, a prickly Virginian wearing his trademark bright red shirt, the Confederates launched a desperate, dramatic charge into Burnside's men and drove them back. McClellan, again fatefully timid, refused to send in his Fifth Corps, fresh troops waiting behind the lines; the demoralized Northerners retreated back across Burnside's Bridge. The day ended with six thousand men dead and seventeen thousand more wounded.

Lee's army was reduced from forty-five thousand to about thirty thousand combat-ready men, but McClellan refused to pursue the attack on September 18. Instead, he allowed Lee to make a retreat back to Virginia. President Lincoln was livid, sensing that his commander had squandered yet another great chance to crush the Confederate Army of Northern Virginia.

The battle was, however, at least a tactical victory for the Union. With the victory he sought, Lincoln issued his Emancipation Proclamation on September 22, although it did not officially take effect until January 1. And after the fall elections, on November 5, 1862, Lincoln finally removed McClellan—a popular Democrat—for good.

The Emancipation Proclamation was scarcely a sweeping blow against slavery. It applied only to slaves in areas of the Confederacy "still in rebellion," and exempted all of the Union slave states and occupied parts of the Confederacy. Ever the politician, Lincoln tried to make a revolution seem like something moderate; seeking to hold on to the political mainstream, he made the Proclamation seem less dramatic than it was. In reality, of course, the most fundamental effect of the Emancipation Proclamation was to change the nature of the war: from January 1, 1863, the Union Army became an army of liberation that made men and women "forever free." The news spread quickly to the slaves, and even more ran away from their plantations. In the first year of the war, slavery began to disintegrate from within; now it was under direct attack by the advancing Union forces. More and more avenues to freedom opened every day. As usual, Lincoln summed it up best: the war was killing slavery by "friction and abrasion." As slavery slowly died, more and more whites—just as Frederick Douglass predicted in 1861—had to face the fundamental issue of freedom.

Union reaction to the Proclamation was, of course, mixed. Abolitionists were overjoyed. Despite the document's limited nature, the president of the United States had placed his government and his huge armies on the side of emancipation. William Lloyd Garrison knew the Proclamation was timid, but "Joy, gratitude, thanksgiving, renewed hope, and courage fill my soul." Republicans generally rallied to emancipation, even if only to help weaken the Confederacy and end the war. Democrats, including General McClellan, united in their opposition to it, and rallied for the fall elections.

In the campaigns of 1862, Republicans downplayed the Proclamation, emphasizing loyalty for the war effort, support for the "boys in the field," and restoration of the Union. As they repeated to voters: not all Democrats are traitors, but all traitors are Democrats. For their part, Democrats attacked Lincoln's conduct of the war and alleged that his inexperience and incompetence had undermined McClellan's efforts in Virginia. A Confederate invasion of Kentucky, which nearly reached the outskirts of Cincinnati, Ohio (the governor called out the state militia to defend the city), was turned back only after a fierce battle at Perryville, Kentucky, in mid-October, and further depressed Northern civilians. Democrats played on voters' growing war weariness and their frustration with mounting casualties. Most of all, they attacked the Proclamation and accused Lincoln and Republicans of promoting "negro equality" and racial "amalgamation": "How long before the manly, warlike people of Ohio," one of the state's congressmen said, "of fair hair and blue eyes, in a large preponderance, would become, in spite of Bibles and morals, degenerate under the wholesale emancipation and immigration favored" by Republicans? New York Democrats appealed more directly to white workers: "A vote for [Democratic gubernatorial candidate Horatio] Seymour is a vote to protect our white laborers against the association and competition of southern negroes."

The voting produced no clear referendum on Lincoln's war leadership. Republicans remained strong in New England and the upper North. They also gained significantly in the border states, where the government barred secessionists from voting and many men were off fighting in the Confederate armies. Democrats, however, gained thirty-four seats in the House of Representatives, nearly all in the lower North tier of states that had provided Lincoln's margin of victory in 1860. After the elections, they controlled the state legislatures in New York, Ohio, Pennsylvania, Indiana, and Illinois, all of which Lincoln had carried two years before. The president was fortunate that Republican governors in Ohio and Pennsylvania did not face reelection until 1863, and those in Indiana and Illinois until 1864.

The Emancipation Proclamation changed the nature of the war. It completed the slow transition from a "limited war" approach that courted Southern Unionists to one that recognized the truly revolutionary potential inherent in a conflict between slaveholding and non-slaveholding states. From this point, no one knew quite what would happen. What if the war ended in the next few months? What would be the fate of runaways, or slaves in the Confederate states, or in the border states? No one simply assumed that slavery was over, but most agreed that it would be difficult to turn back. For African Americans and white abolitionists, the Proclamation represented the chance they had waited for. Of course, the Union still had to win the war.

Abraham Lincoln: The Preliminary Emancipation Proclamation (September 22, 1862)

After the Union victory at the Battle of Antietam, Lincoln announced his decision to emancipate slaves in unoccupied areas of the Confederacy, effective January 1, 1863. Although limited in its immediate legal impact, the Proclamation changed the nature of the war.

That on the first day of January, in the year of our Lord one thousand eight hundred and sixty-three, all persons held as slaves within any State or designated part of a State, the people whereof shall then be in rebellion against the United States, shall be then, thenceforward, and forever free; and the Executive Government of the United States, including the military and naval authority thereof, will recognize and maintain the freedom of such persons, and will do no act or acts to repress such persons, or any of them, in any efforts they may make for their actual freedom.

That the Executive will, on the first day of January aforesaid, by proclamation, designate the States and parts of States, if any, in which the people thereof, respectively, shall then be in rebellion against the United States; . . .

Now, therefore I, Abraham Lincoln, President of the United States, by virtue of the power in me vested as Commander-in-Chief of the Army and Navy of the United States in time of actual armed rebellion against the authority and government of the United States, and as a fit and necessary war measure for suppressing said rebellion, do, on this first day of January, in the year of our Lord one thousand eight hundred and sixty-three, and in accordance with my purpose so to do publicly proclaimed for the full period of one hundred days, from the day first above mentioned, order and designate as the States and parts of States wherein the people thereof respectively, are this day in rebellion against the United States, the following, to wit: . . .

And by virtue of the power and for the purpose aforesaid, I do order and declare that all persons held as slaves within said designated States, and parts of States, are, and henceforward shall be, free; and that the Executive Government of the United States, including the military and naval authorities thereof, will recognize and maintain the freedom of said persons.

And I hereby enjoin upon the people so declared to be free to abstain from all violence, unless in necessary self-defence; and I recommend to them that, in all cases when allowed, they labor faithfully for reasonable wages.

And I further declare and make known that such persons of suitable condition will be received into the armed service of the United States to garrison forts, positions, stations, and other places, and to man vessels of all sorts in said service.

And upon this act, sincerely believed to be an act of justice, warranted by the Constitution upon military necessity, I invoke the considerate judgment of mankind and the gracious favor of Almighty God.

A Group of Contrabands: "Slaves of Rebel General T. F. Drayton, Hilton Head, S.C." (1860–1865ca)

Photograph by H. P. Moore. GLC 5140.01.001 The Gilder Lehrman Collection, courtesy of the Gilder Lehrman Institute of American History, New York.

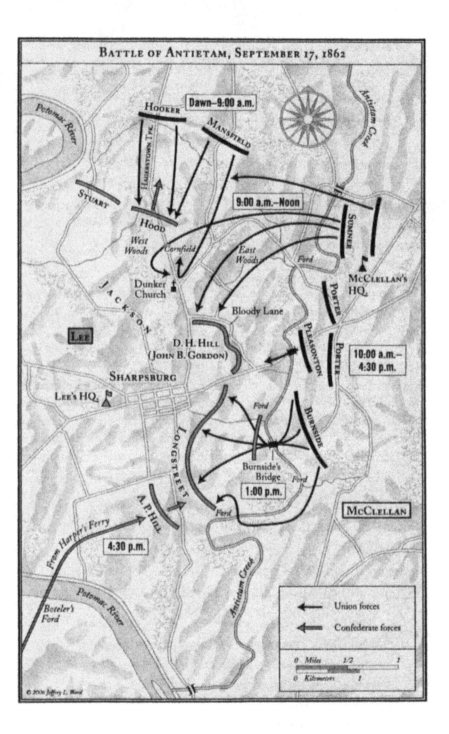

BATTLE OF ANTIETAM, SEPTEMBER 17, 1862

Potomac River

HOOKER

Dawn–9:00 a.m.

MANSFIELD

HAGERSTOWN TPK.

STUART

HOOD

9:00 a.m.–Noon

SUMNER

West Woods

Cornfield

East Woods

Ford

McClellan's HQ.

JACKSON

Dunker Church

Bloody Lane

PORTER

PLEASONTON

PORTER

LEE

D. H. HILL
(JOHN B. GORDON)

10:00 a.m.–
4:30 p.m.

SHARPSBURG

Lee's HQ.

Ford

Ford

BURNSIDE

LONGSTREET

Burnside's Bridge

1:00 p.m.

Ford

McCLELLAN

From Harper's Ferry

A. P. HILL

Ford

4:30 p.m.

Boteler's Ford

Potomac River

Antietam Creek

Antietam Creek

Miles   0   1/2   1
Kilometers   0   1

→ Union forces

→ Confederate forces

© 2006 Jeffrey L. Ward

Meschack P. Larry, Army of the Potomac, to His Sister (February 16, 1863)

Many Northern whites changed (or at least reconsidered) their racial attitudes once they actually met African Americans— many had never known, much less interacted with any black person. This letter, written by a Maine soldier, is similar to many others, particularly those from New England and the Upper North, where abolition and the Second Great Awakening had made the greatest impact on social and racial attitudes.

I think people talk to much about fighting for the negroe, for my part what I *believed* to be the curses of slavery has become knowledge and instead of thinking les of a negroe I have sadly learned to think them beter than many wight meen that hold responsible positions Why blame the negroe for what he can not help why speak of him with scorn and contempt when does all he is alowed to do, god knows that a soldier life is hard, but I do not wish to exchange mine for that of a negroes bond or free. as for liberty I have all that a soldier could expect and sertanly feel as free as a king I agreed to obey orders and therefore no one is to blame but myself if I do not like them can a slave say the same

M. P. Larry

Letters of Meschack P. Larry, Maine Historical Society, Portland, ME. Quoted in Silber and Sievers, eds., 98.

Captain C. B. Wilder and Corporal Octave Johnson on Escaping Slavery (1863 and 1864)

Many African Americans who escaped slavery during the war enlisted in the Union Army, and their stories frequently were recorded. Both of these passages relate the dangers and difficulties involved in escaping and the important role that the Union Army played in motivating men and women to run away.

* * * *

[Interview with Captain C. B. Wilder, Fortress Monroe, Va.]
May 9, 1863.

Question How many of the people called contrabands, have come under your observation?

Answer Some 10,000 have come under our control, to be fed in part, and clothed in part, but I cannot speak accurately in regard to the number. This is the rendezvous. They come here from all about, from Richmond and 200 miles off in North Carolina There was one gang that started from Richmond 23 strong and only 3 got through. . . .

Q In your opinion, is there any communication between the refugees and the black men still in slavery?

A Yes Sir, we have had men here who have gone back 200 miles.

Q In your opinion would a change in our policy which would cause them to be treated with fairness, their wages punctually paid and employment furnished them in the army, become known and would it have any effect upon others in slavery?

A Yes—Thousands upon Thousands. I went to Suffolk a short time ago to enquire into the state of things there—for I found I could not get any foot hold to make things work there, through the Commanding General, and I went to the Provost Marshall and all hands—and the colored people actually sent a deputation to me one morning before I was up to know if we put black men in irons and sent them off to Cuba to be sold or set them at work and put balls on their legs and whipped them, just as in slavery; because that was the story up there, and they were frightened and didn't know what to do. When I got at the feelings of these people I found they were not afraid of the slaveholders. They said there was nobody on the plantations but women and they were not afraid of them.

[Account of Corporal Octave Johnson]
    I was born in New Orleans, I am 23 years of age; I was raised by Arthur Thiboux of New Orleans, I am by trade a cooper. I was treated

pretty well at home; in 1855 master sold my mother, and in 1861 he sold me to S. Contrell of St. James Parish for $2,400; here I worked by task at my trade. One morning the bell was rung for me to go to work so early that I could not see, and I lay still, because I was working by task, for this the overseer was going to have me whipped, and I ran away to the woods, where I remained for a year and a half, I had to steal my food, took turkeys, chickens and pigs; before I left our number had increased to thirty, of whom ten were women; we were four miles in the rear of the plantation house; sometimes we would rope beef cattle and drag them out to our hiding place; we obtained matches from our friends on the plantation; we slept on logs and burned cypress leaves to make a smoke and keep away mosquitoes; Eugene Jardean, master of hounds, hunted for us for three months; often those at work would betray those in the swamp, for fear of being implicated in their escape; we furnished meat to our fellow-servants in the field, who would return corn meal; one day twenty hounds came after me; I called the party to my assistance and we killed eight of the bloodhounds, then we all jumped into Bayou Fanpron; the dogs followed us and the alligators caught six of them, "the alligators preferred dog flesh to personal flesh," we escaped and came to Camp Parapet, where I was first employed in the Commissary office, then as a servant to Col. Hanks; then I joined his regiment.

Both in Ira Berlin, et al., eds., *Freedom: A Documentary History of Emancipation, 1861–1867, Series I, Volume I: The Destruction of Slavery* (Cambridge: Cambridge University Press, 1985).

ELEVEN

Union Families, the Peace Movement, and Northern Politics in 1863

B Y 1863, THE DEMANDS of civil war affected communities and families across the North and South. In the previous year, both sides experienced massive losses and had to use increasingly coercive methods to sustain their armies in the field. In 1862, the Union made significant military progress in the West and along the Confederate coast; in the East, the war was a standoff as Confederates staged a desperate defense of Richmond and won smashing victories in northern Virginia. Finally, the character of the war changed forever when the Union turned back the Confederates at Antietam Creek and Lincoln issued the Emancipation Proclamation in September 1862. In 1863, everything about the war got harder—raising manpower, paying for everything the armies needed, and rallying civilians behind the war effort. Lincoln and Davis struggled to keep their countries united, and sought new and creative means to solve the problems of wartime. Also in 1863, the close relationship between the battlefield and the home front became more evident. The ups and downs of civilian morale, inflation, electoral politics, recruiting, and other issues depended greatly on the fortunes of each army. The timing of events was critical; sometimes a few days made all the difference. The fates of Lincoln, the Republican Party, and the Union war effort, in particular, were tied to the fate of Northern armies.

In the winter-spring of 1862–1863, the Union suffered three stinging defeats, and another brutal encounter was essentially a draw. As a result,

Union morale hit a new low between January and July 1863. After the fall 1862 elections, Lincoln fired McClellan (for the last time) and replaced him with General Ambrose Burnside, whose corps had fought so hard to cross the bridge at Antietam Creek. With more than one hundred thousand men, Burnside invaded Virginia again, moving on the city of Fredericksburg, where he planned to trap Lee's seventy-thousand-man army. The Union plan hinged on crossing the Rappahannock River quickly and assaulting the Confederate position west of the city. On December 13, after taking longer than anticipated to cross the river, Federal troops launched nearly a dozen assaults up a long slope toward the Confederate center on Marye's Heights (the hills west of Fredericksburg). Entrenched below the summit, several thousand Southerners crouched behind a low stone wall and rained lead down on the hapless Yankees. It was a slaughter. As one Confederate said, "A chicken could not live on that field." Emotionally overwrought by the disaster, Burnside tried personally to lead one last suicidal attack. The Union suffered twelve thousand casualties, the Confederates five thousand. In Virginia this was the last action before the armies settled into winter quarters, leaving Lincoln, the army, and the Northern public to chew on the Fredericksburg debacle for four months. Burnside was out, replaced by "Fighting Joe" Hooker.

Also in December 1862, the Union tried to take Vicksburg, the last Confederate stronghold on the Mississippi River. Situated on a high bluff on the river's east bank, the city was ringed by trenches and fortifications, and to the south and west the land was swampy and impassable much of the year. Not conditioned to wait, Grant decided to make a late-season assault. His part of the Union force, however, was delayed by Confederate cavalry. General William Tecumseh Sherman's men made it to the city not knowing of Grant's difficulties. Sherman carried out his attack on December 29 with appalling losses, and Grant decided to wait until spring before making another attempt.

In Tennessee, having maneuvered around one another after the Confederate invasion of Kentucky and the Battle of Perryville, the two armies came together outside Murfreesboro at the end of the year. On December 31, thirty-eight thousand Confederates under General Braxton Bragg attacked nearly forty-five thousand Federals, led by General William Rosecrans. Bragg graduated West Point in 1837 near the top of his class, and served in the Seminole Wars and in Mexico. A favorite of Jefferson

Davis, Bragg alienated other generals who resented that friendship and disparaged his lack of creative leadership. But early on December 31, he caught the Union Army by surprise, and his men pushed back the Union right as confused Yankee troops retreated in chaos toward Stone's River. It was shaping up as another debacle, but General George H. Thomas's brigade held in the center of the Union line and delayed the Confederate advance. Rosecrans himself helped rally the Union troops, riding calmly among the men. Thomas's stand saved the day, and the Union reorganized. Desultory action characterized January 1, but on the next day, Bragg and the Confederates launched another offensive that was also stopped by stiff Federal resistance. The battle was really a draw, and both sides suffered more than one-third casualties—the single highest rate of any battle of the war. Still, the Union had averted disaster, briefly reviving morale.

The last Union defeat, perhaps the most depressing of them all, occurred in Virginia in early May 1863. The Army of the Potomac, 115,000 strong and now under Joseph Hooker, moved on Lee's Army of Northern Virginia, again encamped outside Fredericksburg with about sixty thousand men. Hooker's plan called for part of his force to feint against the Confederates on Marye's Heights (site of the Fredericksburg disaster), but the main attack would come from the west, along the Orange Turnpike and past a crossroads hotel called Chancellorsville. Rather than repeat Burnside's mistakes of the previous December, Hooker intended to take the Confederate main force from behind and then crush it between the two halves of his much larger army. It was a good plan. It forced Lee to divide his army, leaving only ten thousand men to hold Fredericksburg while he moved west to meet the main Union threat. In a series of dramatic gambles, Lee divided his army twice in the face of a superior enemy, violating all conventional logic. In one of the most famous incidents of the entire war, Lee discovered that the west end of Hooker's main line was "in the air," meaning that it was not anchored on any hill, trench, or other natural feature, and was therefore vulnerable to attack. Lee sent "Stonewall" Jackson with twenty-six thousand men on a concealed march—using a small country lane pointed out by a local farmer's son—around the Union line, where they took up position late in the afternoon of May 2. Not wasting the opportunity, Jackson's men crushed the Union flank, which "crumbled like a dry leaf" according to one Confederate.

After dark, Jackson was scouting positions for a morning attack when he was accidentally shot by some of his own pickets. He died a few days later—an event that perhaps changed the course of the war. The next three days featured desperate fighting by the Confederates—on two fronts as the Union Army advanced on Lee's forces from both east and west—and missed opportunities by Hooker, who was injured (probably a severe concussion) by an artillery shell but refused to pass command to another general. It was a four-day battle with more movement, countermarches, and dramatic tactical decisions than nearly any other individual encounter. With their better than two-to-one advantage, Hooker's corps commanders begged him to launch an all-out assault to crush Lee's army between the two halves of the Army of the Potomac. Hooker refused, instead withdrawing back toward Washington. The Battle of Chancellorsville was a humiliating Union defeat. "My God," Lincoln supposedly lamented, "what will the country say!"

Remarkably, spirits in the Army of the Potomac remained quite high, primarily because the men blamed Hooker for the defeat. Union morale at home, however, could not have been lower. In spring and into early summer 1863, Union offensives stalled everywhere: Grant's army had not taken Vicksburg, and by June had settled into a depressing siege during which his men dropped from diseases in the hot Mississippi summer; Hooker's Army of the Potomac did nothing after the Chancellorsville defeat; and in southeastern Tennessee, Rosecrans bogged down in the mountains against stubborn Confederate resistance. These months before July 1863 were a high point for the growing Union peace movement. Many Democrats, of course, had opposed the war from the beginning, and the party divided between peace and war "wings." The peace wing found supporters in the border states and areas along the Ohio River, particularly in southern Illinois, Indiana, and Ohio, and in major cities such as New York. Peace Democrats often were men and women sympathetic to the South, slaveowners, and immigrants, the last fearing emancipation and competition from unskilled African American workers. Added to dissatisfaction and disappointment with the Union war effort were the Emancipation Proclamation and more intrusive draft policies.

On March 3, 1863, the Enrollment Act made Northern men ages twenty to forty-five eligible for service. This measure, modified several times, remained the basic law of Union conscription until the end of the war. Like the Militia Act of 1862, the Enrollment Act was designed to stimulate volunteering by assigning quotas (based on population) to each congressional district. If a locality fell short of its quota, men would be drafted from the militia rolls. As spring turned to summer, few volunteers came forward, and state and local governments offered more and higher bounties. LAST CHANCE FOR BOUNTIES! NOW IS THE TIME! read one typical poster for the First Regiment of New York Rifles. The appeal was obvious: don't take a chance of missing several hundred dollars in bonuses and be drafted for nothing. When a year's wages for working men rarely exceeded five hundred dollars, the cash incentives were tempting. They also led to abuse, as men collected the money and then deserted, moved on and did it again. In July, having failed to stimulate enough volunteers, the federal government made its first official draft call. Eventually four drafts called nearly eight hundred thousand men, although fewer than fifty thousand were actually forced into service, because larger bounties helped bring in volunteers (especially in 1864) and more than three hundred thousand were exempted, primarily for physical disabilities. The most controversial features of the draft laws were substitution and commutation. Men could hire substitutes—as in the Confederate system—from among those not otherwise eligible. To keep the price of substitutes down, men could also pay a three-hundred-dollar fee to "commute" their service responsibility. This hated provision ended in 1864, but it, and substitution (which continued), alienated working-class men and especially immigrants.

The draft laws, when combined with emancipation and mounting losses, helped create a more coherent peace movement. Lincoln and the Republicans were incompetent, the argument ran, and mismanaged the war effort due to inexperience and to their meddling with West Point officers such as McClellan. In desperation the president had issued the Emancipation Proclamation—to distract Northerners from his failed military record—and was now drafting poor men as cannon fodder, all in the name of a radical and misguided racial policy. Thus came together war weariness, racism, and resentment of Republican policies that intruded into the lives of Northern men and women. By mid-1863, in other words, the Union war effort had generated opposition from a diverse but increasingly united group of traditional Democrats in the lower North and in large urban centers. Republicans labeled the Peace Democrats as "Copperheads," for their "poisonous" influence. Perhaps their most vocal leader was Ohio congressman Clement Vallandigham, who attacked emancipation and openly called for draft evasion. The latter led to his conviction for disloyalty, and Lincoln exiled him to the Confederacy, but he found his way to Canada, from where he ran for governor of Ohio in 1863.

Peace Democrats such as Vallandigham also criticized Lincoln for suspending the writ of habeas corpus, and thus allowing military officials to arrest suspected Confederate sympathizers and hold them without charges or trial. Lincoln rarely suspended habeas corpus outside the border states, and the vast majority of those arrested (about fifteen thousand for the entire war) were released within a few hours. But for critics of the administration, here was further evidence of Lincoln's "despotism," which included his Emancipation Proclamation.

Finally, in 1863, Northerners began to feel the effects of paying for the war. The Union generally financed the war successfully, without causing runaway inflation. For the years 1861–1865, inflation in the Union registered about 80 percent (very similar to the rates during World Wars I and II). Lincoln and the Republicans relied on taxes and loans to pay for between 80 and 85 percent of the war effort. The range of things taxed included luxuries such as liquor, tobacco, and yachts; more famous and of lasting impact was the nation's first income tax (more despotism, Democrats said). It applied to a tiny number of people, but represented an important precedent. Most loans were actually bonds (essentially loans from the savings of ordinary citizens), and the most popular were "5 and 20" bonds marketed by investor Jay Cooke. The government paid interest in gold—making the bonds very attractive, including to overseas investors—and promised to redeem the bonds in not less than five but not more than twenty years. Eventually about one-fourth of Union families bought bonds (setting a precedent for larger bond drives during World Wars I and II). Finally, the government printed money, creating the first uniform currency in American history. The Legal Tender Act of February 24, 1862, created "Greenbacks" that (like all paper money in the nineteenth century) fluctuated in value from time to time and place to place, and often was tied to Union military fortunes. Although the Union financed the war successfully—especially from our perspective and compared with the Confederacy—inflation and additional taxes caused hardship and resentment among many Northerners, particularly wage earners and salaried workers whose incomes struggled to keep pace with rising prices. Still, the Northern economy in general—as opposed to many individual workers—benefited from the war, as evidenced by more grain exported to Europe, new technology and modernized industrial production, and an improved transportation infrastructure.

Peace Democrats agitated these related war issues—battlefield failure, emancipation, the draft, and inflation—and fed the growing frustration with Lincoln and the Republicans. In 1863, protests and riots occurred in the border states and in southern Indiana, Illinois, and Ohio, but most spectacular were those in New York City in mid-July, which remain the deadliest riots in American history. They centered in Democratic areas of the city dominated by poor immigrants and were fueled especially by antidraft and antiblack feelings. Screaming "kill the naygars," Irish immigrants, Irish Americans, and others attacked free African Americans, burned the Colored Orphan Asylum, and ransacked mixed-race brothels and saloons. More than a dozen black men were lynched and burned. Also torched were several homes of prominent Republicans and, symbolically, a Brooks Brothers shop that made uniforms for the Union Army. At its height, on July 13, the mob numbered perhaps fifty thousand men and women, according to contemporary estimates. Finally, Union troops arrived by train (most straight off the Gettysburg battlefield) and they coolly stood down the rioters, killing well more than a hundred in several dramatic confrontations. In *The New York Times*, one rioter defended himself in classic language that brought together his mixed motives. "Although we got hard fists, and are dirty without, we have soft hearts, . . . and that's the reason we love our wives and children more than the rich, because we got not much besides them; and we will not go and leave them at home to starve." He concluded: "Why don't they let the nigger kill the slave-driving race and take possession of the South, as it belongs to them." His letter had it all: resentment of the draft, hatred of Southerners and the war, racism, and even a subtle plea to keep free African Americans in the South.

The New York City Riots actually hurt the peace movement and the Democratic Party. The mostly Irish rioters looked like traitors, particularly as they confronted Union troops so recently victorious at Gettysburg. The riots were also followed, on July 18, by the dramatic attack at Fort Wagner, in South Carolina, led by the Fifty-fourth Massachusetts Colored Infantry. The contrast between the white, Democratic rioters and the African American troops could hardly have been more stark.

The enrollment of African Americans into the army was another controversial measure. From the beginning, black men tried to volunteer but were turned away (although they served in the navy). Many whites believed that black men would not fight, or that whites would not fight with them. Lincoln feared a backlash among Northern voters afraid of armed black men marching through the country. Military service also carried with it the implication of legal equality, which concerned many whites even more than emancipation. By late 1862, however, Lincoln considered using African American men to help overcome the Union's growing manpower shortage. Although he publicly denied his intention to do so, he and Secretary of War Stanton quietly authorized commanders in occupied South Carolina to enroll ex-slaves (up to five thousand men) in August 1862. By spring 1863, the difficulty in raising troops became acute, and the Union began widespread enrollment of black men. A logical extension of the Emancipation Proclamation, Lincoln justified it on the same grounds: as a war measure, a strategy to help win the war quickly and save (white) lives. If Northern whites were unsure of black soldiers, Southerners were outraged. Jefferson Davis threatened to sell captured black soldiers into slavery and execute the white officers leading the men—all units were segregated and had only white officers. Lincoln responded by vowing to put one Confederate prisoner at hard labor for any Union man sold into slavery and to execute one Southern prisoner for every Union officer similarly treated.

African American troops received mostly rear-guard assignments and seldom fought in combat. First, there was less risk of capture and slavery, or execution of white officers. Second, deep-seated racism led many whites to question if black men would fight or if whites would support them. When black troops did see action, in May 1863 in the Mississippi Valley, they performed well and received complimentary reports from Grant and other Union officers. On July 18, the widely reported attack at Fort Wagner was led by the Fifty-fourth Massachusetts Colored Infantry. Journalists following several black units reported their actions to readers in the North, and even many skeptical whites grudgingly admitted the men's bravery under fire. Sergeant William H. Carney, of the Fifty-fourth Massachusetts, became the first black man awarded the Congressional Medal of Honor (not until 1908) for his part in the assault on Fort Wagner.

Despite these heroics, black men's military service remained a contentious issue in the changing Union political culture, and helped bring together Democratic opposition. Generally, Democrats were divided by the war but united by racial issues; Republicans united behind the war effort but often disagreed about emancipation, African American troops, or the desirable amount of racial equality.

The close, dramatic sequence of events in July 1863 helped prompt a public letter from President Lincoln that assailed the New York City rioters and particularly Peace Democrats: "You say you will not fight to free negroes," he wrote, although "some of them seem willing to fight for you." He predicted that after the war "some black men" will "remember that, with silent tongue, and clenched teeth, and steady eye, and well-poised bayonet, they have helped mankind on to this great consummation; while, I fear, there will be some white ones, unable to forget that, with malignant heart, and deceitful speech, they strove to hinder it." The sentiments he expressed demonstrated how far Lincoln's thinking had evolved. Within the three basic Republican factions—conservatives, radicals, and moderates—Lincoln was moving from moderate toward radical.

In the fall 1863 elections, Democrats united behind the slogan "No Abolition, No Emancipation, No Negro Equality." The usual images appeared in Democratic publications: Lincoln applauding as black men danced with white women; Republican ministers blessing interracial marriages and baptizing mixed-race children. They continued to attack Lincoln's war leadership. For their part, Republicans defended the Emancipation Proclamation and the decision to use black men in the army. The election results gave Lincoln great hope. Key votes in Ohio, New York, and Pennsylvania brought huge Republican victories; Vallandigham lost by more than one hundred thousand votes in his try for Ohio governor. After the elections, Lincoln traveled to Gettysburg to dedicate the battlefield cemetery. His famous address summarized the war, the nation, and defined citizenship and democracy. "We here highly resolve that these dead shall not have died in vain—that this nation, under God, shall have a new birth of freedom— and that the government of the people, by the people, for the people, shall not perish from the earth." The war, Lincoln avowed in his typically concise, evocative prose, was about freedom for all people, democracy, and majority rule. He had taken Union military strategy a long way from its conservative beginnings in spring 1861; whether or not he and the North could win the war, and implement those high ideals, remained to be seen.

Clement Vallandigham Attacks Lincoln,
Speech in the House of Representatives (January 7, 1863)

*A representative from Ohio, Vallandigham was a leading
Peace Democrat who criticized the war and Lincoln's policies,
particularly emancipation, the draft, and the occasional
suspension of habeas corpus. He was briefly jailed, but
eventually went to Canada, from where he ran for governor
of Ohio in 1863. He returned to help shape the Democratic
campaign in 1864.*

Soon after the war began the reign of the mob was ... supplanted by
the iron domination of arbitrary power. Constitutional limitation was broken down; habeas corpus fell; liberty of the press, of speech, of the person,
of the mails, of travel, of one's own house, and of religion; the right to bear
arms, due process of law, judicial trial, trial by jury, trial at all; every badge
and muniment of freedom in republican government or kingly government—all went down at a blow; ...

And now, sir, I recur to the state of the Union to-day. What is it? Sir,
twenty months have elapsed, but the rebellion is not crushed out; its military power has not been broken; the insurgents have not dispersed. The
Union is not restored; nor the Constitution maintained; nor the laws enforced. Twenty, sixty, ninety, three hundred, six hundred days have passed;
a thousand millions been expended; and three hundred thousand lives lost
or bodies mangled; and to-day the Confederate flag is still near the Potomac and the Ohio, and the Confederate Government stronger, many
times, than at the beginning. ...

You have not conquered the South. You never will. It is not in the nature of things possible; much less under your auspices. But money you have
expended without limit, and blood poured out like water. Defeat, debt,
taxation, sepulchers, these are your trophies. ... The war for the Union
is, in your hands, a most bloody and costly failure. The President con-

fessed it on the 22d of September. . . . War for the Union was abandoned; war for the negro openly begun, and with stronger battalions than before. With what success? Let the dead at Fredericksburg and Vicksburg answer. . . .

But slavery is the cause of the war. Why? Because the South obstinately and wickedly refused to restrict or abolish it at the demand of the philosophers or fanatics and demagogues of the North and West. Then, sir, it was abolition, the purpose to abolish or interfere with and hem in slavery, which caused disunion and war. . . .

Neither will I be stopped by that other cry of mingled fanaticism and hypocrisy, about the sin and barbarism of African slavery. Sir, I see more of barbarism and sin, a thousand times, in the continuance of this war, the dissolution of the Union, the breaking up of this Government, and the enslavement of the white race, by debt and taxes and arbitrary power.

Clement Vallandigham, *Speeches, Arguments, and Letters* (New York: J. Walter and Co., 1864), 418–35.

Abraham Lincoln to James C. Conkling (August 26, 1863)

In this famous letter, Lincoln attacked Peace Democrats for their
opposition to the war, emancipation, and the use of African
American troops. It was published during the height of the 1863
election campaign, and soon after the Union victories at
Gettysburg and Vicksburg.

There are those who are dissatisfied with me. To such I would say: You desire peace; and you blame me that we do not have it. But how can we attain it? There are but three conceivable ways. First, to suppress the rebellion by force of arms. This I am trying to do. Are you for it? If you are, so far we are agreed. If you are not for it, a second way is to give up the Union. I am against this. Are you for it? If you are, you should say so plainly. If you are not for *force*, nor yet for *dissolution*, there only remains some imaginable *compromise*. I do not believe any compromise, embracing the maintenance of the Union, is now possible. All I learn, leads to a directly opposite belief. . . .

But to be plain, you are dissatisfied with me about the negro. Quite likely there is a difference of opinion between you and myself upon that subject. I certainly wish that all men could be free, while I suppose you do not. . . .

You dislike the emancipation proclamation; and, perhaps, would have it retracted. You say it is unconstitutional—I think differently. I think the constitution invests its Commander-in-chief, with the law of war, in time of war. The most that can be said, if so much, is, that slaves are property. Is there—has there ever been—any question that by the law of war, property, both of enemies and friends, may be taken when needed? And is it not needed whenever taking it, helps us, or hurts the enemy? . . .

You say you will not fight to free negroes. Some of them seem willing to fight for you; but, no matter. Fight you, then exclusively to save the Union. I issued the proclamation on purpose to aid you in saving the Union. Whenever you shall have conquered all resistance to the Union, if I shall urge you to continue fighting, it will be an apt time, then, for you to declare you will not fight to free negroes.

I thought that in your struggle for the Union, to whatever extent the negroes should cease helping the enemy, to that extent it weakened the enemy in his resistence to you. Do you think differently? I thought that whatever negroes can be got to do as soldiers, leaves just so much less for white soldiers to do, in saving the Union. Does it appear otherwise to you? But negroes, like other people, act upon motives. Why should they do anything for us, if we will do nothing for them? If they stake their lives for us, they must be prompted by the strongest motive—even the promise of freedom. And the promise being made, must be kept. . . .

Peace does not appear so distant as it did. . . . And then, there will be some black men who can remember that, with silent tongue, and clenched teeth, and steady eye, and well-poised bayonnet, they have helped mankind on to this great consummation; while, I fear, there will be some white ones, unable to forget that, with malignant heart, and deceitful speech, they strove to hinder it.

Marshall Phillips, Harrison's Landing, VA, to His Wife (June 2, 1863), and John Peirce to Clarissa Peirce (January 3, 1864)

These letters suggest the importance of monetary gain for many Union soldiers, particularly after 1862, when bounties rose dramatically in the Union.

Virginia
June 2, 1863

Dear Wife
   A few lines to you privately we have been paied off today two months pay I think I shal send what I send by mail dont open my letters before any one as there is likely to be money in them at any time, I would not open them before our children as they might speek about it I shal not send but a little at a time Diana you sed to me don't go in to another battle for my sake dear Wife I will do any thing that I can do to permote your happiness that will not disg[r]ace me nor my family, but you dont want me if we are called upon to go in to battle to leave the ranks and fall back in the rear if I am able to go with them there is two or three in this regt that has got to be courtmarseld for leaveing the ranks at this last fight one from our com[pany] but he has since diserted Diana all that I can think about wen I am about going in to battle is you and the family but I suppose I have only about eleven months longer to serve if I am permitted to live that length of time I hope I may come home. . . .

January 3, 1864
. . . you say you can spend the money I want you to spend all you want that is what I came here for nothing will pleas me better then to have you enjoy it i hope you will Clara remember I do not want to you to deny your-self of any thing i want you to live well and to dress well and the children to so long as you are provided for I can content myself and you will be so long as I am in Unkel Sams servis that makes me content the capt says we shall get our US pay this week the rest of the bounty is not due till we are

musterd out of the servis i did inspection this afternoon at for at half past two we have got to go out with our knapsacks on tell John the next letter I send will be to him his name on it it is eving we are a going to signe the pay roll to knight we are a going to escort the nineteenth Reg when they come home we think they will come tomorrow good knight Clara when I say good knight it makes me think of old times in 1847 and 1848 darling Clara

Letters of Marshall and Diana Phillips, Maine Historical Society, Portland, ME; Letters of John Peirce, John Peirce Papers, Peabody Essex Museum, Salem, MA. Quoted in Silber and Sievers, eds., 39, 80–81.

Tillie Pierce and the Battle of Gettysburg
(June 26–July 3, 1863)

Tillie Pierce was fifteen years old when she encountered the Civil War firsthand. She ran home from school ahead of Confederate troops and just before the Battle of Gettysburg began; by the end of the battle she was helping to care for thousands of wounded and dying men. Her experience was more typical of Southern girls and women, since most of the fighting took place in the Confederacy and local residents had to care for wounded troops after each encounter.

June 26, 1863

We were having our literary exercises on Friday afternoon, at our Seminary, when the cry reached our ears. Rushing to the door, and standing on the front portico we beheld in the direction of the Theological Seminary, a dark, dense mass, moving toward town. Our teacher, Mrs. Eyster, at once said:

"Children, run home as quickly as you can."

It did not require repeating. I am satisfied some of the girls did not reach their homes before the Rebels were in the streets.

As for myself, I had scarcely reached the front door, when, on looking up the street, I saw some of the men on horseback. I scrambled in, slammed shut the door, and hastening to the sitting room, peeped out between the shutters.

What a horrible sight! There they were, human beings! Clad almost in rags, covered with dust, riding wildly, pell-mell down the hill toward our home! Shouting, yelling most unearthly, cursing, brandishing their revolvers, and firing right and left. . . .

July 3, 1863

Toward the close of the afternoon it was noticed that the roar of the battle was subsiding, and after all had become quiet we started back to the Weikert home. . . .

When we entered the house we found it almost completely filled with the wounded. We hardly knew what to do or where to go. They, however, removed most of the wounded, and thus after a while made room for the family.

As soon as possible, we endeavored to make ourselves useful by rendering assistance in this heartrending state of affairs. I remember Mrs. Weikert went through the house, and after searching awhile, brought all the muslin and linen she could spare. This we tore into bandages and gave them to the surgeons, to bind up the poor soldier's wounds.

By this time, amputating benches had been placed about the house. I must have become inured to seeing the terrors of battle, else I could hardly have gazed upon the scenes now presented. I was looking out of the windows facing the front yard. Near the basement door, and directly underneath the window I was at, stood one of these benches. I saw them lifting the poor men upon it, then the surgeons sawing and cutting off arms and legs, then again probing and picking bullets from the flesh. . . .

Tillie Pierce Alleman, *At Gettysburg, or What a Girl Saw and Heard of the Battle* (Baltimore, MD: Butternut and Blue, 1994; orig. 1888).

New Jersey Recruiting Poster (1863)

By summer 1863, Northern men could collect significant bounties for enlisting. This poster includes the usual mixture of appeals to patriotism and financial self-interest. Husbands often received higher bounties than single men.

Collection of the New-York Historical Society, #AC03085.

Substitute Poster (1863)

Hiring substitutes became more difficult and expensive as the war progressed. Through substitute agents, or brokers, such as the one listed on this broadside, men seeking to avoid the draft could arrange for a substitute without having to negotiate personally or make themselves known publicly.

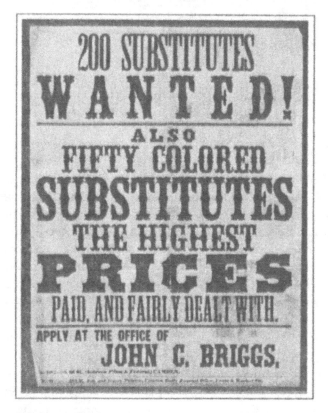

Collection of the New-York Historical Society, #AC03029.

The War in 1863:
Gettysburg, Vicksburg, and Chattanooga

IN THE MIDDLE OF 1863, Republican fortunes looked bleak as the Democratic-led peace movement gained strength. The primary reason was the Union's apparent lack of military progress in subduing the Confederacy. Unsuccessful or stalled offensives in Virginia, Tennessee, and Mississippi discouraged Northerners and called Lincoln's leadership into question, and he knew that only battlefield victories could turn public opinion around. Confederate leaders also watched Union politics closely. As the war dragged on, many believed their best hope to be the Northern peace movement, which might unseat the Republicans or force Lincoln to negotiate a settlement. Jefferson Davis, Robert E. Lee, and the rest of the Confederate military and political leadership weighed their options, with Southern independence hanging on where and how they committed their dwindling resources; and 1863 appeared to be a turning point in the relative abilities of each side to mobilize resources. The Union economy was growing stronger, the men in uniform were better supplied, and even with recruiting problems, the North's vastly greater manpower reserve foretold defeat for the Confederacy if the war continued too long. Davis wanted and needed to embolden the peace movement—but how? Should the Confederacy continue to fight mainly a defensive war, protecting as much territory as possible? Or should they concentrate forces and try for a dramatic victory, perhaps on Union soil, that would shock the Northern public and force Lincoln and the Republicans to consider a cease-fire?

The situation in Mississippi in the spring of 1863 remained unchanged from the previous winter. The Union offensive had stalled north of Vicksburg. Grant's December 1862 invasion was derailed by Nathan Bedford Forrest's Confederate cavalry ranging far behind enemy lines to destroy railroads and telegraph lines. The longer Grant's supply lines became, the more vulnerable he was to Forrest's mounted troops.

Forrest was quite an exception among the famous Southern military leaders who emerged during the war. Born in poverty in backwoods Tennessee, he became a wealthy planter by 1861, mainly by selling slaves and land from his Memphis business. Tough and proud, with dark eyes set above prominent cheekbones, Forrest proved to be a genius with cavalry, moving fast and hitting the enemy hard. He also used bluff and deception to trick the Union repeatedly into thinking he commanded greater forces than he did. His exploits in northern Mississippi had prevented Grant from reaching Vicksburg in December 1862.

For Grant, the other main problem was the terrain around Vicksburg. It sits on a high bluff overlooking the Mississippi River, and the Confederate artillery could punish any Union efforts on the water. Particularly to the west, but also the south, swamps made the terrain practically unusable; the northern approach to the city was guarded by the Chickasaw Bluffs, where Sherman's men made their unfortunate attack. That left the east. The question Grant faced was how to get enough of his men southeast of the city in order to make a move over the more accessible terrain. In spring 1863, the Union tried several schemes to cut canals west of the river and thereby avoid the Confederate guns entrenched in Vicksburg. They also deliberately flooded the swampy area to make a huge lake. None of these plans worked.

Frustrated and impatient, Grant finally decided to risk the river and take as many men as possible south of Vicksburg, cut loose from his supply and communication lines, and campaign into central Mississippi. Nearly everyone else, including Sherman and Lincoln, opposed the novel, risky idea. But Grant's stubbornness carried the day. On a moonless night in mid-April, he floated his men on twelve ships past the city. Within range of Confederate guns for more than three miles, the ships were battered and many set on fire, but only one sank. After another two weeks Grant had most of his army landed outside Port Gibson, and with about forty-five thousand men he set off toward Jackson. Confederate troops in the vicinity numbered about thirty-three thousand, commanded by General John C. Pemberton. Davis ordered him to hold Vicksburg at all costs, which led him to move cautiously and stay close to the river city. A Pennsylvanian and West Pointer decorated in Mexico, Pemberton feared public criticism of his loyalty—after agonizing about the choice, he stayed with his Virginia-born wife when the war began—which reinforced his disinclination to take chances.

As Grant charged into central Mississippi, Pemberton vacillated and eventually retreated his large force to Vicksburg rather than try to halt the Union advance on open ground. In the next three weeks, Grant secured his place in military history with a brilliant, lightning-fast, hard-hitting series of moves that overwhelmed the Confederates. Rather than moving straight north toward Vicksburg, which would have meant crossing the Big Black River in uncertain terrain, Grant went east and took Jackson on May 14. Much of the city burned. He then turned sharply west, toward Vicksburg, winning three separate battles against the overmatched Pemberton. By May 17, Confederate forces were trapped inside Vicksburg, with the river and swamps on one side and Grant's army surrounding the other. Complicating matters, however, was a new Confederate army under Joseph E. Johnston advancing from eastern Mississippi. Johnston ordered Pemberton to fight his way out of the city and link up with him. Unsure of his position, Pemberton chose to follow Jefferson Davis's primary directive to stay and defend Vicksburg.

Grant's men made two disastrous assaults on the fortress in mid-May, and contrary to his own aggressive nature, he was forced to begin a long siege of the city. Grant feared disease in the semitropical Mississippi summer, as well as Johnston's smaller Confederate force catching him off guard. The siege was brutal for the men and civilians inside Vicksburg. By mid-June little food remained, and eventually the residents ate mule meat, rats (which were "hung and dressed" in the market, according to one resident), water-soaked leather, and dirt paste. Union artillery rained down on the terrified civilians, many of whom lived primarily in underground caves dug into the hillsides. As the siege dragged into late June, the Northern public read only depressing accounts of camp diseases that threatened to cripple Grant's army. Casual observers considered it another failed Union offensive. In reality, the Confederate defenders were close to the end.

The desperate situation outside Vicksburg helped spark the most dramatic campaign and battle of the entire war. Partly to relieve pressure on Confederates in Mississippi and Tennessee, Lee proposed to invade Pennsylvania with the largest Southern army ever assembled. Over objections from other Southern politicians, Davis approved the idea. Lee and Davis hoped to relieve Virginia's hard-pressed farmers—the Confederates could live off the land up north for a while—and perhaps revive the possibility of European intervention. Most of all, of course, they hoped to win a dramatic victory in the Union, embarrass Lincoln, strengthen the Peace Movement, and end the war quickly. By late June, most of Lee's army crossed the Potomac River and headed, generally, toward Harrisburg, Pennsylvania; Lee's plan was to force the Union to attack him. For much of the campaign, Lee and the Confederates suffered from the same problems that normally plagued Union invasions: poor intelligence and communication, lack of familiarity with the local terrain, and unfriendly civilians. Confederates also "repaid" Union tactics in Virginia by destroying Northern railroad and telegraph lines and seizing property and people, that is, free African Americans, who were sent into slavery.

Lee had about seventy-five thousand men divided into three large corps under Generals James "Old Pete" Longstreet, A. P. Hill, and Jubal Early (who replaced Jackson). Longstreet became Lee's most trusted subordinate after Jackson's death, and Lee referred to him as "my old war horse." Another West Point graduate (nearly at the bottom of his class in 1842) wounded in Mexico, Longstreet earned a reputation for being somewhat moody and aloof, attributes worsened by the deaths of three of his children early in the war. By July 1863, he also disagreed with many Southerners in arguing that the Confederacy should conserve resources and fight primarily on the defensive, and he pioneered several innovations in defensive entrenchments. Longstreet had performed brilliantly in nearly every major battle in Virginia; Hill and Early were new corps-level commanders.

The Union Army of the Potomac was hastily reorganized on June 28, when Hooker resigned and George Gordon Meade took command. Born in Spain (his father was a naval agent), Meade graduated West Point in 1835 and fought in Florida and Mexico. He was dour, prickly, and gruff, and his legendary temper earned him a most colorful nickname among the men: "that damned goggle-eyed old snapping turtle." Meade was cautious and new to command, but he demonstrated a tactical superiority in the heat of battle. For nearly a week, both sides probed the countryside searching for one another. On July 1, some of the advance Confederate troops marched toward Gettysburg, apparently on reports of a warehouse full of shoes. On the northwest edge of the town, they encountered Union cavalry under John Buford, who recognized the importance of holding the high ground along the ridge of a long slope running back into Gettysburg. Ordering his men to dismount and fight as infantry, Buford held up the Confederates until the Union's First Corps arrived. Led by General John F. Reynolds, these were some of the best Federal troops, and many veterans on both sides considered Reynolds one of the finest officers in either army. Although Reynolds was killed by a sharpshooter, his men held off the Confederates until late in the day. Finally, the outnumbered Union men retreated south through the town and took a position on Cemetery Hill, southeast of Gettysburg (see map on p. 174).

The course of the Battle of Gettysburg was, in many ways, determined by the terrain and the outcome of this first day's fighting. The hills and connecting ridges south of the town provided a perfect defensive position, something both commanders recognized. Late on July 1, Lee vaguely ordered Jubal Early to take Cemetery Hill "if practicable." In one of the most debated moments in Civil War history, Early decided against an attack on the crucial position. Would Jackson have moved more decisively? Almost certainly, and Lee's order may have reflected his habit of relying on Jackson's personality and leadership. What if Lee had given Early a more precise order? No one knows, but the result meant that the Union held the high ground. Overnight and into the next morning, Longstreet strongly urged Lee to withdraw and find a better position, and thus force Meade to attack them. Lee refused. He had the largest army in Confederate history, nearly at equal strength with that of the Union (Meade had just under ninety thousand men), and he felt it might be the South's last great opportunity to win the war. In the first of several bad mistakes, Lee ordered an all-out attack on the Union left flank for the morning of July 2.

Longstreet disagreed with the plan, and he stalled—his critics say pouted—for much of the morning as he tried to persuade Lee to authorize a flanking movement to the Confederate right (Union left), where he hoped to occupy the hills known as Little Round Top and Big Round Top. A colossal Union blunder gave the Confederates this opportunity. General Daniel Sickles, commander of Meade's Third Corps, had moved his men forward off Cemetery Ridge, thus exposing the two Round Tops. (Sickles was a New York machine politician most famous for killing his wife's lover.) Still Lee refused to alter his plans, and as the Confederates debated, the Union occupied Little Round Top in the nick of time.

What followed was perhaps the most famous day of fighting in American history (rivaled only by D-Day, eighty-one years later). In brutal contests at the base of Cemetery Ridge and then Little Round Top, men from both armies slugged it out in the Peach Orchard, the Wheatfield, the Devil's Den, and the Slaughter Pen. The climax, perhaps, occurred near the summit of Little Round Top. The sharp hill was strewn with large boulders up to its flat top, and offered ideal defensive terrain for the Union. The last unit in line—the extreme left flank of the Union Army— was the Twentieth Maine, a regiment of farmers and lumbermen that had about 350 men when the battle started. Led by Colonel Joshua Lawrence Chamberlain, a professor of rhetoric from Bowdoin College, the Twentieth Maine suffered over 50 percent casualties before turning back the last Confederate push. When his men ran out of ammunition, Chamberlain ordered his exhausted troops to charge down the hill into the attacking Southerners. The bold move worked, and Chamberlain was given the Congressional Medal of Honor. By the end of the day, the Union lines had buckled, but held.

Again Longstreet urged Lee to withdraw, and again Lee refused. On day three he insisted on another infantry charge, this time against the Union center at the top of Cemetery Ridge. This terrible decision led to the second defining moment of the battle: Pickett's charge. George E. Pickett had never commanded men in battle, but he loved the pomp and circumstance of war. He relished the challenge, but Longstreet knew better and could scarcely bring himself to give Pickett the final order to attack. Confederate artillery shelled the Union forces but failed to inflict significant damage. Pickett's men marched over a mile and a half of mostly open ground, their ranks ripped apart by Union artillery. At the center of the Union line waited the elite Second Corps, led by Winfield Scott Hancock, one of the North's most respected officers. A few Confederates reached the Union lines, but nothing more. Pickett's division suffered 60 percent casualties (5,600 men), two of three brigadier generals were killed, and all thirteen colonels were killed or wounded. Pickett never forgave Lee.

On July 4, the Confederates braced for a Union counterattack that could have ended the war. Wounded severely, Hancock begged Meade to send in nearly twenty thousand unused reserves, but Meade refused. Lincoln again was livid, believing he had lost yet another chance to destroy Lee's army. Meade offered to resign, but Lincoln dared not accept, considering that Northerners were reveling in their first major victory in the East and that Meade was something of a hero. The Union suffered twenty-three thousand casualties, one-fourth of the army; Confederates recorded twenty-five thousand casualties, one-third of their forces. Nearly seven thousand men were killed over the three days; perhaps another five thousand of the wounded died soon after. It was the costliest battle of the war and in all of American history.

The Union prevailed because for once the two armies reversed trends: Confederate commanders, particularly Lee, Early, and the cavalry legend J.E.B. Stuart, made mistakes; Southerners got lost, didn't know the terrain, and mistimed their attacks; the Union finally had the right men in the right places, and they made all the right decisions; and most of all, the Yankees held all the best ground.

Also on July 4, the garrison at Vicksburg finally surrendered. Out of food and facing a revolt by civilians and his own men, Pemberton turned the city over to Grant. Four days later, the Confederate outpost at Port Hudson also fell to the Union, which then controlled the entire Mississippi River. The losses at Gettysburg and Vicksburg sent Confederate morale to a new low. In just "one brief month," wrote a high-placed Confederate official in late July, Southern fortunes went from "the point of success" to nearly "absolute ruin." "The Confederacy totters to its destruction," he concluded.

Dramatic encounters such as Gettysburg, of course, were exceptional moments in soldiers' lives. By the middle of 1863, there was a rhythm and similarity to everyday army life—Union or Confederate. Veterans became accustomed to long months of boredom in camp, particularly during the months of "winter quarters." Many men spent time playing cards, gambling, drinking, and playing baseball, which received a dramatic boost in popularity (especially among Northerners); and every army attracted a following of prostitutes, often desperate women whose lives had been shattered by the war. On the other hand, religious revivals were common, drawing on the antebellum movement that had energized American evangelicals, and on the fears of men engaged in the deadliest war anyone had ever seen. The men also sent and received thousands of letters and read all the newspapers they could get, a reflection of Americans' unusually high rate of literacy. (Union and Confederate troops were the first mass, literate armies in world history.) Northern troops, in particular, held debates in which they discussed the goals of the war, emancipation, and religion, among many topics. Because Union armies enjoyed vastly greater resources, the men often had photography studios, newspapers, and multiple churches from which to choose. They also had more chances to go home on furlough. Southern troops endured greater material hardships, particularly a lack of shoes and, during certain times, food. Federals and Confederates also fraternized and traded with one another; probably the most common exchange was Union coffee for Southern tobacco. With mandatory reenlistment for life after April 1862, Southern troops had few chances to see their families, a particular form of suffering that they sometimes relieved with selective or seasonal desertion, usually for short periods of time.

Both armies also represented a reasonably accurate cross section of the free population, despite the resentment among poor men (from both sections) toward certain provisions of conscription. The country's major occupational groups—farmers, skilled and unskilled workers, and white-collar professionals—seem to have been fairly represented in the Union and Confederate armies. Only men from the Northern middle class avoided military service in disproportionate numbers, a result of substitution and commutation, and the Union's greater reserve of manpower. Also underrepresented in Northern armies were Catholics, primarily a measure of their Democratic Party loyalty. Among Confederates, all social classes seem to have served in proportionate numbers, including planters and professionals.

The most important motives for men to join the armies changed over time. In 1861 there was great idealism on both sides: Northerners wanted to preserve the Union and uphold democracy and the rule of law; Southerners fought for independence, slavery, honor, and because Yankees were invading their homes. Over time, many Northerners joined to avoid the draft and collect recruiting bounties, particularly immigrants and other poor working men, and more Southerners were conscripted or forced to volunteer in order to avoid conscription. As the war dragged on, a growing number of men on both sides fought because they didn't want to admit defeat or because their hatred of the enemy had grown so intense that they wanted to see the war to its conclusion. Finally, to what extent white Northerners embraced emancipation as a cause remains controversial. Certainly a large number of Union soldiers, as they encountered African Americans for the first time, became convinced that slavery was wrong, even if they never believed in racial equality (which almost no whites did). Furthermore, modern readers—overwhelmingly cynical and distrustful, especially of great moral crusades—may tend unfairly to doubt the idealism frequently expressed by nineteenth-century men and women. Regardless of Northern whites' sincerity about the war's great racial questions, the vast majority agreed that emancipation and enrolling black men would shorten the war and potentially save lives—goals they all could support.

The final Union victory of 1863 was in Tennessee. Since February 1862, when Union forces captured Forts Donelson and Henry and occupied Nashville, the two sides had fought a war of position in the rugged mountains of southeast Tennessee. The Union objective was Chattanooga, a major railroad center and the gateway to Georgia since it controlled a gap in the Appalachian Mountains. Throughout July and August 1863, Union commander William Rosecrans pushed Braxton Bragg's Confederates south toward Chattanooga. Ringed by mountains and straddling the Tennessee River, the city presented a real danger for any occupying force since it could be easily surrounded and cut off. In early September, Rosecrans maneuvered enough troops south of the city so that Bragg feared a repeat of Vicksburg, and on the ninth he abandoned Chattanooga. Rather than continue the retreat, however, the Confederates mounted a surprising counteroffensive. They moved Longstreet and twelve thousand troops from Virginia—over nearly a thousand miles of hobbled railroads—and in heavy fighting on September 18–20 (the Battle of Chickamauga), they pushed the Federals back to Chattanooga. Longstreet and his men performed well, and the Confederates nearly won a major victory. But the Union was saved by inspired battlefield leadership from George H. Thomas (the hero of Stone's River), who several times rallied his men and averted a complete collapse. His calm presence allowed the Union to make an orderly retreat to Chattanooga and earned Thomas the best nickname of the war: "the Rock of Chickamauga."

The Union still occupied Chattanooga, but now *they* faced slow starvation from a Confederate siege. Although one tenuous mountain road allowed a trickle of supplies into the city, Northern troops were suffering by October. On the seventeenth, Grant arrived personally to take command. He replaced Rosecrans with Thomas, and the two generals devised a plan to fight their way out of the siege. (They were aided when Davis unwisely ordered Longstreet to move north and try to retake Knoxville, Tennessee, thereby weakening the Southern force besieging Chattanooga.) The Confederate line ran roughly northeast to southwest, just east of the city. It was anchored by large mountains at each end—with the imposing Lookout Mountain on the south—and connected by Missionary Ridge, a low sloping hill that ran between them. On November 24, the Union captured Lookout Mountain, although Sherman's men failed to take the north end of the line. Apparently stalled, the Union offensive suddenly revived when Thomas's men staged a remarkable assault on the Confederate center along Missionary Ridge. Grant believed the position too strong to attack and had ordered only a diversionary feint, but when the Union veterans surged into the first Southern trenches, they were inspired, and pushed spontaneously up the hill. Grant and Thomas stared in disbelief as the cheering Federals overwhelmed the stunned defenders, who retreated in chaos toward Georgia. The two sides settled into winter quarters, and the Union secured Chattanooga and southeast Tennessee.

The three great Union victories in 1863 dealt the Confederacy a severe blow. Losses were staggering for both armies, but Southerners had fewer reserves at home and could not replace the men lost at Gettysburg and elsewhere. Lee's daring invasion gamble failed in every respect, and cost him a third of his army. Poor Confederate strategic decisions contributed to the military turnaround, and Davis and Lee squandered scarce resources in Pennsylvania and Tennessee. Northerners were confident heading into 1864, and even Lincoln expressed some rare optimism. How would Confederates respond? Much depended on how Southern civilians could endure shortages and dislocations that accompanied the increasingly brutal war and expanding Union occupation.

Colonel Joshua Lawrence Chamberlain's Report of the Battle of Gettysburg (July 6, 1863)

Chamberlain commanded the Twentieth Maine Infantry, which held a key position on Little Round Top during the brutal, desperate fighting that took place on July 2 at the extreme left end of the Union line. These portions of his official report touch on some of the critical moments, giving a sense of the terrain and the desperate nature of the Union defense.

✶ ✶ ✶ ✶

Somewhere near 4 p.m. a sharp cannonade, at some distance to our left and front, was the signal for a sudden and rapid movement of our whole division in the direction of this firing. . . . We took a farm road crossing Plum Run in order to gain a rugged mountain spur called Granite Spur, or Little Round Top. . . .

Colonel Vincent [the brigade commander] indicated to me the ground my regiment was to occupy, informing me that this was the extreme left of our general line, and that a desperate attack was expected in order to turn that position, concluding by telling me I was to "hold that ground at all hazards."

In order to commence by making my right firm, I formed my regiment on the right into line, giving such direction to the line as should best secure the advantage of the rough, rocky, and stragglingly wooded ground.

The line faced generally toward a more conspicuous eminence southwest of ours, which is known as Sugar Loaf, or Round Top. . . . The artillery was replaced by a vigorous infantry assault upon the center . . .

In the midst of this, an officer from my center informed me that some important movement of the enemy was going on in his front . . . Mounting a large rock, I was able to see a considerable body of the enemy moving by the flank in rear of their line engaged, and passing from the direction of the foot of Great Round Top through the valley toward the front of my left. The close engagement not allowing any change of front,

I immediately stretched my regiment to the left, by taking intervals by the left flank, and at the same time "refusing" my left wing, so that it was nearly at right angles with my right, thus occupying about twice the extent of our ordinary front, some of the companies being brought into single rank when the nature of the ground gave sufficient strength or shelter. . . . We were not a moment too soon; the enemy's flanking column having gained their desired direction, burst upon my left, where they evidently had expected an unguarded flank, with great demonstration.

We opened a brisk fire at close range, which was so sudden and effective that they soon fell back among the rocks and low trees in the valley, only to burst forth again with a shout, and rapidly advanced, firing as they came. They pushed up to within a dozen yards of us before the terrible effectiveness of our fire compelled them to break and take shelter.

They renewed the assault on our whole front, and for an hour the fighting was severe. Squads of the enemy broke through our line in several places, and the fight was literally hand to hand. . . .

The enemy seemed to have gathered all their energies for their final assault. We had gotten our thin line into as good a shape as possible, when a strong force emerged from the scrub wood in the valley, as well as I could judge, in two lines in echelon by the right, and, opening a heavy fire, the first line came on as if they meant to sweep everything before them. We opened on them as well as we could with our scanty ammunition snatched from the field.

It did not seem possible to withstand another shock like this now coming on. Our loss had been severe. One-half of my left wing had fallen, and a third of my regiment lay just behind us, dead or badly wounded. I feared that the enemy might have nearly surrounded the Little Round Top, and only a desperate chance was left for us. My ammunition was soon exhausted. My men were firing their last shot and getting ready to club their muskets.

It was imperative to strike before we were struck by this overwhelming force in a hand-to-hand fight, which we could not probably have withstood or survived. At that crisis, I ordered the bayonet. The word was enough. It ran like fire along the line, from man to man, and rose into a shout, with which they sprang forward upon the enemy, now not 30 yards away. The effect was surprising; many of the enemy's first line threw down their arms and surrendered. . . .

Four hundred prisoners, including two field and several line officers, were sent to the rear . . . One hundred and fifty of the enemy were found killed and wounded in our front.

I have the honor to be, your obedient servant,

Joshua L. Chamberlain, Colonel,

Commanding Twentieth Maine Volunteers.

The War of the Rebellion: A Compilation of the Official Records of the Union and Confederate Armies, 130 Volumes (Washington, DC: Government Printing Office, 1880–1900), Series I, Volume 27.

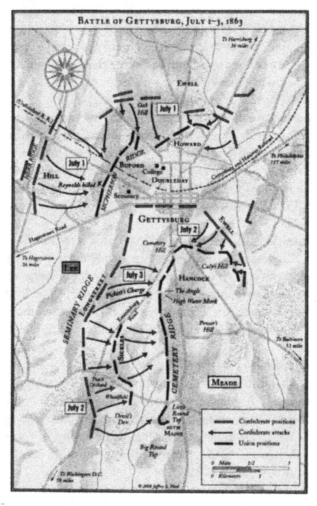

General John Imboden Describes the Confederate Retreat After Gettysburg (July 4, 1863)

*Robert E. Lee's Army of Northern Virginia was in a desperate
position as it retreated south after the battle, as this passage
suggests. Many men—Northern and Southern, and especially
President Lincoln—wondered why Union commander
Meade did not attack the decimated Confederates.*

The column moved rapidly, considering the rough roads and the darkness, and from almost every wagon for many miles issued heart-rending wails of agony. For four hours I hurried forward on my way to the front, and in all that time I was never out of hearing of the groans and cries of the wounded and dying. Their torn and bloody clothing, matted and hardened, was rasping the tender, inflamed, and still oozing wounds. Very few of the wagons had even a layer of straw in them, and all were without springs. The road was rough and rocky from the heavy washings of the preceding day. The jolting was enough to have killed strong men, if long exposed to it. From nearly every wagon as the teams trotted on, urged by whip and shout, came such cries and shrieks as these:

"O God [!] why can't I die!"

"My God [!] will no one have mercy and kill me!"

"I am dying! I am dying! My poor wife, my dear children, what will become of you?"

John Imboden, "The Confederate Retreat from Gettysburg," in Clarence Buel and Robert Johnson, eds., *Battles and Leaders of the Civil War, Volume IV* (New York: T. Yoseloff, 1956; orig. 1888).

"Hotel de Vicksburg" (July 1863)

*This scrap, presumably written by a Vicksburg resident during
the siege, was discovered after the surrender and reprinted in
various newspapers across the country. In comic form the "bill of*

fare" conveys the desperation and near-starvation that men and women in Vicksburg faced.

* * * *

THE CONFEDERATE READER

HOTEL DE VICKSBURG

Bill of Fare for July, 1863.

SOUP
Mule Tail.

BOILED
Mule bacon with poke greens.
Mule ham canvassed.

ROAST
Mule sirloin.
Mule rump stuffed with rice.

VEGETABLES
Peas and Rice.

ENTREES
Mule head stuffed a-la-Mode.
Mule beef jerked a-la-Mexicana.
Mule ears fricassed a-la-gotch.
Mule side stewed, new style, hair on.
Mule spare ribs plain.
Mule liver, hashed.

SIDE DISHES
Mule salad.
Mule hoof soused.
Mule brains a-la-omelette.
Mule kidney stuffed with peas.
Mule tripe fried in pea meal batter.
Mule tongue cold a-la-Bray.

JELLIES
Mule foot.

PASTRY
Pea meal pudding, blackberry sauce.
Cotton-wood berry pies
China berry tart.

DESSERT
White-oak acorns.
Beech nuts.
Blackberry leaf tea.
Genuine Confederate Coffee.

★ ★ ★

Southern Punch, August 22, 1863.

Confederate Carlton McCarthy on Disillusionment Among the Troops

Speaking for many men on both sides, McCarthy describes how soldiers became disillusioned with the romantic, gallant notions of war that they had held in 1861. This passage also recounts some of the usual boredom of camp life and Southern assumptions about Yankee troops.

It is amusing to recall the disgust with which the men would hear of their assignment to the rear as reserves. They regarded the order as a deliberate insult, planned by some officer who had a grudge against their regiment or battery, who had adopted this plan to prevent their presence in battle, and thus humiliate them. How soon did they learn the sweetness of a day's repose in the rear! . . .

Another fancy idea was that the principal occupation of a soldier should be actual conflict with the enemy. They didn't dream of such a thing as camping for six months at a time without firing a gun, or marching and countermarching to mislead the enemy, or driving wagons and ambulances, building bridges, currying horses, and the thousand commonplace duties of the soldier. . . .

Everybody remembers how we used to talk about "one Confederate whipping a dozen Yankees." Literally true sometimes, but generally speaking, two to one made hard work for the boys. . . .

Wounds were in great demand after the first wounded hero made his appearance. His wound was the envy of thousands of unfortunates who had not so much as a scratch to boast, and who felt "small" and of little consequence before the man with a bloody bandage. Many became despondent and groaned as they thought that perchance after all they were doomed to go home safe and sound, and hear, for all time, the praises of the fellow who had lost his arm by a cannon shot, or had his face ripped by a sabre, or his head smashed with a fragment of shell. . . . Wisdom, born of experience, soon taught all hands better sense, and the fences and trees and ditches and rocks became valuable and eagerly sought after . . .

Only the wisest men, those who had seen war before, imagined that the war would last more than a few months. The young volunteers thought one good battle would settle the whole matter; and, indeed, after "first Manassas" many thought they might as well go home! . . .

The newspaper men delighted in telling the soldiers that the Yankees were a diminutive race, of feeble constitution, timid as hares, with no enthusiasm, and that they would perish in short order under the glow of our Southern sun. Anyone who had seen a regiment from Ohio or Maine knows how true these statements were. . . . Sherman's army, marching through Richmond after the surrender of Lee and Johnston, seemed to be composed of a race of giants, well-fed and well-clad. . . .

The pride of the volunteers was sorely tried by the incoming of conscripts—the most despised class in the Army—and their devotion to company and regiment was visibly lessened. They could not bear the thought of having these men for comrades, and felt the flag insulted when claimed by one of them as his flag. . . .

As the companies became decimated by disease, wounds, desertions and death, it became necessary to consolidate them, and so the social pleasures received another blow. Men from the same neighborhoods and villages, who had been schoolmates together, were no longer in companies, but mingled indiscriminately with all sorts of men from anywhere and everywhere.

Carlton McCarthy, *Detailed Minutiae of Soldier Life in the Army of Northern Virginia* (Richmond, VA: B. F. Johnson, 1908; orig. 1882).

Abraham Lincoln: The Gettysburg Address
(November 19, 1863)

Asked to help dedicate the cemetery for soldiers killed at Gettysburg, Lincoln spoke for just a few minutes, eloquently defining the war as a struggle to preserve democracy and freedom—all without mentioning slavery or emancipation.

✳ ✳ ✳ ✳

Fourscore and seven years ago our fathers brought forth, on this continent, a new nation, conceived in Liberty, and dedicated to the proposition that all men are created equal.

Now we are engaged in a great civil war, testing whether that nation, or any nation so conceived, and so dedicated, can long endure. We are met on a great battlefield of that war. We have come to dedicate a portion of that field, as a final resting-place for those who here gave their lives, that that nation might live. It is altogether fitting and proper that we should do this.

But, in a larger sense, we can not dedicate—we can not consecrate—we can not hallow—this ground. The brave men, living and dead, who struggled here, have consecrated it, far above our poor power to add or detract. The world will little note, nor long remember what we say here, but it can never forget what they did here. It is for us the living, rather, to be dedicated here to the unfinished work which they who fought here have thus far so nobly advanced. It is rather for us to be here dedicated to the great task remaining before us—that from these honored dead we take increased devotion to that cause for which they gave the last full measure of devotion—that we here highly resolve that these dead shall not have died in vain—that this nation, under God, shall have a new birth of freedom—and that government of the people, by the people, for the people, shall not perish from the earth.

THIRTEEN

European Diplomacy, the Union Blockade, and Confederate Families at War in 1863

IN 1863, CONFEDERATE ARMIES SUFFERED massive casualties in desperately fought but, in the end, unsuccessful major battles across the country. The year started with high expectations as the Union looked inept in Virginia, Tennessee, and Mississippi, but it ended with a succession of Northern triumphs in each theater. The year was perhaps harder for Southern women and children. Even as more and more of them mourned the loss of husbands, brothers, and fathers, the Union blockade of Southern commerce tightened, creating shortages and destabilizing the economy. In addition, as more Southern territory came under Union control, civilians had to accommodate (or not) the realities of occupation. These two great underlying factors—occupation and the prolonged, widespread absence of most adult white men—affected everything else on the Confederate home front. With four-fifths of the adult free men gone to war or already dead, people struggled to maintain a coherent society and economy, and the Confederate government struggled to make effective policies. How to take advantage of their dwindling resources? How would they pay for the war? Finally, how would slaves react to the massive dislocations that had shattered Southern white society and to news of the Emancipation Proclamation? No matter how valiant the Confederate Army, by 1863 it was unclear how, or if, Southern civilians could maintain the economy and society needed to sustain the war.

From the beginning of the war, as we have noted, Confederates' military strategy conflicted with their long-term resources. Their best chance seemed to be prolonging the conflict until Northerners lost their commitment or foreign intervention led to a Southern victory—the "American Revolution" plan. A longer war, however, allowed the Union to take advantage of its manpower and industrial superiority, and exposed the Confederacy's corresponding weaknesses. Confederate leaders also expected the South's cotton-based export economy to pay for the war effort; in turn this depended on the Union blockade proving ineffective or on the British navy intervening to break it ("King Cotton diplomacy"). By 1863, these Southern expectations remained unfulfilled and the Confederate economy and social order were showing serious cracks.

The Confederate plan to use cotton as an economic and diplomatic weapon had limitations. In 1861, Confederates tried a self-imposed, internal blockade on exports. The supposed resulting shortage—a "cotton famine"— was expected to pay dividends in the long run as British manufacturers would demand that their government import Southern cotton. But Southerners failed to account for two things. First, their record production of the late 1850s meant that British manufacturers had a glut of raw cotton in 1861 and textile mill owners in Britain were happy to use it up. Second, the British had the world's greatest empire, and as the American Civil War dragged on they simply cultivated new sources of raw cotton, particularly in Egypt and India. This development would profoundly affect the postwar Southern economy, and during the war it meant that the British could replace Southern cotton without resorting to military intervention. British manufacturers faced one brief shortage, late in 1862, but that passed by 1863 as new imperial sources provided more cotton.

Besides the economic illusions in the King Cotton theory, there were plenty of additional reasons for the British (and the French, who determined to follow the British lead) not to intervene on behalf of the Confederacy. First, the Confederacy was a rebel government, and the British had plenty of potential rebels in their own worldwide empire. Why recognize and encourage rebellion? Second, British leaders remained more concerned with European crises (particularly in Poland and Denmark) than with the American war. They also wanted to establish the diplomatic principle that naval blockade was a legitimate weapon of war, something that paid dividends for the Royal Navy during World War I, when the United States was forced to abide by the British blockade of Germany. Third, the United

States was a stabilizing influence in the Western Hemisphere, and many British leaders began to see it as a potential ally with a common heritage and values. Fourth, the British economy did not suffer during the war; in fact, what they lost in cotton imports was nearly balanced by increased purchases of Union wheat and other grains. Fifth, the Confederacy never won quite enough battles to convince the majority of Britain's leaders that it could win the war. The South's best string of success, in mid- and late 1862, raised Confederate hopes of formal recognition from London and Paris, but the Union victory at Antietam Creek checked European admiration for Lee and his ragged troops. Finally, and most important, the Emancipation Proclamation changed the nature of the war to one clearly for or against slavery. As the world's leading antislavery government, Great Britain would not intervene to help a Confederacy fighting to maintain slavery. The U.S. minister in London, Charles Francis Adams, wrote perceptively that Lincoln's proclamation in September 1862 "has done more for us here than all our former victories and all our diplomacy."

Without British intervention, the Union blockade slowly strangled Southern exports and imports, and eventually crippled the Confederacy's ability to pay for the war and meet some basic needs. The blockade was a daunting task, of course, given the Confederacy's size and long coastline (consider the difficulty of controlling illegal drug shipments into the United States today, even with modern technology). The Union Navy began with fewer than a dozen patrol ships and ended the war with more than five hundred vessels on duty as part of the blockading fleet. The primary strategy was to close each major port by controlling the waters surrounding it, which was more important than taking physical possession of the city. For example, Savannah was closed to blockade runners in April 1862, although the city itself was not taken by land forces until Christmas 1864. When the Union essentially closed Charleston, South Carolina, by late 1863, it left only Mobile, Alabama, Galveston, Texas, and Wilmington, North Carolina, as significant ports open to the blockade runners that came in from the Caribbean. Using small, fast ships, blockade runners usually took on cargo, sent from Europe in larger merchant vessels, in Jamaica or other Caribbean islands and then tried to run the Union blockade into the Confederacy. Once the British agreed to allow Union warships to stop neutral merchant ships (mostly British) traveling between neutral ports (such as London and Havana) if the Union believed the cargo was *eventually* heading for the Confederacy, the Caribbean trade slowed. This was known as the "doctrine of continuous voyage (or transportation)," and it demonstrated Britain's long-term perspective. Establishing international diplomatic and legal principles of benefit to them as owner of the world's most powerful navy was Great Britain's primary goal. The short-term effect on the American Civil War—in this case strengthening the Union blockade—was secondary.

The blockade's effectiveness remains a matter of perspective. Most blockade runners got through, probably more than four-fifths. Perhaps the Confederacy's greatest success, for the course of the war, was importing six hundred thousand rifles from Europe. On the other hand, small blockade runners carried much less than antebellum merchant ships. Between 1856 and 1860, the future Confederate states exported more than ten million bales of cotton; in the four war years they shipped only about one million bales to Europe or the North. That was not enough to fund the massive Confederate war effort, and in that regard the Union Navy's blockade was central to the North's winning the war. Furthermore, most blockade runners carried luxury items such as silk, bourbon, or cigars, which brought big prices from wealthy Confederates who could pay in gold. Bulky items such as shoes were desperately needed by the army, but Jefferson Davis's government had limited success in forcing blockade runners to import necessities.

The smaller Confederate Navy could not realistically hope to break the Union blockade of any port. Instead, Confederate naval efforts focused on two broad strategies: ocean commerce raiding, and inland defense of rivers and harbors using gunboats. Commerce raiders achieved some spectacular successes and destroyed dozens of Union ships on the high seas. Most famous were the exploits of Captains Raphael Semmes of the *Alabama* and James Waddell of the *Shenandoah*. Semmes and the *Alabama* wreaked havoc on Union merchants from 1861 until late 1864, when the ship finally was sunk. It had captured and destroyed at least fifty-five merchant ships. The *Shenandoah* was not commissioned until October 1864, and was never captured. It entered Liverpool, England (after sailing to Australia and New Zealand), in November 1865, the last Confederate force of any kind still in service. Commerce raiders particularly affected Union merchants by forcing many to transfer their vessels' ownership to neutral countries in order to avoid capture. Confederate river gunboats operated effectively at several key points, especially around Richmond, where they held off the Union flotilla on the James River.

Despite these successes, the Union blockade hindered Jefferson Davis's economic policy and crippled his ability to pay for the war. Without significant cotton exports, the Confederacy scrambled to raise money for a war of such unanticipated scale and duration. As in the Union, Confederates tried three basic approaches to fund the war: borrowing, taxing, and printing paper money. The disparity between the Union's and the Confederacy's abilities to finance their war efforts underscored the vast differences in their respective economies. In the end, it demonstrated that the Southern agricultural economy simply could not sustain such a long, draining war. When the conflict began, most Confederate capital was invested in land and slaves, and therefore not easily converted to cash. Most Confederates gave what gold they had in the country's first bond drives in 1861, but that largely emptied the public savings of Southern civilians. Thus, although Davis's government tried a range of taxes very similar to those levied in the Union, Southerners had little gold with which to pay the new duties. By April 1863, the Richmond government had enacted an income tax and various luxury taxes, including taxes on salt, wine, tobacco, liquor, and cotton. There were license taxes on virtually every occupation. Eventually the government also tried a controversial "tax-in-kind" of 10 percent on agricultural produce, which farmers greatly resented because it was a higher rate than other levies.

Confederate civilians complained about all taxes, in part because Southern rates had been so low before the war, but also because the taxes were unevenly collected as the war progressed. Occupied areas, of course, were beyond the reach of Confederate agents, and remote places such as Texas or western North Carolina presented difficulties for the hard-pressed Confederate bureaucracy. In areas more easily accessed by agents—central Virginia or Georgia, for instance—farmers had to pay over and over. In the end, taxes paid for less than 5 percent of the war effort.

Loans were slightly more successful. The Confederacy negotiated several direct loans, including a one-hundred-million-dollar loan collected in 1861 that came mostly from planters. The most famous European loan came through Emile Erlanger, a Frenchman sympathetic to the Confederacy (his son was romancing the daughter of Confederate diplomat John Slidell). The European line of credit soon dried up, however, another consequence of the Confederacy's lack of diplomatic recognition. Davis's government also tried bonds, a tactic that was helping the Union so tremendously. But the Confederacy could not pay interest in gold, making their bonds unattractive for overseas investors. And of course, who knew if the Confederacy would be around in five or ten years to pay them off? Finally, the Confederacy tried "produce loans" in an effort to utilize its most valuable commodity, cotton, as a sort of substitute currency. The idea was that Davis's government would purchase cotton in exchange for bonds, ship it through the blockade and then hold the cotton in Europe until the price went up enough to realize a huge profit. Unfortunately for the Confederacy, many planters preferred to sell their cotton to blockade runners or to smuggle it through Union lines to the North, both of which brought greater profits than the government-backed produce loans. In short, many planters' selfishness undermined the use of cotton for loans or bonds, which together only financed about a third of the Confederate war effort.

The last option, printing paper money, supplied nearly two-thirds of Confederate wartime spending. The national government, state governments, and city governments (even some individuals) all printed money, practically around the clock, using it to pay for all the things that troops and civilians needed. State and local governments alone printed over $112 million worth of paper money. Not surprisingly, runaway inflation followed. By early 1863, most paper already was worth less than one-third of its face value. The vast variety of paper presented another set of problems. How much was a note from the state of Alabama worth in Richmond? What about something from Virginia's Bank of Philippi in Savannah? Most Confederate paper fluctuated with the fortunes of Southern armies, although the long-term trend was sharply downward. By the end of 1863, inflation was bad enough that the Confederacy drifted toward a barter economy. According to one Confederate official, butter was four dollars a pound and plain fabric nearly five dollars per yard in late 1863.

Inflation took a toll on all Confederates, but wage workers fared worst, and families of servicemen who relied on soldiers' meager pay became embittered. When the pay arrived at all it remained fixed at eleven dollars per month for privates. Urban dwellers did not have land to farm, and many women and children in cities faced starvation by 1863. On April 2 of that year, several hundred Richmond women rioted for bread. Many of them relied on the wages earned by husbands working in the Tredegar Iron

Works—wages that had fallen far behind the rate of inflation. One desperate young woman informed a wealthy resident that the swelling crowd intended "going to the bakeries and each of us will take a loaf of bread. This is little enough for the government to give us after it has taken all our men." Governor John Letcher failed to satisfy the growing mob, which marched on the city's retail district and looted beef and whatever they could carry off. It was stopped only when Jefferson Davis himself appealed to the people's patriotism, and then threatened to have the city's reserve troops shoot them down. The next day, Confederate infantry patrolled the streets. That same year, residents in more than a half dozen other cities also rioted; in Mobile, Alabama, the crowd carried signs reading BREAD OR BLOOD. Conditions got worse, but even by 1863, Southern civilians experienced widespread shortages and suffering. Local relief efforts simply could not match the level of need. Normally "states' rights" advocates called for more, not less, government action.

The blockade and inflation affected nearly all Southerners, but the impact of Union invasion and occupation naturally varied. By 1863 large sections of the Confederacy were under Union control: northern and western Virginia; most of Tennessee and Louisiana; coastal South Carolina, Georgia, and Florida; parts of Arkansas. In these places Southern civilians had to decide whether, or how, to accommodate the enemy. Most civilians first registered shock and fear when the Yankees came, and most stayed inside their homes as much as possible. Persistent rumors about the rough and lewd behavior of Union soldiers worried Southern women and presented Confederate men with a dilemma. Soldiers from occupied areas faced either doing their duty for the country and their comrades or going home to make sure their wives and children were safe. Following the 1862 invasion of Virginia by Union general John Pope, who authorized strong measures against civilians and Southern property, Southern fears intensified. As more and more women, resentful at the lack of male protection, directly asked men in the army where their "true" duty lay, Southern generals and politicians wondered how their soldiers would react.

The Union armies advancing into the Confederacy after January 1, 1863, also freed slaves under the terms of Lincoln's Emancipation Proclamation. News of the edict quickly spread among slaves, who ran away in even greater numbers. Throughout 1863, rumors of slave rebellions and "disrespectful" behavior spread among Southern whites. Always fearful of slave violence, whites tried greater measures to control the black population. The Confederacy's four million slaves allowed the South to mobilize a high percentage of white men, but the war also exposed how inflexible slavery was. The system existed on fear and torture, and even with the twenty-slave rule ensuring that a minimum number of young white men remained at home, slaves had greater latitude and more chances to escape. And reaching the advancing Union Army was much easier than getting to the North or Canada before the war. As Union forces penetrated Southern territory they attracted thousands of runaways, many of whom stayed to work for the Yankees. More and more ex-slaves also enlisted. The Emancipation Proclamation and Union military success, then, further destabilized slavery, depriving the Confederacy of valuable manpower; eroded civilian confidence in their government's war effort; and prompted more Confederates to desert the army. In July 1863, one conscription officer estimated that between fifty thousand and one hundred thousand men were "evading duty," and at least forty thousand men were absent without leave. By September, another conscription inspector in North Carolina reported organized groups of deserters, several hundreds strong, hiding in mountainous regions inaccessible or too dangerous for his men to patrol.

Union occupation also forced Southern civilians to decide whether or not to do business with the Union Army, which became the most valuable source of income in occupied areas. Southerners who questioned secession more willingly took a loyalty oath, although they feared reprisal if or when the occupying forces moved on. Occupation also meant that local men were beyond the reach of Confederate or state conscription officers, something many of them, and their families, appreciated. But other men resented the lack of "enthusiasm" among these "idlers." Why wasn't every man trying to get through the Union lines to serve the Confederacy? When the Union Army left, some of these men faced retribution from resentful neighbors. In short, Union occupation forced Confederate men and women to make difficult decisions about their position on the war and their relationship to the government. All of these considerations helped divide Southern civilians, spreading suspicion and uncertainty that hurt the overall war effort.

In 1863, the Confederacy faced greater manpower shortages and difficulty raising troops. Centralized conscription, including mandatory reenlistment, generated stiff opposition, accentuated by the continued exemption for slaveowners. Resentment of military service among poor folks added to growing problems of inflation and long absences of husbands, fathers, and sons. Widespread volunteering and conscription had devastated most local economies by the end of 1862, and in rural areas where few owned slaves, women were forced to do much of the hardest work. More and more men asked how long they would be expected to ignore the needs of their families, particularly when wealthy planters seemed to have ways to avoid military duty. The unexpected length and destructiveness of the war, in other words, exposed cracks in the supposedly unified Southern class system. The discriminatory features of conscription and the floundering economy turned poor men and women increasingly against the war effort. "I am fearful," one North Carolina soldier wrote to his governor, "we will have a revolution unless something is done as the majority of our soldiers are poor men with families who say they are tired of the rich mans war & poor mans fight, [and] they wish to get to their families."

All of these economic, social, and political problems played out against the backdrop of the Confederacy's faltering military effort late in 1863. Southerners in most Confederate states faced some direct threat from Union forces, and extensive physical damage had destroyed large areas of farmland, railroads, roads, and bridges. Numerous cities had suffered massive damage. In short, the war "was asking" much more of Southern men and women than they had expected, and many reconsidered whether or not to continue supporting the Confederate effort. It was Jefferson Davis's task to inspire his people and mobilize the remaining, increasingly scarce resources, all without alienating so many civilians that men in uniform questioned where their primary duty lay. By the end of 1863, it seemed that Davis's best chance of winning independence was, once again, the Northern peace movement.

A Confederate Soldier Criticizes the "rich mans war & poor mans fight" (February 27, 1863)

By 1863 many Southerners, particularly non-slaveowners, complained about Confederate policies that seemed to favor planters at the expense of poorer folks. This letter, written to the governor of North Carolina, summarizes this growing disaffection.

* * * *

Fayetteville, North Carolina

Dr Sir

Please pardon the liberty which a poor soldier takes in thus addressing you as when he *volunteered* he left a wife with four children to go to fight for his country. He cheerfully made the sacrifices thinking that the Govt. would protect his family, and keep them from starvation. In this he has been disappointed for the Govt. has made a distinction between the rich man (who had something to fight for) and the poor man who fights for that he will never have. The exemption of the owners of 20 negroes & the allowing of substitutes clearly proves it. Healthy and active men who have furnished substitutes are grinding the poor by speculation while their substitutes have been discharged after a month's service as being too old or as invalids. By taking too many men from their farms they have not left enough to cultivate the land thus making a scarcity of provisions and this with unrestrained speculation has put provs. up in this market as follows Meal $4 to 5 per Bus, flour $50 to 60 per Brl, Lard 70 cents per lb by the brl, Bacon 75 cents per lb by the load and every thing else in proportion.

Now Govr. do tell me how we poor soldiers who are fighting for the "rich mans negro" can support our families at $11 per month? How can the poor live? I dread to see summer as I am fearful there will be much suffering and probably many deaths from starvation. They are suffering now. A poor little factory girl begged for a piece of bread the other day &

said she had not had anything to eat since the day before when she eat a small piece of Bread for her Breakfast.

I am fearful we will have a revolution unless something is done as the majority of our soldiers are poor men with families who say they are tired of the rich mans war & poor mans fight, they wish to get to their families & fully believe some settlement could be made were it not that our authorities have made up their minds to prosecute the war regardless of all suffering since they receive large pay & they and their families are kept from suffering & exposure and can have their own ends served. There is great dissatisfaction in the army and as a mans first duty is to provide for his own household the soldiers wont be imposed upon much longer. If we hear our families are suffering & apply for a furlough to go to them we are denied & if we go without authority we are arrested & punished as deserters. . . .

I would also request in behalf of the soldiers generally (for I know it is popular with the army) for you to instruct our representatives in Congress to introduce a resolution as follows. That all single young men now occupying salaried positions as Clerks Conductors or Messengers in the Depts of Govt & State & Rail Road & Express Cos. be discharged immediately & sent into services and their places filled by married men & men of families who are competent to fill the positions. . . .

Governor's Papers, North Carolina Division of Archives and History, Raleigh, NC.

A Southern Woman Protests Inflation and Suffering at Home (April 9, 1863)

Runaway inflation threatened to destroy the Confederate economy in 1863. Hardest hit were women and families who depended on their soldier-husbands' small paychecks. This letter, written to the governor of North Carolina, describes the desperation felt by many women trying to feed their hungry children.

✳ ✳ ✳ ✳

Mcleanesville N c
Aprile 9th 1863

Gov Vance

I have threatend for some time to write you a letter—a crowd of we Poor wemen went to Greenesborough yesterday for something to eat as we had not a mouthful meet nor bread in my house what did they do but put us in gail. . . .

I have 6 little children and my husband in the armey and what am I to do. Slone wont let we Poor wemen have thread when he has it we know he has everything plenty he say he has not got it to spair when we go but just let thes big men go they can git it withou aney trouble. . . . We wemen will write for our husbans to come . . . home and help us we cant stand it the way they are treating us they charge $11.00 Per bunch for their thread and $2.50 for their calico—They threatend to shoot us and drawed their pistols over us that is hard.

Jim Slone sid he would feed we poor weman on dog meet and Roten egges. . . .

Governor's Papers, North Carolina Division of Archives and History, Raleigh, NC.

A Confederate Officer Details Widespread Desertion and Evasion of Duty (September 2, 1863)

This letter discusses the difficulties faced by those men trying to enforce Confederate conscription. Conscription officers dared not even enter many parts of the South—such as the wooded, mountainous portion of North Carolina described here.

✳ ✳ ✳ ✳

OFFICE OF INSPECTOR OF CONSCRIPTION,
Salisbury, N.C., September 2, 1863.

. . . The utter inadequacy now of any force that we can command without potential aid from armies in the field will become apparent when it is realized that desertion has assumed (in some regions, especially the central and western portions of this State) a very different and more formidable shape and development than could have been anticipated. It is difficult to arrive at any exact statistics on the subject. The unquestionable facts are these: Deserters now leave the Army with arms and ammunition in hand. They act in concert to force by superior numbers a passage against bridge or ferry guards, if such are encountered. Arriving at their selected localities of refuge, they organize in bands variously estimated at from fifty up to hundreds at various points. These estimates are perhaps exaggerated in some cases. . . .

While the disaffected feed them from sympathy, the loyal do so from fear. The latter class (and the militia) are afraid to aid the conscript service lest they draw revenge upon themselves and their property . . .

Letters are being sent to the Army stimulating desertion and inviting the men home, promising them aid and comforts. County meetings are declaring in the same spirit and to hold back conscripts. As desertion spreads and enjoys impunity, in the same proportion do the enrolled conscripts hang back from reporting where there is not force enough to compel them, and the more dangerous and difficult becomes the position of our enrolling officers. . . .

The War of the Rebellion: A Compilation of the Official Records of the Union and Confederate Armies, 130 Volumes (Washington, DC: Government Printing Office, 1880–1900), Series VI, Volume 2, 783–86.

FOURTEEN

The War and Union Politics in 1864:
Sherman, Grant, and Lincoln

AFTER THE UNION VICTORIES in 1863, many Northerners predicted a quick end to the war. For the first time, Lincoln also had a
commanding general who agreed with him about how the Union should
pursue the war. In March 1864, Lincoln named Ulysses S. Grant as general-
in-chief of all Union forces. Both men believed they should press the
Confederates on all fronts simultaneously, taking advantage of their own
numerical superiority. Lincoln summarized with a metaphor from farm
life: "Those not skinning can hold a leg," a phrase Grant particularly enjoyed. Both Lincoln and Grant also believed that Confederate forces—
especially Lee's Army of Northern Virginia, which was the most powerful
symbol of Southern resistance—should be the Union's objectives, not nec-
essarily strategic points on the map. By 1864, they reasoned that Southerners could not replace lost manpower, while the Union could, at least up
to a point. However, as the year dragged on—toward the presidential election in the fall—Lincoln and the Republicans worried about Northerners'
resolve in the face of ever-mounting casualties. Could they have fought so
long and hard only to lose the war at the ballot box? Confederate leaders
watched closely, too, and tried everything to encourage the peace movement. Military events and Union politics again intersected, and together
they reached the war's last critical moment.

Grant and the Union began with four major forces and a basic plan to
coordinate their offensives. The Army of the Potomac, with about 115,000

men and still led by George Gordon Meade, would move south generally toward Richmond, but with Lee's Army of Northern Virginia (about sixty thousand strong) as its chief target. Rather than stay in Washington (partly to avoid the political intrigue and controversy that had engulfed McClellan), Grant made his headquarters in the field and became the de facto commander; Meade served as chief bureaucrat, something at which he excelled. The two generals worked well together. Second, the Army of the James (about thirty thousand) was supposed to work its way up the Yorktown peninsula and join with the larger force at Richmond, where they would crush Lee's army. Third, in northern Georgia were William Tecumseh Sherman's combined forces, with about one hundred thousand men. Sherman's objectives were Atlanta and Joseph E. Johnston's fifty thousand Confederates. Finally, from New Orleans came another Union force (about twenty-five thousand) under Nathaniel Banks, who intended to move east, take Mobile, Alabama, and then join Sherman's men somewhere in southern Georgia. Nearly a separate war took place in Texas and southern Arkansas, where the Trans-Mississippi Department of the Confederacy operated without orders from Richmond. In that theater, the Union made little progress against stubborn Southern resistance.

Overall, the Union had twice as many men under arms as the Confederacy, and they were possibly the best-supplied troops in world history. But Southern troops were mostly battle-tested veterans—unlike the Union, which continued to bring in new men, including lowly regarded substitutes and draftees. Among the South's remaining troops, morale remained fairly high and men were adequately supplied. Most shortages, in fact, fell first on Confederate civilians. Furthermore, to conserve resources, Southern commanders and troops knew they would be fighting on the defensive nearly all of the time. This allowed them to choose advantageous terrain and build fortifications, conserve manpower, and exploit the technological superiority of fighting on the defensive. From 1861, the widespread use of rifled guns and artillery made it possible for a small number of determined men, well supplied and in a strong position, to defeat a much larger attacking force. Over and over Confederates proved this truism—overlooking the Stone Bridge at Antietam Creek or from behind the stone wall at Fredericksburg, for instance.

By 1864, the nature of Civil War combat evolved as each side sought to gain an advantage, looking for innovations to shift the balance. The war produced iron-plated warships, repeating rifles and crude machine guns, submarines, and airborne observation balloons. More widespread was the use of railroads to move troops, changing strategy and the course of individual battles, and the telegraph for nearly instant communication. These developments foreshadowed the twentieth-century world wars, and beg the question of whether or not the Civil War was a "modern" conflict. Of course it depends on one's perspective. And the debate certainly involves more than on-field technology: conscription; industrial mass production and the impact of grinding economic and financial attrition; decisive naval power at sea and on inland rivers; and finally, targeting the enemy's civilian morale and willingness, rather than their ability, to continue the war. These were all important strategic characteristics of World Wars I and II and, according to most military experts, defining features of modern warfare. But the Civil War was also profoundly shaped by "pre-modern" factors: both sides relied primarily on animal transport and muzzle-loading, single-shot rifles; weather—especially rain and mud—and terrain determined the armies' movements and the campaign season; cavalry and horses were critical for gathering intelligence and protecting the infantry; and neither side normally targeted civilians intentionally.

A final factor—perhaps the most important one—that signified the war's pre-modern qualities was the impact of disease. Overall, perhaps twice as many men died from disease as from wounds in battle. (Not until World War II did more Americans die from combat wounds.) The ratio of disease deaths to battlefield deaths was considerably higher for the Union: they had more men stationed behind the lines on guard duty and in camps; and men from the northern climates had fewer immunities to some of the semitropical diseases they encountered in the deep South. Diseases spread rapidly among men encamped together by the thousands, sharing food and utensils, taking drinking water from the same source where raw sewage was disposed, and with lice, flies, mosquitoes, and vermin everywhere. Doctors had some notion of sterilizing medical instruments and disinfecting wounds, but they had no real understanding of germ theory or of infections. Often, surgeons would use fire or alcohol only once per day to sterilize their scalpels and bone saws, or use the same rags to wipe off the blade in between amputations. Naturally these practices spread diseases rapidly. "Childhood" diseases, especially measles, mumps, chicken pox, and influenza, killed thousands; some evidence suggests that men from the rural Midwest fared worst in this regard, lacking the exposure to these germs that city kids more routinely encountered. "Camp diseases" such as typhoid, diarrhea, and dysentery killed even more, and were particularly devastating in prisons.

Both the Union and Confederacy recruited doctors; probably fifteen thousand served during the war. While they did not significantly advance the overall state of medical knowledge or care, surgeons became more adept at removing lead and making efficient amputations. The general rule was to amputate quickly in order to save the patient's life: "The sum of human misery will be most materially lessened," advised the *American Journal of Medical Science*, "by permitting no ambiguous cases to be subjected to the trial of preserving the limb." The number of amputations will never be accurately calculated, particularly if "minor" ones such as one or two fingers are included. The *Official Records* list more than thirty thousand "major" amputations—at least one hand or foot—but most experts consider that number a small fraction of the actual total. One Union private described a field hospital in 1863: "A large hole was dug in the yard, about the size of a small cellar, and into this the legs and arms were thrown as they were lopped off by the surgeons." Because they had greater resources, the Union pioneered some important innovations. In 1862, General McClellan organized the first modern ambulance corps in history, and nearly all European nations copied his system during World War I. The Union also made significant improvements to hospital facilities.

The U.S. Sanitary Commission coordinated the efforts to treat wounded men in the Union. Organized under the War Department, the Sanitary Commission employed thousands of salaried bureaucrats (nearly all men) and oversaw tens of thousands of volunteers (mostly women) who rolled bandages, collected food, wrote letters, and comforted dying men with kind words and passages from the Bible. In 1862 the Commission came under control of General William A. Hammond, a progressive surgeon who moved the Commission toward a more professional approach. Antebellum reformer Dorothea Dix—known for her investigation of insane asylums—worked with the army to coordinate women volunteer nurses, whom she required to be "plain looking" and middle-age. Other famous women who served were author Louisa May Alcott and Clara Barton, a teacher who raised private money, volunteered, and received permission to deliver supplies to the front. Barton later founded the American Red

Cross, in 1881. For the entire war, about 3,200 women and 10,000 men served as paid nurses.

The records for Confederate medical care are less reliable. There was no organization to match the Union's Sanitary Commission, and army commanders did not have the luxury of detailing men for a separate ambulance corps. Instead, Southern leaders primarily relied on the local population—wherever a battle took place—to take care of the wounded. Women took on the chief responsibility of caring for wounded men, Confederate or Union, left behind after battle. As the war progressed, Confederate care fell farther behind. Shortages of food and medicine increased death rates from wounds and disease. Confederates also used many slaves—again, mostly women—to care for the wounded. Civilians in certain areas, most obviously Virginia, felt the pressure more than others, and thousands of women ended the war simply exhausted and numb from the carnage.

In 1864, both sides had to make full use of their medical personnel and facilities. The Army of the Potomac moved into northern Virginia in late April, beginning more than a month of nearly continuous fighting that matched Grant and Lee in a classic duel of legends. Grant's plan was to move gradually south and east, toward Richmond and Petersburg, inflicting as many casualties as possible on Lee's smaller army. He hoped to lure Lee into the open for a decisive battle that would end the war. Lee countered Grant's moves and refused to be drawn into one great final encounter. He used the terrain and rivers of northern Virginia to slow the Union advance, and his men took a dreadful toll on their attackers. On May 5–7, the two armies fought the Battle of the Wilderness (roughly over the same ground as the Battle of Chancellorsville in May 1863), a confused struggle in which both sides celebrated prematurely. Confederate general Longstreet was accidentally shot by his own men and needed five months to recuperate. It was another Union tactical defeat, and veterans of the Army of the Potomac expected to turn back toward Washington. Grant, however, ordered them south toward Richmond. And in one of the war's classic scenes, Union veterans cheered and waved their hats in support of their new commander as a genuinely appreciative Grant rode past them. At the Wilderness, the Union lost seventeen thousand men, the Confederates eleven thousand (17 percent of Lee's forces).

Next came Spotsylvania (May 8–12), another crossroads in the middle of Virginia's dense forests. Grant tried to flank Lee's army to the east and south, but the Confederates beat the Federals to Spotsylvania and established a strong defensive position. On May 12, the climax of this encounter, the two sides fought for nearly twenty hours in pouring rain (including through the night), a battle that was particularly brutal on the Confederate right end, known as the "Bloody Angle." Each side suffered more than seven thousand casualties in one day. The two armies continued moving south and east toward Richmond. One of the most famous attacks of the entire war occurred on the morning of June 3. Lee had established a formidable defensive line between the Chickahominy River and Totopotomy Creek, but Grant ordered a frontal assault anyway. At this Battle of Cold Harbor, the Union lost seven thousand men in about forty-five minutes; it was the only attack that Grant later said he regretted.

Grant's forces were also hindered by the lack of success of other Union forces in Virginia. General Butler's Army of the James failed in its efforts to pressure Lee's army from the south, not taking Petersburg or cutting the railroads that supplied the Army of Northern Virginia. To the west, in the Shenandoah Valley, Union general Franz Sigel was confounded by Confederates under General Jubal Early. Early's men even reached the outskirts of Washington on July 10–11, firing on the stunned defenders. Finally, Grant had to send his top cavalry man, diminutive general Philip Sheridan, to the Valley in order to rout the Confederates. The unsuccessful campaigns by Butler and Sigel allowed the Confederacy to shift men from those areas and reinforce Lee's hard-pressed army.

In early June, after another flanking move, Grant beat Lee to the outskirts of Petersburg, but his commanders could not push out the Confederate defenders (fewer than three thousand men) led by General Beauregard. Lee then moved the bulk of his army into Richmond and Petersburg, the cities connected by a good railroad, and surrounded them with a network of trenches linked by small rivers and creeks. Grant was reluctant to attack such well-entrenched veteran troops. Instead, he settled in for a quasi-siege of the two cities; Confederates still got some supplies from the Southside and Weldon Railroads that ran west and south out of Petersburg. In three months, Grant's campaign cost sixty-four thousand Union casualties; Northern editors vilified him as "Butcher Grant," and public morale hit yet another new low. In July, the Union also faced the loss of thousands of three-year veterans—almost half of Grant's combat troops. But after appeals to their patriotism and offers of large bounties and thirty-day furloughs, a majority of the men signed back up to try to "see it through" to the end. The Confederates had lost about thirty thousand men in these Virginia battles, but added to their ranks the clerks in Richmond and Petersburg, and whomever they could find, and were now dug in.

The Union's best chance to break Confederate defenses came on July 30, 1864, at the infamous battle of "the Crater." The Forty-eighth Pennsylvania Infantry held one spot on the Union line. Most of them coal miners, they convinced their officers they could dig a long tunnel under the Confederate defenses, pack it with explosives, and blow a massive hole in the enemy's line. Grant approved the plan, and on July 30 a tremendous blast ripped a gaping breach in the Confederate line. Bewildered Southerners stood in shock or fled in panic, the Union had an open path to divide the Confederates and take Petersburg. From that point, everything went wrong. Unprepared white Union troops ran *into* the crater rather than advancing around it—an African American regiment had trained specially for the attack, but Grant pulled them at the last minute because he feared being accused of getting them all killed in such a wild maneuver. More Union troops (including the black troops that had trained for the attack) poured into the hole, making it a seething mass of humanity. The Confederates recovered and began firing into the crater with artillery and rifles, shooting down the hapless Yankees. It turned into a horrendous slaughter. Grant resigned himself to a long siege.

The other major Union offensive, in Georgia, fared only somewhat better. General Sherman and his counterpart, Joseph E. Johnston, preferred a war of movement in the mountains north of Atlanta. The Confederates skillfully used the mountains and gave ground slowly, although outnumbered two to one. Sherman tried one frontal assault, at Kennesaw Mountain on June 27, but suffered huge losses. By July 10, the two armies reached Peachtree Creek, outside Atlanta. Then, on July 17, Jefferson Davis made one of the war's most controversial command decisions: he replaced Johnston with John Bell Hood. The public wanted a more vigorous Confederate defense, and newspapers criticized Johnston's slow, retreating approach. Hood vowed to attack and drive the Yankees back. A celebrated corps commander, Hood had fought ferociously at Antietam Creek and Gettysburg, among many other encounters. By July 1864, he was down to one leg and one arm, and had to be helped into the saddle each morning.

On July 18, 20, and 28, Hood's men attacked the Union north and east of Atlanta. They suffered huge losses—thirteen thousand against "only" six thousand Federals—and made no gains. Hood retreated to Atlanta, and Sherman moved to lay siege to the city. He was bedeviled by Confederate cavalry under Nathan Bedford Forrest, which repeatedly cut the Union's long supply lines that meandered back to Chattanooga and Nashville.

The incomplete nature of Sherman's accomplishment dealt another blow to Lincoln and the Republicans. On July 18, Lincoln had called for another five hundred thousand volunteers, and Peace Democrats rejoiced. By September 1, the Union had suffered more than one hundred thousand casualties since May, and the Confederates still held Richmond, Petersburg, and Atlanta. The Union Army under Nathaniel Banks was stalled in southern Mississippi, Benjamin Butler never got up the peninsula in Virginia, and Confederates controlled Texas and most of Arkansas. After starting the year with such high hopes, Union voters now despaired. The July 1864 draft call produced the most no-shows of any single Union draft—more than sixty-six thousand men simply failed to report. Nearly another thirty thousand men furnished substitutes, another wartime high.

With the presidential election coming in November, some Radical and some Conservative Republicans tried to replace Lincoln. Movements to consider Salmon Chase, John C. Frémont, Grant, and others all failed, and Lincoln won the nomination. Even after that, however, powerful New York editor Horace Greeley and other Republicans tried to dump Lincoln, believing he could not be reelected, given the worsening military situation. Most Republicans, though, defended their war record, and the Republican platform included a ringing endorsement of Lincoln and, in particular, the Emancipation Proclamation and use of African American men in combat. The proclamation, Republicans said, was "a deathblow at this gigantic evil" of slavery, and they approved, "especially, . . . [of] the employment as Union soldiers of men heretofore held in slavery."

The Democrats met in convention in late August, and nominated George McClellan. Still divided between peace and war wings, the Democrats never quite meshed a perfect strategy for the campaign. Ex-general McClellan favored winning the war first, then negotiating a peace. The party platform, however, called for peace first, Union second, if possible. Most controversial was a passage that declared the war effort a "failure," something written into the document by arch-Copperhead Clement Vallandigham. Thus, although they agreed on matters of slavery and race, the Democrats could not present a united front on the war. As before, they attacked Lincoln and Republicans as radical advocates of racial equality and as tyrants who deprived their critics of civil liberties through the suspension of habeas corpus.

A new issue in 1864 involved prisoners of war, but actually reflected the racial division between the parties. Until 1863, few men became prisoners as both sides adhered to an informal (later formalized) policy of "exchange," in which equal numbers of prisoners captured after a battle were traded one for one. Any "extra" on one side swore an oath not to reenlist until an equivalent number of men from the other side were captured and similarly "paroled." This quaint arrangement benefited the Confederacy, of course, since it was so short of manpower. In 1863, with the controversy over black troops in combat and the white officers who led them, the prisoner exchange system broke down. Grant also urged an end to exchange since it undermined the Union strategy of attrition. In 1864, Democrats attacked Lincoln for "forcing" racial equality—insisting that African American prisoners be treated equally—at the expense of white prisoners who suffered in miserable Confederate prisons. The notorious Georgia prison Andersonville peaked at almost 33,000 inmates; nearly one-third of the men sent there died, a result of poor sanitation, disease, and shortages of food and medical care. Union prisons, however, were also deadly, despite their much greater resources. North and South there were about 150 prisons, in which almost 60,000 men died.

Republicans made one fateful change to their ticket, replacing Hannibal Hamlin with Andrew Johnson of Tennessee as the vice president. This appealed to Unionist, prowar Democratic voters. A former slaveowner, Johnson was the only Confederate-state senator who did not resign his office when the war started. In late August, the election prospects looked bleak for Republicans. On August 23, Lincoln sent his Cabinet members a memo that encouraged them to cooperate with the incoming administration; Mary Todd Lincoln packed many of their personal belongings for the expected move back to Illinois. On August 24, Lincoln wrote a "Peace Letter" to Davis in which he insisted on the Union but offered "future negotiations" on slavery and emancipation. It was the only time Lincoln seemed to waver on the question of emancipation. He never mailed the letter.

Finally the Union armies made some progress. On August 23, the Union Navy took the last Confederate fort surrounding Mobile, Alabama, effectively closing the city to blockade runners. Much more important, Sherman's men marched into Atlanta on September 3, after Hood's ragged Confederates abandoned the city rather than be trapped and have to surrender. Would Joseph Johnston have been able to hold on to Atlanta through the elections? Without the capture of Atlanta, would Lincoln have won reelection? Of course we'll never know. In early October, Lincoln carried Pennsylvania, Ohio, and Indiana in their traditional early voting. Those victories gave him some momentum, and the election actually delivered a huge Republican landslide. Lincoln won the Electoral College 212 to 21; Republicans controlled the Senate 42 to 10 and the House of Representatives 145 to 40. Union soldiers voted overwhelmingly for Lincoln—the men who actually had to do the fighting wanted to see the war to its end. Lincoln and Secretary of War Edwin Stanton furloughed home thousands of soldiers in order to allow them to vote in closely contested states, and in Democratic-controlled states, such as Indiana, that would not allow absentee voting. Close analysis suggests that soldiers helped Lincoln and the Republicans carry New York and Connecticut, and possibly Indiana and Maryland. In a supremely symbolic act, venerable abolitionist William Lloyd Garrison cast his first ever vote for president when he supported Lincoln.

Almost certainly the election of 1864 represented the Confederacy's last great chance to win the war, in this case through a Democratic victory and negotiated settlement. Lincoln's reelection ensured that the war would be fought to the end. After the results became public, a stream of deserters left Confederate armies. The winter of 1864–1865 witnessed the final collapse of the Southern war effort, both on the home front and on the battlefield.

John Peirce, Washington, DC, to Clarissa Peirce
(June 23, 1864)

The financial motives that prompted John Peirce to enlist are evident in this letter to his wife. He also expressed anger that his wife had not yet received the state portion of his enrollment bounty.

★ ★ ★ ★

My Dear Wife

I got your letter and was glad to hear that you was all well at home i feel mad to think that they do not pay you the state wages if they do not send it to you you hade better take the order and get some one to go with you to Boston i think you wold be sure to get it it is to bad not to pay a Soldier as the state agreed to the State Treasuer told me in Salem that the wages wold be sent to you with out any troubel it is a shame to decieve a man in that way i never wold enlisted but I was pro[m]ised 32 from the state aid and Wages the wages every two months

when i know my famely is not provided for I shell be of littel use to the government i have felt first rate becaus i thought you hade enough to get along with at home if you do not get the order again that you gave to the town Treasuer i will send you a nother i sent you a letter the 22d with 10 dollars i send you some in this. i am well and enjoy as good health as ever I did in my life about the state pay makes me mad if writing will get it it will come some of the mens Wifes have been to Boston and got it it is bad to go to have that troubel when it ought to be paid to you without going after it.

Letters of John Peirce, John Peirce Papers, Peabody Essex Museum, Salem, MA. Quoted in Silber and Sievens, eds., 149–50.

Democratic Party Platform (1864)

*The Democrats nominated George McClellan, from the war
wing of their party, but the platform came from the peace wing,
led by Clement Vallandigham. The most notorious section
of the platform was this one, declaring the war a "failure."*

. . . *Resolved,* That this convention does explicitly declare, as the sense of the American people, that after four years of failure to restore the Union by the experiment of war, during which, under the pretense of a military necessity, or war power higher than the Constitution, the Constitution itself has been disregarded in every part, and public liberty and private right alike trodden down, and the material prosperity of the country essentially impaired,—justice, humanity, liberty, and the public welfare demand that immediate efforts be made for a cessation of hostilities, with a view to an ultimate convention of the States, or other peaceable means, to the end that, at the earliest practicable moment, peace may be restored on the basis of the Federal union of the States. . . .

Republican Party Platform (1864)

*The Republicans defended emancipation, the use of African
American troops, and Lincoln's war leadership. On all of these
"race issues," their platform demonstrated how far the party
had moved since the beginning of the war. It also revealed the
growing power of Radical Republicans within the party.*

. . . 3. Resolved, That as slavery was the cause, and now constitutes the strength of this Rebellion, and as it must be, always and everywhere, hostile to the principles of Republican Government, justice and the National safety demand its utter and complete extirpation from the soil of the Republic; and that, while we uphold and maintain the acts and proclamations by which the Government, in its own defense, has aimed a deathblow at this gigantic evil, we are in favor, furthermore, of such an amendment to the Constitution, to be made by the people in conformity with its provisions, as shall terminate and forever prohibit the existence of Slavery within the limits of the jurisdiction of the United States. . . .

5. Resolved, That we approve and applaud the practical wisdom, the unselfish patriotism and the unswerving fidelity to the Constitution and the principles of American liberty, with which ABRAHAM LINCOLN has discharged, under circumstances of unparalleled difficulty, the great duties and responsibilities of the Presidential office; that we approve and endorse, as demanded by the emergency and essential to the preservation of the nation and as within the provisions of the Constitution, the measures and acts which he has adopted to defend the nation against its open and secret foes; that we approve, especially, the Proclamation of Emancipation, and the employment as Union soldiers of men heretofore held in slavery; . . .

7. Resolved, That the Government owes to all men employed in its armies, without regard to distinction of color, the full protection of the laws of war—and that any violation of these laws, or of the usages of civilized nations in time of war, by the Rebels now in arms, should be made the subject of prompt and full redress.

8. Resolved, That foreign immigration, which in the past has added so much to the wealth, development of resources and increase of power to the nation, the asylum of the oppressed of all nations, should be fostered and encouraged by a liberal and just policy.

9. Resolved, That we are in favor of the speedy construction of the railroad to the Pacific coast.

Democratic Party Campaign Poster (1864)

Democrats tried to portray McClellan as a soldier-statesman "above the fray" of partisan politics. This poster—showing McClellan flanked by Washington and Jackson—typified this strategy.

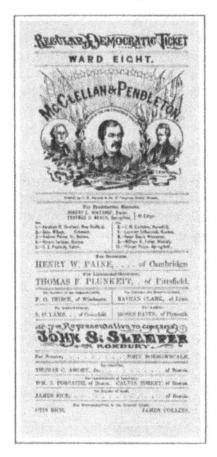

Library of Congress.

Abraham Lincoln: Second Inaugural Address (March 4, 1865)

Anticipating the end of the war, Lincoln called for compassion and national healing in his second inaugural address. He also reviewed the momentous changes in the country since 1861, focusing, of course, on emancipation, and reiterated that slavery was the cause of the war.

✻ ✻ ✻ ✻

. . . On the occasion corresponding to this four years ago all thoughts were anxiously directed to an impending civil war. All dreaded it, all sought to avert it. While the inaugural address was being delivered from this place, devoted altogether to *saving* the Union without war, urgent agents were in the city seeking to *destroy* it without war—seeking to dissolve the Union and divide effects by negotiation. Both parties deprecated war, but one of them would *make* war rather than let the nation survive, and the other would *accept* war rather than let it perish, and the war came.

One-eighth of the whole population were colored slaves, not distributed generally over the Union, but localized in the southern part of it. These slaves constituted a peculiar and powerful interest. All knew that this interest was somehow the cause of the war. To strengthen, perpetuate, and extend this interest was the object for which the insurgents would rend the Union even by war, while the Government claimed no right to do more than to restrict the territorial enlargement of it. Neither party expected for the war the magnitude or the duration which it has already attained. Neither anticipated that the *cause* of the conflict might cease with or even before the conflict itself should cease. . . .

The Almighty has His own purposes. "Woe unto the world because of offenses; for it must needs be that offenses come, but woe to that man by whom the offense cometh." If we shall suppose that American slavery is one of those offenses which, in the providence of God, must needs come, but which, having continued through His appointed time, He now wills to remove, and that He gives to both North and South this terrible war as the woe due to those by whom the offense came, shall we discern therein any departure from those divine attributes which the believers in a living God always ascribe to Him? Fondly do we hope, fervently do we pray, that this mighty scourge of war may speedily pass away. Yet, if God wills that it continue until all the wealth piled by the bondsman's two hundred and fifty years of unrequited toil shall be sunk, and until every drop of blood drawn with the lash shall be paid by another drawn with the sword, as was said three thousand years ago, so still it must be said "the judgments of the Lord are true and righteous altogether."

With malice toward none, with charity for all, with firmness in the right as God gives us to see the right, let us strive on to finish the work we are in, to bind up the nation's wounds, to care for him who shall have borne the battle and for his widow and his orphan, to do all which may achieve and cherish a just and lasting peace among ourselves and with all nations.

FIFTEEN

Confederate Families at War in 1864–1865

IN THE LAST YEAR of the war, many Confederate civilians suffered from shortages of food, clothes, and shoes; tens of thousands of women and children were homeless refugees facing starvation. Of course both white and black families faced the same problems. By 1864, several hundred thousand slaves had run away from farms and plantations, or been liberated by the Union Army; many of them drifted along with Northern troops and tried to find work. Major sections of the South were devastated from intense fighting: crops and farmland were burned or run-down from neglect; bridges, buildings, and homes were destroyed from artillery shells and subsequent fire; and tens of thousands of men hid out as deserters, roamed the countryside looking for family members, property to steal, or—for those too severely crippled to stay in service—work and food. Much of this devastation occurred as a by-product of the war; some of it the Union Army visited on the population intentionally. In short, in the war's last months the physical and psychological effects of more than three years of war brought Confederate civilians to the breaking point. How would they react? And more important, what would men in Southern armies do? Jefferson Davis and other Confederate leaders tried to rally their citizens by appealing to Southern pride and patriotism. They also passed increasingly activist, and divisive, legislation to try to mobilize the country's dwindling resources.

By 1864, the wartime problems that had affected Southern civilians since 1861 became even more pressing. Most evident was inflation. Soldiers' families could not expect to survive solely on a military paycheck. Pay for privates remained eleven dollars per month, and in Richmond, by the fall of 1864, flour was about three hundred dollars per barrel and shoes cost more than one hundred dollars. State and local governments tried to provide direct relief for destitute families, although that normally entailed printing more paper money, which only worsened inflation. It hurt town residents and anyone working for a salary the most; rural folks at least could eat. Farm families (like virtually everyone else), however, faced the same shortages of cloth, shoes, boots, and anything else manufactured. Merchants closed their doors rather than accept Confederate paper money; desperate Southerners occasionally looted stores anyway. By the end of the war, the Confederate economy functioned largely through barter.

An issue related to inflation that further angered Confederate civilians was "impressment," or the forced seizure of livestock, food, and other items needed for Southern troops. The Confederate Congress approved the Impressment Act early in 1863, and protests started late in that year. Local agents surveyed farmers' crops and merchants' stock, assessing the value of anything taken for the army. State boards were supposed to adjudicate disputes. There seemed to be three basic problems: First, the government paid for merchandise in devalued Confederate bills or with an IOU, neither of which appealed to people losing their livestock or crops. Second, the government set prices far below market value. This was done partly to control prices and inflation, but also to get the merchandise cheaply. Finally, much of what impressment agents took never reached the men in uniform, partly due to poor management but also as a consequence of a floundering transportation system. As a result, local residents lost their property and then watched it sit at the local depot for months. Taken together, inflation and impressment prompted many farmers and merchants to blame government corruption or incompetence (or both) for the Confederacy's crumbling economy.

In 1864, the disintegration of slavery also accelerated. As the Union Army advanced into new areas, slaves flocked to their lines and became "forever free," as the Emancipation Proclamation phrased it. Their precise legal status remained ambiguous, considering that only Lincoln's wartime authority lay behind his historic decree. Regardless of the constitutional particulars, however, slaves knew freedom when they saw it. For whites, the internal collapse of their "peculiar institution" forced them—even if subconsciously—to confront the reality that their fleeing slaves were neither happy nor content. When Sherman marched out of Atlanta toward Savannah and his army picked up refugees, perhaps as many as fifty thousand of them were slaves.

As more slaves escaped or were liberated by the advancing Union Army, the damage to the Confederate war effort and economy increased. Slaves allowed the Confederacy to enroll over 80 percent of white men ages eighteen to forty-five, and also to use the vast majority of soldiers directly for front-line duty. Slaves were impressed by Southern armies (like other property), and dug fortifications, moved materiel, cooked, and performed a hundred other tasks. The slave population that remained on the home front helped feed and supply the Confederacy, and produced most of the cotton. One of the most famous instances of slaves powering the Confederate war effort was at Richmond's Tredegar Iron Works. The South's only large foundry, Tredegar used roughly equal numbers of skilled white and black (mostly slave) workers throughout the war. The disintegration of slavery reduced the available manpower that could help the Confederate Army directly, and also undermined food production, which hurt the troops indirectly. Most immediately, however, it affected Southern civilians, particularly white women, who took on even greater burdens as the Confederacy's forced-labor pool drained away.

By 1864, many Confederate white women openly questioned the war. Farm women whose families had no slaves struggled with traditionally male duties such as planting, weeding, and harvesting in order to keep the farms producing and keep themselves and their children fed. In this way Confederate women contributed immeasurably to the war effort. By 1864, though, many had had enough—enough field work and enough dead and disfigured family members. They wrote thousands of letters to husbands, fathers, sons, and sweethearts, often making explicit appeals for their men to leave the army and come home. Others simply described their desperate condition—an implicit plea for help. Mary Cooper's agonizing letter to her husband, Edward, used typical—if particularly heartrending—language. "I would not have you do anything wrong for the world, but before God, Edward, unless you come home, we must die. Last night I was aroused by little Eddie crying. I called and said, 'What is the matter, Eddie?' And he said, 'O mamma! I am so hungry.' And Lucy, Edward, your darling Lucy, she never complains, but she is getting thinner and thinner every day. And before God, Edward, unless you come home, we must die." How many husbands and fathers could ignore appeals like that? Public spokesmen lectured women: "Do not write GLOOMY letters," one Alabama editor implored. "Say nothing that will embitter their thoughts or swerve them from the path of duty." Others reminded women that desertion was punishable by death.

No matter how much of it women prompted, desertion from Confederate ranks accelerated late in 1864 and early in 1865. Most estimates suggest more than half of Confederate troops were absent without leave by March 1865. This loss of manpower, of course, crippled Southern armies. Some evidence suggests that earlier in the war, desertion often was seasonal, spiking in early spring (for planting) and early fall (for harvesting), and that Confederate generals (to an extent) accommodated it. Clearly, however, by late 1864 and early 1865, thousands of men who left had no intention of returning to their posts. In mountainous parts of the South, men hid nearly with impunity. Conscription agents simply avoided most of western North Carolina, northern Alabama and Mississippi, and unoccupied Tennessee or Arkansas. Confederate leaders appealed to the men's pride, patriotism, and shame, but by the end of the war none of these tactics proved very effective. Too many men no longer trusted Davis's government or believed that the Confederacy could win the war, and they resented policies that worked unfairly against poorer men and their families.

By 1864–1865, the impact of Confederate policies touched more and more Southerners of all classes. The most unpopular remained conscription, which in 1864 expanded to include men ages seventeen through fifty. Though substitution and most work-related exemptions had ended, Southerners continued to resent the mere fact of conscription, and as the prospects for victory dimmed, more and more men simply failed to show when called. Conscription, the tax in kind, and inflation all affected poor farm and working families most adversely and turned them increasingly against the Confederate government and the war. These policies violated a sort of "unwritten agreement" that kept antebellum white Southerners united across class lines. Small, non-slaveowning farmers cast their votes for planters and allowed the wealthy to hold high office and set policy; in return, planters kept government small and taxes low. The war made that compromise impossible to maintain, and poorer Confederates lost faith in their planter-politicians. Impressment and the government's efforts to control the trading and selling of cotton, on the other hand, tended to alienate planters and merchants. By 1864, then, the most far-reaching, intrusive, and centralized Confederate policies managed to arouse the enmity of men and women from all classes.

Many of Davis's wartime policies also violated the principle of states' rights, on which many Southerners believed the Confederacy was founded. Critics of the Richmond administration assailed conscription, in particular, and some governors worked actively to frustrate it. The most persistent of Davis's adversaries was Georgia governor Joseph E. Brown, a strict adherent to states' rights who disputed Davis's wartime expansion of powers. Nothing raised Brown's ire more than conscription. Believing that defending their state and their families was his and their first priority, he exempted thousands of Georgia men, claiming that they were militia officers, and helped others avoid Confederate service when possible. The governor exchanged long letters with Jefferson Davis, debating the finer points of constitutional theory, even as the war effort crashed down around them. Late in the war, Brown even considered trying to negotiate a separate peace treaty with the Union. Most state leaders supported Richmond, but by 1864 many governors questioned the wisdom of sending so many of their remaining men to Virginia or Georgia. Mississippi's Charles Clark, elected late in 1863, supported Davis, but vowed that his state would "repel" and "not conduct" any more invasions. How much did these states' rights "obstructionists" cost the Confederate effort? It is impossible to determine, but with such a small margin for error, any lost resources could prove fatal.

By 1864, Jefferson Davis himself had become the object of much Confederate anger. Never personally popular, he began the war with a tremendous amount of prestige and goodwill. Most of his modern critics fault him for failing to inspire Southerners toward a greater sense of Confederate nationalism. Though Davis could stir crowds with his oratory, as president he failed to provide any positive, unifying symbols for the Confederacy. What could he have done? That is unclear, but for the four years of its existence, the Confederacy's coalescing images were generals such as Lee, Jackson, and Stuart—and slavery. Confederate currency, for instance, often included images of the cotton gin and slaves carrying the great staple. By 1864, Davis's government essentially used race and fear to keep the war effort going—fear of emancipation, racial mixing or race war, and fear of Yankee occupation. Davis's prickly personality became more grating for those who had to work with him. Vice President Alexander Stephens called Davis "timid, petulant, peevish, [and] obstinate," and "ambitious as Lucifer." Certainly, Davis expanded the authority of his government far beyond what most Southerners expected, but like his Northern counterpart, Davis discovered that running a massive war effort required greater central authority than most people anticipated or wanted.

Davis also encountered greater political opposition after mid-1863, when military defeats and unpopular policies took an even greater toll on Southern unity. The 1863 national Confederate elections returned about 40 percent of congressional representatives hostile to Davis. Confederates sacrificed greatly, and some of the faltering support for the cause fell on Davis. Still, he did not get much help from an ineffective Confederate Congress and a mediocre Cabinet. (Lincoln, on the other hand, enjoyed a Republican-controlled Congress filled with veteran legislators and a Cabinet distinguished by some truly brilliant members.) Lastly, many of Davis's fellow planters undermined his efforts: trading cotton through Union lines and the blockade rather than allowing the government to use it as an economic weapon; practicing price gouging; using exemptions from conscription or combat duty; and hoarding supplies. At the least, planters helped divide Southern whites along class lines because of the widespread *perception* that they were acting selfishly. Whatever blame Davis deserves for falling civilian morale, many of the problems he confronted simply defied any political solutions.

Finally, in late 1864 and early 1865, the Union's success on the battlefield—highlighted by Sherman's "March to the Sea"—sapped morale among even the most optimistic Southerners. After Sherman occupied Atlanta, he paused, planning a campaign southeast toward Savannah and Charleston. Throughout 1864, Sherman's forces had been vexed by Confederate cavalry as they advanced through north Georgia toward Atlanta, and to avoid that distraction he decided to cut loose from his supply and communication lines—as Grant had done in Mississippi—and "live off the land." He vowed to "make Georgia howl" by destroying all property that could be used to support the Confederate war effort. This was an extension of the argument Lincoln used to promote emancipation: slaves helped support the Southern war effort, so freeing them would end the war. Sherman, more than any other Union general, articulated a more complete version of what we now call "total war"—destroying your enemy's ability to wage war.

When Confederates objected, Sherman chastised them in terms that pleased the most Radical of Republicans. On September 11, Atlanta's mayor protested Sherman's order to vacate the city. "How is it possible for the people still here (mostly women and children) to find any shelter? And how can they live through the winter in the woods?" He concluded, "what has this *helpless* people done, that they should be driven from their homes, to wander strangers and outcasts, and exiles, and to subsist on charity?" Sherman's contempt was barely concealed in his lengthy response: "You cannot qualify war in harsher terms than I will. War is cruelty, and you cannot refine it; and those who brought war into our country deserve all the curses and maledictions a people can pour out." He continued, lecturing that the "terrible hardships of war" were "inevitable." Southerners could have peace only "by admitting that [the war] began in error and is perpetuated in pride." The Union did not want slaves or Southerners' homes, "but we do want and will have a just obedience to the laws of the United States. That we will have, and if it involves the destruction of your improvements, we cannot help it." Sherman was even less forgiving when Confederate general Hood made a similar request for leniency. "You who, in the midst of peace and prosperity, have plunged a nation into war," Sherman wrote, "Who dared and badgered us into battle, insulted our flag . . . talk to the Marines, but not to me."

Sherman's army cut a swath of destruction fifty miles wide as it marched leisurely through Georgia without any meaningful Confederate resistance. The men destroyed nearly all property in their path, famously twisting railroad tracks around tree trunks—"Sherman neckties"—so they would never be usable again. One Illinois soldier noted that Rebel papers called on citizens to resist the Union Army. "Let them do it if they dare. We'll burn every house, barn, church, and everything else we come to; we'll leave their families houseless and without food; their towns will *all* be destroyed." The Union forces collected refugees by the thousands—both white and black Southerners now homeless and destitute. They occupied Savannah on December 21, 1864, and Sherman wired Lincoln to offer him the city as a "Christmas present." Sherman's March had a devastating psychological effect on Southern civilians, many of whom wrote Davis and begged him to end the war. Early in 1865, Sherman and his army turned north and happily wreaked havoc in South Carolina, the birthplace of secession.

By the end of 1864, Confederate civilians were in a desperate condition. Homeless and starving women and children searched for family or friends who could take them in. Union forces occupied large sections of the South, freeing slaves as they advanced. The Confederate economy collapsed under the combined weight of occupation, inflation, the Union blockade, and a massive labor shortage. Confederate armies continued to fight as the war approached four years, but the end was in sight.

Christian M. Epperly to Mary Epperly (May 8, 1864)

*In 1864 the number of desertions from Confederate ranks rose
dramatically. This letter describes the execution of fourteen
North Carolinians caught after deserting, as well as the writer's
disgust with the punishment.*

✳ ✳ ✳ ✳

I haven't any news to write to you at this time, only the sad and awful
Execution which taken place in our Brigade yesterday which was too cruel
for mortal man to behold. There was 14 North Carolinians shot to Death
yesterday with musketry. 10 belonging to the 58 North Carolina and 4 to
the 60 Regt. Their cries and groans, how sad they did sound. They were
tied to stakes by their Captains and then cruelly murdered by the order of
a few wicked men and had done nothing . . . but left the army and went
home to see their Families and Friends. . . . God forbid that I Should witness another such deed committed by men.

The Gilder Lehrman Collection, GLC 2715.91, the Pierpont Morgan Library,
New York, NY.

A Union Soldier Describes Sherman's March to the Sea (November 1864–March 1865)

*This passage from the Illinois lawyer and soldier James
Connolly includes vivid accounts of the destruction wrought by
Sherman's massive, unstoppable army as it marched through
Georgia and the Carolinas. Connolly also conveys a sense
of the Union Army's confident attitude toward the dwindling
Confederate forces and hapless Southern civilians.*

✳ ✳ ✳ ✳

Near Sand Town, Ga., November 19, 1864 . . .
Our men are foraging on the country with the greatest liberality. Foraging parties start out in the morning; they go where they please, seize wagons, mules, horses, and harness; make the negroes of the plantation hitch up, load the wagons with sweet potatoes, flour, meal, hogs, sheep, chickens, turkeys, barrels of molasses, and in fact everything good to eat, and sometimes considerable that's good to drink. Our men are living as well as they could at home and are in excellent health.

Near Murder Creek, Ga., November 21, 1864 . . .
Every "Gin House" we pass is burned; every stack of fodder we can't carry along is burned; every barn filled with grain is destroyed; in fact anything that can be of any use to the rebels is either carried off by our foragers or set on fire and burned.

Near Milledgeville, Ga., November 25, 1864 . . .
We burn their houses, barns, fences, cotton and everything else, yet none of the Southern braves show themselves to punish us for our vandalism. . . .

Near Sandersville, Ga., November 26, 1864 . . .
The rebel papers we get hold of from Augusta also call on all the citizens to turn out and fall timber across the roads—destroy their forage and provisions, and do everything possible to harass us and retard our march. Let them do it if they dare. We'll burn every house, barn, church, and everything else we come to; we'll leave their families houseless and without food; their towns will *all* be destroyed, and nothing but the most complete desolation will be found in our track. This army will not be trifled with by citizens. If citizens raise their hands against us to retard our march or play the guerrilla against us, neither youth nor age, nor sex will be respected. Everything must be destroyed.

Fayetteville, N.C., March 12, 1865 . . .
The army burned everything it came near in the State of South Carolina, not under orders, but in spite of orders. The men "had it in" for the State and they took it out in their own way. Our track through the State is a

desert waste. Since entering North Carolina the wanton destruction has stopped.

Paul M. Angle, ed., *Three Years in the Army of the Cumberland* (Bloomington, IN: Indiana University Press, 1959), 314–24, 384.

William Gilmore Simms on the Burning of Columbia, South Carolina (1865)

The writer and historian William Gilmore Simms witnessed the destruction of Columbia by Sherman's forces. Like other reflective Southerners, he began to consider the reasons for their defeat, and tried to articulate the feelings of a beaten people.

It has pleased God, in that Providence which is so inscrutable to man, to visit our beautiful city with the most cruel fate which can ever befall States or cities. He has permitted an invading army to penetrate our country almost without impediment; to rob and ravage our dwellings, and to commit three-fifths of our city to the flames. . . . The schools of learning, the shops of art and trade, of invention and manufacture; shrines equally of religion, benevolence and industry; are all buried together, in one congregated ruin. Humiliation spreads her ashes over our homes and garments, and the universal wreck exhibits only one common aspect of despair.

William Gilmore Simms, *Sack and Destruction of the City of Columbia, S. C.: to which is added a list of property destroyed* (Columbia, SC: Power Press of Daily Phoenix, 1865).

1865: Emancipation, Surrender, and Assassination

THE LAST MONTHS OF THE WAR included some of its most dramatic events and poignant scenes. Though Confederate forces were vastly outnumbered and in disarray, the men fought on stubbornly; many of them simply could not conceive of surrender. Sensing victory, Union leaders started arguing about what the end of the war would mean and what would follow it. Many Radical Republicans began to fear a cease-fire and peace negotiations, wanting nothing less than a decisive military victory and the South's utter capitulation. Perhaps most important, what would be the fate of African Americans? The Emancipation Proclamation did not apply everywhere—could the war end and slavery survive in some form? If and when the Union won the war, what would become of Southerners? Of the Southern states? The answers to all of these questions depended significantly on the interplay among, and relative power of, the three major Republican factions—Radicals, Moderates, and Conservatives. The party had such a huge majority in Congress that it could pass any legislation it wanted, although its members hardly agreed on all issues—particularly those related to race. Depending on the issue at hand, relations between congressional Republicans and Lincoln ranged from cooperative to strained to openly hostile.

By winter 1864–1865, three main Confederate forces remained east of the Mississippi River: Lee's army entrenched in Richmond and Petersburg; Hood's army from Georgia, which had evacuated Atlanta; and various forces collected under Joseph E. Johnston in North Carolina. In late November 1864, John Bell Hood's army moved into Tennessee rather than pursue Sherman across Georgia. Hood apparently intended to link with Lee somewhere in western Virginia, but nothing much about his plan or movements made sense. In Tennessee he faced superior, well-supplied forces, and cold weather at a time when many of his men had no shoes. On November 30, he ordered disastrous attacks on Union forces at Franklin, Tennessee, losing three times as many men as did the Union, but instead of retreating, he advanced toward Nashville and took a position south of the city, daring the Union to attack him. Union general George H. Thomas obliged, finally advancing on the frozen, haggard remnants of the once-powerful Army of Tennessee on December 15. Though Hood's men fought desperately, they gave way inevitably to Thomas's superior forces and retreated all the way to Mississippi. Hood resigned, and most of his army melted away as the weary, demoralized men drifted home.

In South Carolina, Sherman continued his march of destruction. In February 1865, his men captured Charleston, the home of secession, and burned Columbia, the state capital. Along the way they continued to practice their special version of Union conquest, destroying homes, barns, crops, and railroads. Northern troops recorded the miserable state of civilians and the general desperation of the Confederacy: "I was perfectly sickened by the frightful devastation our army was spreading," wrote Illinois's James Connolly. "Every house [in our path] except the church and the negro cabin was burned to the ground; women, children, and old men turned out into the mud and rain and their houses and furniture first plundered, then burned." In March, Sherman's men reached North Carolina. "This state is filled with deserters from the rebel army. . . . Hundreds of them have gathered up their families and, with a little bundle of bedding stowed away in an ox car or mule cart, they toil along after our trains." Facing torrential rains, flooded rivers, and swamps, the Union Army just kept going. The men built their own roads and bridges when necessary. A separate Union force also won a major victory by capturing Fort Fisher, off the North Carolina coast, which closed Wilmington to blockade runners—it had been the last significant Confederate port open to them. General Joseph Johnston, back in command thanks to Robert E. Lee (who had taken over responsibility for all Confederate forces in early February), scraped together about twenty thousand men to try to stop Sherman's destruction. It didn't work. Reinforced to nearly one hundred thousand men, Sherman's army marched on toward Richmond and a meeting with Lee and Grant.

The siege of Richmond and Petersburg continued through the summer, fall, and winter of 1864–1865. Union forces moved continually south and then west around Petersburg, working to cut the Confederates' remaining supply lines. On August 18, 1864, Grant's forces cut one of the two main railroads that supplied the two Virginia cities. Confederates rallied, however, and a series of counterattacks in the fall prevented the Union from capturing the Southside Railroad. This kept a tenuous supply line intact through the winter and allowed Lee's men to maintain their position. In February, Grant began moving west again, forcing Lee to stretch his already thin lines in order to protect the last road and railroad into Petersburg. By March, Lee decided that he needed to try to fight his way out of the two cities to avoid being crushed between the converging armies of Grant, Sherman, and Sheridan. Lee began his withdrawal to the west in the last days of March, hoping to combine with Johnston's scattered forces from North Carolina. The Union began its final assault on Petersburg on April 2, and took possession of both Petersburg and Richmond the following day. Casualties for the last six months of the siege and campaign were typically appalling: for the Union, more than forty thousand; at least twenty-eight thousand Confederates. Among the last to be killed was Confederate general A. P. Hill, one of the heroes of Antietam Creek, a battle that by then seemed a lifetime ago for many Southerners.

Throughout these last campaigns, peace negotiations continued but ultimately failed. The most famous attempt was the so-called Hampton Roads Peace Conference of February 3, 1865. Lincoln and Seward met personally with Confederate vice president Alexander Stephens and two other Southern commissioners on a Union steamship in the waters off Hampton Roads, Virginia. Considering the military situation, Lincoln stated very generous terms: the South could have peace if it accepted reunion and emancipation, which might be enacted gradually. He even offered possible compensation for slaveowners. Incredibly, Davis (through the commissioners) rejected the terms out of hand because Lincoln would not agree to a cease-fire in advance. Thus, for Davis's stubbornness, arrogance, and failure to grasp reality, the war continued.

Early in 1865, the Union Congress also passed the Thirteenth Amendment, preparing the way for the end of slavery. Invigorated by the contributions of African American troops and driven by the growing power of Radical Republicans, the abolition amendment gained support throughout 1864. The Republicans had included a plank calling for the amendment's passage in their platform of that year, and the election landslide of November gave the party more than the three-fourths majority it needed in the new Congress, but Lincoln urged the amendment's approval before those men took their seats. A bipartisan effort would be preferred, he thought. On January 31, 1865, just enough Democrats broke ranks to help the Thirteenth Amendment pass the House of Representatives. Republicans rejoiced, closing Congress for the rest of the day in honor of the historic moment. Black men and women alternately sobbed and screamed in unmatched exultation. All Northern states except New Jersey, Delaware, and Kentucky approved the amendment in the spring of 1865.

As an ironic counterpoint to the Thirteenth Amendment, the Confederate Congress approved arming slaves to fight for the Southern cause. Discussed as early as 1864, the radical idea was rejected by most Confederate leaders as counter to everything their Confederacy stood for. Howell Cobb, a popular Georgia politician, famously summarized that if "slaves will make good soldiers our whole theory of slavery is wrong." He was correct, of course, in that most Southerners had based the defense of slavery on the notion that African Americans were inevitably inferior and childlike. A vigorous debate ensued in the Southern press, with most spokesmen seemingly opposed to arming black men. Public opposition, however, succumbed to the prestige and power of Robert E. Lee, who supported using slaves if it would help win independence. On March 13, the Confederate Congress approved the plan (although without guaranteeing freedom for slave-soldiers, as Lee advocated), but no slaves were enrolled.

No slaves ever entered the Confederate armies, because those armies had surrendered in April. On the ninth, Lee's army failed in a last-ditch effort to outrun Grant's pursuing forces. The Confederates were surrounded at Appomattox Courthouse. After several notes were exchanged, Lee and Grant met in the town house of Wilmer McLean, a Virginian who had fled his farm outside Manassas in 1861 because he wanted to avoid the First Battle of Bull Run. His home was used as a Confederate headquarters during that first major battle. Now he hosted the most dramatic moment in American history since 1776. Lee arrived first, impeccably dressed in "a new uniform of Confederate gray, buttoned up to the throat, and at his side he carried a long sword of exceedingly fine workmanship, the hilt studded with jewels." Grant came straight from the battlefield, unkempt as usual, "wearing an open blouse, a slouch hat, trousers tucked into heavy, mud-stained boots, and with only the four tarnished gold stars to indicate his office!" The two leaders spoke briefly about their service in Mexico, and then Grant wrote out the terms of surrender. Following Lincoln's charge to "give them the most liberal and honorable terms," he allowed Confederates to retain "their private horses or baggage" in order "to work their little farms"—after all, it was planting season. The two men walked outside and Grant "stepped down from the porch, and, moving toward [Lee], saluted him by raising his hat." Grant then ordered twenty-five thousand rations be distributed to Lee's hungry men.

The Army of Northern Virginia was to surrender formally on April 12 by marching past a body of Union troops and laying down their guns and flags. Chosen to lead the Northern delegation was Joshua Lawrence Chamberlain, the college professor from Maine and hero of Gettysburg. When the first Confederate column approached, Chamberlain "thought it eminently fitting to show some token of our feeling, and I therefore instructed my subordinate officers to come to the position of 'salute' in the manual of arms as each body of the Confederates passed before us." Confederate general John B. Gordon—shot five times at Antietam—recognized the magnitude of the gesture "and instantly assumed the finest attitude of a soldier," wheeling his horse around and swinging its head down "with a graceful bow." On April 26, Joseph Johnston surrendered his remaining forces to Sherman; the last significant Confederate surrender came on May 26, when Edmund Kirby Smith delivered Southern forces west of the Mississippi River. Two weeks earlier, Jefferson Davis had been captured in Georgia.

Northerners rejoiced, particularly with the news of Lee's surrender. The Army of Northern Virginia had become the most important symbol of Confederate resistance, and Lee a nearly superhuman nemesis to the Union. While many Southerners, including Jefferson Davis, had vowed to continue fighting, as guerillas in the mountains if necessary, Lee, a professional soldier for too long, refused to consider this and told his men to accept the defeat and go home. With Lee's army no longer a threat, the Union held a celebration at Fort Sumter on April 14. Major Robert Anderson returned to command the harbor fortress that he had surrendered four years earlier. The audience included abolitionists William Lloyd Garrison and Henry Ward Beecher. Occupying Charleston were the Third and Fourth South Carolina Union regiments, composed of ex-slaves drawn from the surrounding area. For white Southerners it seemed that the world had ended. What would come next was anyone's guess.

The reunification of the Union and reintegration of seceded states was unchartered territory in American history. Who was in charge? The president? Congress? Republicans faced these questions as early as 1863, when Louisiana and Tennessee were largely occupied by Union forces. Lincoln's plan—which he announced on December 8, 1863—called for Southern states to reenter the Union quickly and easily, and under control of Southern whites. There would be a general amnesty for Southerners who took an oath of future allegiance to the Union, and they would keep all property except slaves. When 10 percent of a state's voters (based on the 1860 census) took the oath, then that state could reestablish its government and hold elections. Republicans were divided sharply over Lincoln's plan, which outraged Radicals. In a rare moment of political miscalculation, Lincoln had underestimated the growing power of Radical Republicans, sympathy for ex-slaves, and hatred for Southerners.

Congressional leaders responded with their own plan for Reconstruction: the Wade-Davis Bill, which Congress passed on July 2, 1864. This measure required 50 percent of voters to take an "ironclad" oath of *past* and future loyalty to the United States. Presumably, of course, this would disenfranchise nearly all adult Southern white men. In each state, the new voters would also need to write a constitution before holding any elections. Lincoln pocket-vetoed the measure, splitting the party and jeopardizing his own reelection. But he could not accept what he considered a plan so harsh that it was likely to embitter white Southerners, perhaps for years to come. When the fighting stopped, Lincoln and congressional Republicans remained at an impasse. New governments in Louisiana and Tennessee had been organized under Lincoln's plan, but Congress refused to recognize them (or count their electoral votes in the 1864 election). In April 1865, therefore, white Southerners did not know which plan for Reconstruction would be imposed. Just two days after Lee's surrender, Lincoln spoke in favor of suffrage for some black men, signaling movement toward the Radicals. But he also urged Northerners not to persecute the defeated

Confederates; he still hoped for a quick, peaceful reunion, "with malice toward none; with charity for all," as he said in his second inaugural address.

Lincoln did not have the chance to fight the battle for Reconstruction, of course, because on April 14, John Wilkes Booth, a frustrated actor and Confederate sympathizer, murdered him. Exhausted from the last months of war, Lincoln and his wife attended a play at Ford's Theatre in Washington. General Grant and his wife were supposed to sit with the Lincolns, but chose to visit their children in New Jersey instead. With only limited security—despite numerous death threats during the last four years—Lincoln was sitting in his box when Booth entered and fired a pistol point-blank into his head. Unconscious through the night, Lincoln died the next morning. Booth had conspirators, one of whom also stabbed Secretary of State Seward, who eventually recovered, and another of whom failed to strike Vice President Andrew Johnson. After the nation's greatest manhunt, Union troops killed Booth on April 26 in a barn in Virginia. At news of Lincoln's death, Northerners wept in the streets; African Americans were particularly distraught. In Lincoln, many black men and women envisioned the Christ-Moses figure of deliverance whom they had sung about and prayed for as slaves. Standing over the president's coffin in Washington, Grant broke down and "tears streamed down his cheeks in a steady stream." Lincoln's funeral train headed for Springfield, and millions of grieving men and women watched it pass through cities and small towns. Mary Todd Lincoln never recovered and spent most of her remaining years in a darkened room in Springfield. Andrew Johnson, former slaveowner and Democrat from a Confederate state, became president of the United States.

Northerners called for vengeance, including mass trials and executions of high-ranking Confederates. Some believed that Jefferson Davis had masterminded the assassination. But, ironically, Lincoln's death also evoked sympathy for his Reconstruction program and for the attitude of forgiveness and "charity for all" that he embodied. Lincoln wanted the Union reunited quickly and white Southerners to become citizens again. His understanding and compassion for others was legendary, but whether enough Northerners could muster such forgiveness remained uncertain.

The effects of the war cannot be overstated. In many ways it made America a modern country. Emancipation inaugurated a revolution in social and economic relations beyond our comprehension; the revolution in attitudes is still ongoing. Southern states took at least a hundred years (if it has even happened today) to recover from the legacies of slavery and the financial costs of emancipation. Literally, with the stroke of a pen, 250 years' worth of investment evaporated when four and a half million slaves, worth well more than one thousand dollars each, became freedmen. Because of slavery, however, nearly all of them entered the free workforce without skills or literacy. The war's human cost was at least 630,000 dead, the vast majority of them white men between ages seventeen and fifty. One in four Southern men of those ages did not survive. Tens of thousands of children had no fathers, wives no husbands, communities no leaders.

To cope with defeat and the inconceivable losses, Southern whites invented the "Lost Cause" mythology. The Old South had been a great society, they argued, and the war a worthwhile effort to prevent its unfortunate destruction. But while their men had "fought the good fight," they had succumbed to the Union's superior numbers and industry. The Lost Cause attempted to deal with the psychological costs that white men faced, having failed to defend their society, their homes, and their families. All those deaths had to be worthwhile, and a generation of Southern white women, in particular, wrote poems and novels about the greatness of white Southern manhood and the glory of a Lost Cause "Gone With the Wind."

For the nation, the Civil War enhanced the power and prestige of the federal government, tipping the balance in its favor at the expense of states' rights. Throughout the antebellum years, theories of states' rights, nullification, and secession were constitutional options. The war cemented the national government's superiority and the Union's inviolability. During the war, the federal government—and Davis's government, for that matter— had conscripted men into the army, established the first national currency and nearly a central banking system, imposed a national income tax, and essentially nationalized crucial wartime industries. More than a million men served in the Union Army, creating a generation of Republican voters and political leaders. Not until the 1920s and 1930s did American politics really escape the power of Civil War veterans and the shadow of service in the Grand Army of the Republic. Finally, the war shifted the balance of economic power dramatically in the North's favor. The South had lost roughly two-thirds of its wealth, in addition to men, livestock, and infrastructure. Not until the post-1960s boom in the deep South (thanks to air-conditioning) did those states recover a share of the wealth they had lost between 1861 and 1865.

In the spring and summer of 1865, no one knew what would happen next. Much depended on how white Southerners reacted to the defeat and to emancipation. Many Northern whites, like their deceased president, appeared willing to move forward without a long, harsh peace. But the war left deep scars, and the Union had lost 360,000 men. Under the veneer of magnanimity was a reservoir of hatred waiting to spill over. Perhaps most important, a growing body of Radical Republicans wanted to remake the defeated South and effect lasting changes to the social, economic, and cultural fabric of the region. In April 1865, however, Radicals still were a minority in the North.

A Northern Girl Describes the End of the War
(April 10, 1865)

For Northerners the news of Lee's surrender brought forth unrestrained joy and relief. Many in the Union could hardly believe that their great Confederate nemesis had actually surrendered, and many did not believe it for several weeks.

Monday Morning, April 10
'Whether I am in the body, or out of the body, I know not, but one thing I know,' Lee has surrendered! and all the people seem crazy in consequence. The bells are ringing, boys and girls, men and women are running through the streets wild with excitement; the flags are all flying, one from the top of our church, and such a 'hurrah boys' generally, I never dreamed of.

Caroline Richards, *Village Life in America, 1852–1872* (New York: H. Holt and Co., 1913).

A Union Soldier on Lincoln's Assassination
(April 18, 1865)

Like the man who wrote this letter, many Northerners wanted vengeance for Lincoln's murder.

Father we have heard that President Lincoln has been killed by some traitor in Washington. If that is true I say that we ought to hang every damn rebel in the Southern Confederacy. I go in for killing every one and burn every traitor up north by a stake. I think instead of taken Lee's Army prisoners it would have been better to have hoisted a black flag and butchered every one but now they have paroled them and what are they doing. They are awaiting an opportunity to kill some of our best men. . . .

I say they ought to hang every one. I tell you it is a very hard blow for this nation to lose our President at this present time but I still hope it is not true but I fear it is for there are many traitors up North that are first the ones that would kill him.

The Gilder Lehrman Collection, GLC 08618, the Pierpont Morgan Library, New York, NY.

Newton Scott, St. Charles, AR, to Miss H. M. Cone (May 24, 1865)

This Iowa soldier expressed the bitterness felt by many Northerners at the end of the war. The last major Confederate surrender occurred two days after this letter was written, on May 26, in New Orleans, when General Edmund Kirby Smith surrendered all Southern forces west of the Mississippi River.

. . . I hope we may have no News of much Interest to write from here at this time Everything is Quiet here Except that the Rebs Still continue to Come in & Surrender themselves & take the Oath. There is no Rebs of any Consequence <u>North of the Arkansas River & West of the Miss River</u> now They haveing all or nearly So Come in to our Forces & Taken the Oath . . .

but I Suppose that Kirby Smith & Mcgruder & Price will Still oppose the government until They are Driven out & there Country Burned and If they Do not Surrender I hope to God that our Government will Exterminate the whole Crew of those General Officers & leading men for they cant but know that there case is a hopeless one & have no reason for Continuing the war longer . . .

Believe me as ever
Yours verry Respectfully
Newton Scott
Co. A. 36th Regt Iowa vols

Available at http://www.civilwarletters.com/scott_5_24_1865.html.

Charleston, SC, April 1865

This photograph captures the condition of many Southern cities—and the Southern infrastructure in general—when the war ended. (The surviving building is the Mills House.)

Library of Congress.

John Albee: "A Soldier's Grave"

Break not his sweet repose—
Thou whom chance brings to this sequestered ground,
The sacred yard his ashes close,
But go thy way in silence; here no sound
Is ever heard but from the murmuring pines,
    Answering the sea's near murmur;
    Nor ever here comes rumor
Of anxious world or war's foregathering signs.
    The bleaching flag, the faded wreath,
    Mark the dead soldier's dust beneath,
    And show the death he chose;
Forgotten save by her who weeps alone,
And wrote his fameless name on this low stone:
    Break not his sweet repose.

Edmund Clarence Stedman, *An American Anthology, 1787–1900* (Boston, Houghton Mifflin, 1900).

A Dead Soldier

This young man was one of more than 630,000 who died in the Civil War. Killed in the trenches around Petersburg in 1865, he probably died during the last big Federal attack on April 2. His home was South Carolina.

Library of Congress.

SEVENTEEN

From Presidential to Congressional Reconstruction: 1865 and 1866

DURING THE TENSE MONTHS AFTER LINCOLN'S assassination the threat of violence hung over nearly every encounter between occupying Union troops and defeated white Southerners, testing the uneasy peace. Numerous incidents did lead to violence, and some former Confederates advocated fighting on as guerillas in the mountains, or even from Mexico. A significant number—estimates range from five thousand to twenty thousand—simply left the United States for Brazil, where African slavery remained legal (until 1886). But most white Southerners stayed and worked for the best peace settlement they could get. Their immediate antagonists were ex-slaves and Union soldiers, who remained in some areas of the South until 1877. Each of these two constituencies had its own agenda, as did other Northern whites, including Democrats and business leaders, and African Americans who had been free before the war. Within the dominant Republican Party, Radicals, Moderates, and Conservatives jostled in Congress; and a sharper division existed between the White House, now occupied by Andrew Johnson, and Congress. For Americans in May 1865, nothing was certain, except that nearly every decision had history-changing implications. The course of Reconstruction would be determined largely by the attitudes and actions of these several groups vying for power in the South and in Washington.

The most basic question of all was "how much change?" Would the postwar South be primarily the Old South without legalized slavery?

Would more radical changes—land redistribution to ex-slaves, political power for black men, permanent disenfranchisement for white Confederates—take place? These possibilities, and more, were all seriously considered. But the question of how much change was not utterly unstructured. At least five distinct issues shaped Reconstruction: First, at the national level, did the president or Congress have jurisdiction? Lincoln had argued, as did Johnson, that secession was illegal, which meant that the ex-Confederate states remained states. Therefore, Reconstruction was basically an extension of the war, and the president's war powers gave him the authority to set the course of policy. Congressional leaders argued, in effect, that secession had actually happened and the Southern states were now "conquered territories," which made them Congress's responsibility. This dispute existed during the war and continued after it ended.

Second, who would control Reconstruction in the Southern states—Southern whites (meaning largely ex-Confederates), Southern Unionists, ex-slaves, or transplanted Northerners? These questions only begged more questions: Who was a Unionist? Someone who opposed secession, or someone who had turned against the war in 1864? Or 1863? What did "against the war" mean? Relying on ex-slaves to control Reconstruction would, of course, require suffrage for black men, which some Radical Republicans advocated as early as 1864. It was "too radical" for most Northern whites, even in 1865, although Lincoln endorsed "limited" black male suffrage in one of his last speeches. Republicans also were politicians, and they had barely won the presidency in 1860 with less than 40 percent of the popular vote. Thus, as they looked ahead, Republicans recognized that they needed a Southern wing to the party if they hoped to defeat a reunified, national Democratic organization.

A third major question involved the relationship between the federal government and the states, a complex discussion that went back to the Constitution. Most Democrats wanted to reassert the principles of localism and even states' rights as quickly as possible; most Republicans were more willing to use the federal government as an agent of change, to promote democracy, the economy, and even civil rights. The Confederacy's defeat answered the question of secession, but more broadly, the basic conundrum of American federalism remained.

Fourth, to what extent would the Southern economic power structure be overturned? Radical Republicans wanted to remake the Confederate states by installing a new class of landowners—ex-slaves, if possible, but certainly someone other than antebellum planters. A new economic elite, they reasoned, would mean new political and cultural leadership. Finally, what would freedom mean for ex-slaves—legal equality, political rights, economic rights, or civil rights? These great issues had no clear-cut solutions; some, of course, were not resolved for more than a hundred years.

When the war ended in spring 1865, Congress was out of session, on its long break from March to December. President Johnson decided not to call the members into special session, and instead he proceeded with his own plan (much like Lincoln's) for Reconstruction. Born in North Carolina, Andrew Johnson became a tailor and moved to Tennessee, where he prospered and entered politics. He was a Jacksonian Democrat who championed poor folks from the mountainous parts of Tennessee, but also defended slavery without reservation. He opposed secession, however, and stayed in the U.S. Senate when Tennessee left the Union in 1861. For that loyalty, he was named Lincoln's vice presidential candidate in 1864, a move obviously designed to attract Union Democratic votes. When he assumed the presidency, many Republicans, even Radicals, admired his staunch Unionism and his blunt criticism of the planter-politicians who had led the Old South and the Confederacy. Soon, however, he ran afoul of most Republican leaders. He grudgingly accepted emancipation, but refused to consider any further rights for African Americans. Furthermore, a diehard advocate for states' rights, he had opposed many wartime Republican policies that expanded the federal government's role in American life. Johnson and leading Republicans also came from radically different social and cultural backgrounds. Self-educated, as a young man Johnson became literate but (unlike Lincoln) never became a polished orator—although he was a popular stump speaker, his language often peppered with profanity—or gifted writer. The contrast between him and party leaders such as Charles Sumner (Harvard-educated *Law Review* editor and author) or William Seward (college-educated with honors and a successful lawyer) proved uncomfortable for both sides. Finally, of course, Johnson had been a Democrat his whole life and a slaveowner, and he came from a Confederate state. Many, perhaps most, Union men never quite trusted him.

In the summer of 1865, believing that a Southern Republican Party could be built with unconditional Unionists like himself and some reformed Rebels, Johnson continued Lincoln's plan for a quick, relatively easy Reconstruction. He issued a general proclamation of amnesty that pardoned most ex-Confederates who took an oath of future loyalty to the Union, although high-ranking officers and wealthy planters had to apply personally to Johnson for amnesty. He approved the appeals liberally. Southern states could then reorganize their governments, provided they ratified the Thirteenth Amendment and nullified their secession ordinances. Johnson appointed provisional governors who had been unquestioned Unionists—men such as Mississippi's William Sharkey. There was a limited number of unconditional Unionists, however, and given the president limiting suffrage to white men, ex-Confederates naturally found their way back into public office. Some state conventions also refused to ratify the Thirteenth Amendment or nullify their ordinance of secession. Disappointed and disgusted, Radical Republicans overwhelmingly opposed Johnson's plan and the new governments organized under it.

Despite opposition from Radicals, however, Johnson still enjoyed goodwill among white Northerners in the summer of 1865. Black suffrage did not have enough support to pass a national test, and it even failed in far North, staunch Republican states such as Wisconsin and Minnesota. Conservative Republicans, particularly in the border states, supported Johnson, and most Moderates adopted a wait-and-see attitude. The Radical program seemed dead in the water. But it was about to be rescued, and the history of Reconstruction and America changed forever. The Radicals' saviors turned out to be Southern whites.

Immediately after the fighting, most Southerners (especially ex-soldiers) were resigned to the defeat and to Republican Reconstruction. Many seemed to want nothing more than to recover some part of their previous lives and to wallow in a consuming hatred of everything Yankee. Buoyed by Johnson's lenient policies, however, ex-Confederates soon regained their fighting spirit—in politics, first, but later in the more traditional sense through the Ku Klux Klan. The first real evidence came in the fall elections held by new Southern governments. Voters supported a full complement of ex-Confederate generals, congressmen, and governors; most notable was the selection of Alexander Stephens to the U.S. House of Representatives from Georgia. Worse, from the Northern point of view, was Johnson's willingness to allow Southern states to re-form their militias. By late summer 1865, Northerners began to lose faith in Johnson and prepared for a harder stance against the defeated South. The combination of white Southern actions and Johnson's own shortcomings (from the Radical perspective) doomed his Reconstruction leadership.

The last straw for most Republican moderates were the "Black Codes" passed in many states in the fall and winter of 1865. Enacted in various forms, the Black Codes regulated public behavior generally, but targeted ex-slaves specifically. The laws' intent was to limit the freedom and economic power of black men and women, thereby reestablishing the "proper" racial hierarchy that emancipation had destroyed. The laws provided flimsy pretexts to arrest African Americans, impose fines they could not pay, and "hire out" the prisoners as "vagrants." In fact they were sold at public auction. Mississippi's "vagrant law" of November 1865 provided that any "freedman, free negro, or mulatto" who refused to pay the fine shall be "hire[d] for the shortest time . . . to any one who will pay . . . giving preference to the employer, if there be one." The last clause, designed to help white employers keep control of their workforce, was critical. Among the codes were prohibitions against black men and women leaving their current employer "without good cause," owning firearms, or preaching without a license. In a final catch-all provision, Mississippi's new government allowed that any African Americans "committing riots, routs, affrays, trespasses, malicious mischief, cruel treatment to animals, seditious speeches, insulting gestures, language, or acts, or assaults on any person . . . shall . . . be fined . . . and may be imprisoned at the discretion of the court." If the person could not pay, he or she "shall be hired out by the sheriff . . . at public outcry, to any white person who will pay said fine and all costs." Johnson supported these governments and, at least implicitly, the Black Codes.

In the winter of 1865–1866, the Northern majority rejected the legitimacy of these actions and the Johnson state governments, and Moderate Republicans converted to the Radicals' program. Less than six months after the war in which 360,000 Union boys had died, Southern whites seemed unwilling to accept defeat, reelecting their wartime leaders and re-instituting slavery in another name. When Congress reconvened in December 1865, its members (who control who sits in the chambers) refused to seat the Southern representatives. They moved to take control of Reconstruction through the Joint Committee on Reconstruction, dominated by Radicals, including Charles Sumner, Benjamin Wade, George Julian, and Thaddeus Stevens. Quickly, they resumed the Wade-Davis Plan of

1864—most important, the 50 percent "ironclad" oath for voters, which determined when states could be readmitted to the Union. This provision meant that one of two things would happen: either Southern states would remain out of the Union for a generation, awaiting enough young men who did not fight in the war to come of age and qualify to vote; or there would have to be new voters, most obviously black men. Of course Radical Republicans preferred the latter, and they began to pick up support for black male suffrage throughout 1866.

Five main factors helped generate support. First, military service traditionally gave men a "claim" on the country for legal equality and political benefits. Already, in 1864, the Union government had equalized pay and death benefits for African American troops. About two hundred thousand black men served in the Union Army or Navy, and by 1866, many Northerners felt they deserved citizenship and the right to vote more than ex-Confederates did. Second, the actions of free black men in Louisiana forced many Northern whites to reassess their racist assumptions. When Lincoln's wartime Reconstruction government rejected black suffrage in 1864, free African Americans petitioned the president, and their appeals were publicized in the North. The men came largely from New Orleans's unique free colored community, comprising wealthy (some were slaveowners themselves) and well-educated blacks. The Louisiana protests shocked many Northern whites, most of whom had never encountered an educated black man. Third, the behavior of Southern whites (discussed above) convinced Northerners that they would never "do right" by freedmen. Fourth, American faith in political power led Northerners to believe that suffrage was all that black men needed—if you have the ballot and legal equality, then the rest is up to you. Finally, Republican leaders saw ex-slaves as the foundation of their new Southern wing. Johnson and conservative Republicans preferred white Unionists, but Radicals (and now most Moderates) decided that African Americans would be more loyal, and more deserving, party members. Thus, a combination of practical and principled motives led to greater Republican support for black male suffrage.

Other events in 1866 made that year the turning point when Johnson lost control of Reconstruction to Congress. In February, Republicans voted to extend the Freedmen's Bureau, a relief agency created during the war to help slaves make the transition to freedom. The Bureau provided not only food and clothing, but also legal help and education, among many other services. It also helped white Southerners, and it became widely popular in the immediate postwar South. Objecting to the expanded power of the federal government that the Bureau represented, as well as to the cost of the direct relief it dispensed, Johnson vetoed it. (In July, Congress would override that veto.) Second, in March, Congress passed the Civil Rights Act of 1866, granting citizenship to black men and women (anyone born in the United States). Johnson vetoed it, and Congress overrode the veto. Finally, the citizenship provisions of the Civil Rights Act became the Fourteenth Amendment, as Radicals hoped to make the act permanent and immune to future congressional action.

Throughout the year, Johnson moved closer to Southern whites and further alienated Northern moderates. In February, he spoke on Washington's birthday, denouncing Sumner and Stevens and calling Radical Republicans the "new rebels." In May and July, deadly race riots in Memphis and New Orleans further convinced Northerners that Southern whites would not honor the freedom or even the basic safety of African Americans. Johnson encouraged Southerners to reject the Fourteenth Amendment during the summer of 1866, and consequently it did not have the support of two-thirds of the states and did not become part of the Constitution. All of these events drove Moderates from Johnson and handed power to Radical Republicans. The fall 1866 elections returned even larger Republican majorities in both houses of Congress, yet another indication of the growing impatience with Southern white defiance. While some Southern whites recognized that their course of resistance was provoking Northerners, most aligned with Johnson's stubborn intransigence.

By the end of 1866, then, Radical Republicans largely controlled the Northern Reconstruction agenda. Most Northern moderates initially had little sympathy for the Radical program, in particular civil rights measures beyond emancipation. Many Northerners seemed frankly exhausted by the war—just happy it was over and the Union victorious—and willing to let Johnson and Southern whites chart a course for a quick reunion of the country. But the actions of ex-Confederates aroused the Northern public, unwilling to allow the deaths of so many men to have happened in vain.

Mississippi's Black Codes (1865)

The "Black Codes" were actually a series of laws designed to limit the freedom of ex-slaves. Mississippi's laws became something of a model for some other states. These particular sections focused on giving law enforcement grounds to arrest African Americans for "vagrancy" and hold them in jail when they could not pay the fines levied.

Vagrant Law
[November 24, 1865]
Sec. 1. . . . That all rogues and vagabonds, idle and dissipated persons, beggars, jugglers, or persons practicing unlawful games or plays, runaways, common drunkards, common night-walkers, pilferers, lewd, wanton, or lascivious persons, in speech or behavior, common railers and brawlers, persons who neglect their calling or employment, misspend what they earn, or do not provide for the support of themselves or their families, or dependents, and all other idle and disorderly persons, including all who neglect all lawful business, habitually misspend their time by frequenting houses of ill-fame, gaming-houses, or tippling shops, shall be deemed and considered vagrants, under the provisions of this act, and upon conviction thereof shall be fined not exceeding one hundred dollars, with all accruing costs and be imprisoned at the discretion of the court, not exceeding ten days.

Sec. 7. . . . If any freedman, free negro, or mulatto shall fail or refuse to pay any tax levied according to the provisions of the sixth section of this act, it shall be *prima facie* evidence of vagrancy, and it shall be the duty of the sheriff to arrest such freedman, free negro, or mulatto or such person refusing or neglecting to pay such tax, and proceed at once to hire for the shortest time such delinquent tax-payer to any one who will pay the said tax, with accruing costs, giving preference to the employer, if there be one.

Civil Rights of Freedmen

Sec. 1. . . . That all freedmen, free negroes, and mulattoes may sue and be sued, implead and be impleaded in all the courts of law and equity of this state, and may acquire personal property, and choses in action, by descent or purchase, and may dispose of the same in the same manner and to the same extent that white persons may: *Provided,* that the provisions of this section shall not be construed as to allow any freedman, free Negro, or mulatto to rent or lease any lands or tenements, except in incorporated cities or towns. . . .

Sec. 7. . . . Every civil officer shall, and every person may, arrest and carry back to his or her legal employer any freedman, free Negro, or mulatto who shall have quit the service of his or her employer before the expiration of his or her term of service without good cause. . . .

Certain Offenses of Freedmen

Sec. 2. . . . Any freedman, free Negro, or mulatto committing riots, routs, affrays, trespasses, malicious mischief, cruel treatment to animals, seditious speeches, insulting gestures, language, or acts, or assaults on any person, disturbance of the peace, exercising the function of a minister of the Gospel without a license from some regularly organized church, vending spirituous or intoxicating liquors, or committing any other misdemeanor the punishment of which is not specifically provided for by law shall, upon conviction thereof in the county court, be fined not less than $10 and not more than $100, and may be imprisoned, at the discretion of the court, not exceeding thirty days.

Sec. 5. . . . If any freedman, free Negro, or mulatto convicted of any of the misdemeanors provided against in this act, shall fail or refuse, for the space of five days after conviction, to pay the fine and costs imposed, such person shall be hired out by the sheriff or other officer, at public outcry, to any white person who will pay said fine and all costs, and take said convict for the shortest time.

A Freedman Describes Conditions in Mississippi
(December 16, 1865)

African Americans appealed to the Freedmen's Bureau and the Union Army for help in confronting heavily armed Southern whites. This letter, from Private Calvin Holly to General Oliver O. Howard, recounts incidents of violence and abuse suffered by African Americans.

✳ ✳ ✳ ✳

Vicksburg, Miss.

Sir   Suffer me to address you a few lines in reguard to the colered people in this State, from all I can learn and see, I think the colered people are in a great many ways being outraged beyound humanity,   houses have been tourn down from over the heades of women and Children—and the hold Negroes after they have worked there till they are 70 or 80 yers of age drive them off in the cold to frieze and starve to death.

One Woman come to (Col) Thomas, the coldest day that has been this winter and said that she and her eight children lay out last night, and come near friezing after She had paid some wrent on the house   Some are being knocked down for saying they are free, while a great many are being worked just as they ust to be when Slaves, without any compensation, Report came in town this morning that two colered women was found dead side the Jackson road with their throats cot lying side by side,   I see an account in the Vicksburg. Journal where the (col[ored]) peple was having a party where they formily had one. And got into a fuss and a gun was fired and passed into a house.   they was forbidden not to have any more but did not heed.   The result was the house was fired and a guard placed at the door   one man attempted to come out but was shot and throed back and burned   five was consumed in the flames, while the balance saught refuge in a church and it was fired and burned.   The Rebbles are going a bout in many places through the State and robbing the colered peple of arms money and all they have and in many places killing.

So, General, to make short of a long story I think the safety of this country depenes upon giving the Colered man all the rights of a white

man, and especially the Rebs. and let him know that their is power enough
in the arm of the Govenment to give Justice, to all her loyal citizens . . .

Calvin. Holly., colered

Quoted in Ira Berlin, et. al., eds., *Free at Last: A Documentary History of Slavery,
Freedom, and the Civil War* (New York: The New Press, 1992), 523.

Harper's Weekly (January 12, 1867)

*This drawing by the famous cartoonist Thomas Nast depicts the
Black Codes in action: "vagrants" sold at "public outcry"
(auction) and corporal punishment of ex-slaves (which was
legal under the Black Codes), all carried out before a blindfolded
"lady justice." Radical Republicans used Northern outrage over
the Black Codes to push their reform agenda, including suffrage
for black men.*

Library of Congress.

From Congressional Reconstruction to Redemption: 1867 to 1877

I N 1866 AND 1867, congressional Republicans took control of Reconstruction and began to enact an agenda designed to remake the South into a new society. Many longtime Radicals pursued their vision with the zeal of religious reformers. Men such as Charles Sumner and Thaddeus Stevens had been abolitionists, and remained genuinely committed to civil rights after 1865. They led the Radical faction that was strongest in New England and the upper North, including Michigan, Minnesota, and Wisconsin. Republicans who swung to the Radical position because of Southerners' actions in 1865 and 1866 often had other motives, particularly creating a Southern wing of the party and punishing ex-Confederates. But whatever their motives, a strong majority of Republicans came together in 1867, causing Radicals to spy an opportunity, albeit a potentially brief one. What would happen when the wave of outrage over the Black Codes and race riots subsided? How long could supporters sustain sympathy for African American veterans? Would whites' ingrained racism reemerge to overwhelm the movement for civil rights?

In March 1867, congressional Republicans officially began their own program with the Military Reconstruction Act. This measure divided ten ex-Confederate states (Tennessee had ratified the Fourteenth Amendment and therefore was exempted from military reconstruction) into five military districts, each headed by a Union general (see map on p. 256). It also provided that these states would be officially readmitted after approving new state constitutions that included universal adult male suffrage, and ratifying the Fourteenth Amendment. Extending suffrage to black men was a major victory for Radicals. Still, the Military Reconstruction Act fell short of what most Radicals wanted because it did not include land reform to help ex-slaves establish economic independence and it kept the Johnson-approved state governments in place, although subject to military authority. A later measure provided for military supervision of voter registration, of loyalty oaths, and of the actual voting. Johnson vetoed each of these acts, but his vetoes were easily overridden. Finally, congressional leaders moved to limit Johnson's power and shield Republicans who supported the Radical agenda. The Tenure of Office Act prohibited Johnson from firing any government official or Cabinet member without Senate approval, on the theory that the appointments were Senate-confirmed in the first place. Radicals' primary objective was to protect Secretary of War Edwin Stanton, whom they needed to enforce Military Reconstruction. Congress also provided that Johnson could not issue orders directly to the army (even though he was commander-in-chief), but had to go through General of the Army Ulysses Grant, a recent "convert" to the Radicals' agenda. These measures certainly violated the separation of powers inherent in the Constitution, and Johnson vetoed them all, but to no effect, his vetoes by then having become moot protests.

Frustrated and still not convinced that he had lost control of Reconstruction and the country, Johnson fired Secretary Stanton in August 1867, while Congress was out of session. In response, Johnson was impeached by the House of Representatives on February 24, 1868; the vote was 126 to 47. This set the stage for the actual impeachment trial, held in the Senate, which opened on March 30, 1868.

Lead prosecutor was Benjamin Butler, the former Union general, and the team included arch-Radical Thaddeus Stevens. Johnson's defense was led by Benjamin Curtis, a former associate justice of the Supreme Court. The current chief justice, Salmon P. Chase, presided; Johnson never appeared. Most of the eleven charges dealt with his violation of the Tenure of Office Act (which was almost certainly unconstitutional); another accused him of "inflammatory speeches" during his speaking tour the previous year, when he had called Radicals the "new rebels." The testimony and evidence lasted nearly six weeks, during which time several Moderate Republicans developed reservations about removing a president on flimsy and obviously partisan grounds. Conviction would set a dangerous precedent for future relations between the president and Congress and threaten the hallowed separation of powers. Lastly, many Republicans blanched at the prospect of controversial Benjamin Wade, president pro tem of the Senate, becoming president (since Johnson had no vice president). Behind closed doors, an informal compromise was reached with Johnson, who basically agreed to enforce Military Reconstruction and stay quiet for the remaining months of his term. This helped, but the outcome remained in doubt until the very end, with conviction coming short by one vote. In the long run, the failed attempt to remove Johnson actually hurt Radicals and emboldened a more moderate coalition of Republicans.

While Johnson battled with congressional Republicans, black suffrage, and the effort to organize a Southern Republican party, moved forward. Under the terms of the Military Reconstruction Act, black men voted in the 1868 elections, under Union Army supervision. The coalition that Republicans hoped to build in the South, however, was a naturally unstable one, combining ex-slaves, returning African Americans, transplanted Northern whites (called "carpetbaggers" by most Southerners), and some white Southerners ("scalawags"). Under these circumstances, black men provided the majority of votes, but whites kept most leadership positions. The Democrats initially mounted a weak opposition. While many ex-Confederates returned to politics, others remained disaffected and stayed home. So many white Southern men were dead or refused to take the loyalty oath that, in this fluid political culture, Democrats had difficulty regaining power. These years were the true era of Radical Reconstruction or, as white Southerners termed it, "Black Reconstruction." As individual states satisfied the requirements of Military Reconstruction and formally reentered the Union, nearly all of them did so under Republican control (see map on p. 256). The readmitted states also provided the necessary support that officially added the Fourteenth Amendment to the Constitution, in 1868.

These Republican governments faced staggering problems: a massive labor shortage due to emancipation and one-fourth of young white men dead; the infrastructure in many cities severely damaged or destroyed; no money and the regional economy in shambles; tens of thousands homeless; and an absence of basic public services—especially schools—for the vast majority of the population. To meet these needs, Republican-controlled state governments raised taxes, further alienating the traditionally conservative, libertarian ex-Confederate Democrats. Of course most whites were appalled by black men voting and, although only a small number did, holding office. Even though most Republican elected officials were white, their opponents blamed black men for the problems they associated with Reconstruction. According to Southern Democrats, these "Black Reconstruction" governments were riddled with corruption and ineptitude, which they attributed to the "folly" of granting political power to "childlike" ex-slaves.

Despite black male suffrage in the Southern states, the Radical program lost momentum midway through 1868, thanks mainly to the failed attempt to convict Johnson. At the Republican convention, moderate Ulysses S. Grant won the nomination unanimously. Another moderate, Schuyler Colfax of Indiana, was named Grant's running mate. The party platform even waffled on the issue of universal male suffrage, congratulated Southern states on their new constitutions, and contained a vague commitment to end military occupation. Republicans, of course, touted their wartime record, underscored by Grant's candidacy, and the successes, as they saw them, of Reconstruction. Many Northern Democrats, they reminded voters, had opposed the war and disrupted the draft—something underscored by the Democratic nominee, New York's wartime governor and Peace Democrat Horatio Seymour. And, of course, Republicans noted that Democrats had led the South out of the Union in 1861. Grant won a solid victory, although the results demonstrated the faltering national position of the Republican Party. Democrats made strong gains in the lower North and far West as Seymour carried New York, New Jersey, and Oregon, as well as former slave states Delaware, Maryland, and Kentucky. As more Southern whites reentered politics or rejoined the party, their national position would only be enhanced—Seymour had already won Georgia and Louisiana. Only three years after the war, Republicans confronted a reunified and rejuvenated Democratic Party.

Faced with this Democratic resurgence and the embarrassing fact that though the Military Reconstruction Act allowed black men to vote in the South, they were barred from doing so in much of the North, more Republican leaders embraced the Fifteenth Amendment and universal male suffrage. African American voters, they reasoned, would provide not only a Republican base in the South but also a boost to the Northern wing, particularly in closely contested Midwest and upper South states. Thus, congressional Republicans passed the Fifteenth Amendment in February 1869, and began "selling" it to Northern voters. Even Radicals such as Charles Sumner touted the amendment's political benefits. "You need [Republican] votes in Connecticut, do you not? There are three thousand fellow citizens in that state ready . . . to take their place at the ballot box." New president Grant supported the legislation, and congressional leaders made ratification a further condition for the remaining Southern states— Virginia, Texas, and Mississippi—that had not yet been readmitted to the Union. Enough states voted for universal male suffrage by March 1870 that it became part of the Constitution. Ironically, because many party leaders believed that the Fifteenth Amendment completed legal equality for African Americans and so marked the end of Reconstruction, this success helped stall the Radicals' agenda on more potentially far-reaching proposals such as land redistribution.

As Republicans worked to maintain their hold on national power, Southern Democrats moved to take control of individual states in the former Confederacy. Democrats called this "redeeming" the states from "Black Republican" rule. The redeemers relied on two basic strategies: white unity and violence. Because white voters outnumbered potential black voters in nearly every state and in most congressional districts, if Democrats could get all whites to vote for them then they could reclaim political power. Democrats appealed to white Southerners' deep-seated racism and hatred of Yankees in order to strip away white voters from the Republicans. South Carolina Democrats protested their new state constitution in 1868 as "the work of Northern adventurers, Southern renegades and ignorant negroes," and threatened that "the white people of our State will never quietly submit to negro rule." These unifying themes provided the foundation of Southern Democrats' identity well into the twentieth century.

When appeals to white unity failed, Democrats and their allies turned to violence. The Ku Klux Klan, formed in 1866 (or 1865, according to some sources) in Pulaski, Tennessee, was the most famous and influential organization, but hardly the only one. The Klan started as a veterans' organization for former Confederate soldiers, raising money to help with material needs. Soon it evolved into a paramilitary unit, nearly a wing of the Democratic Party. The group's tactics included intimidation of Republican candidates, beatings and other physical assaults, and untold murders of African Americans. Against white Republicans—both "carpetbaggers" and "scalawags"—the Klan tended to use intimidation and beatings rather than murder. One favorite tactic was a "fake obituary" that appeared in the local newspaper, usually several days before an election, which warned Republican candidates to drop out or risk death. Thousands of black men, and probably hundreds of women, were killed by the Klan and other secret societies.

The violence was slowed by several "Ku Klux Klan" acts in the early 1870s, which Grant personally urged Congress to pass. The acts targeted the wearing of costumes in public, for instance, but the most important one empowered Grant to suspend the writ of habeas corpus and declare martial law, using the U.S. Army to protect African Americans' civil rights. The laws worked, and by 1872 the Klan was largely finished as a significant organization. By mid-decade, however, many Northern whites lost interest in Reconstruction and lost faith in African Americans. Moderates believed that they had "given" black men equal rights before the law, and that the rest was up to them. How long could the U.S. Army stay in the South and supervise voting? Many Northerners thought that a decade was enough.

More fundamental was the slow collapse of the Republican Party's Southern coalition. In most states, white Southerners typically left first. Many "scalawags" had been Unionists, either before or during the war, and they worked with black voters as long as whites maintained leadership and control of the party. But when African Americans demanded an equal share of public offices, many whites balked and then withdrew from politics. Some returned as Democrats, but many simply stayed home. Black Republicans endured countless beatings, but many struggled on and risked lynching every day. As the U.S. Army withdrew from the South, though, the violence took a toll. Georgia's Republicans basically gave up in 1871, overwhelmed by a wave of death that gutted the party's state leadership. In Yazoo County, Mississippi, more than 4,500 men cast Republican votes in the 1874 elections; two years later, seven Republican votes were counted. Between 1873 and 1875, massacres in Vicksburg and Clinton, Mississippi; Hamburg, South Carolina; and Colfax, Louisiana, left hundreds more black men dead. Yet when Mississippi governor Adelbert Ames called for federal protection of black voters in 1875, he was refused.

The combined force of white unity and violence resulted in all but three former Confederate states being "redeemed" by 1876. In that year, the presidential election pitted Democrat Samuel J. Tilden, a lawyer from New York, against Rutherford B. Hayes from Ohio. The voting was very close, and Tilden led with 184 electoral votes to 165 for Hayes (including three from the new state of Colorado, which Republicans rushed through Congress just before the election). There were twenty disputed votes, including nineteen from the three Southern states that Republicans still controlled: South Carolina, Florida, and Louisiana. In these states, Democrats intimidated Republican voters, and there was sporadic violence; Republicans, for their part, manipulated the returns, disallowing thousands of Democratic votes. Complicating things further, while Congress counts the electoral votes, the Constitution does not specify *who* does the counting. Democrats controlled the House of Representatives, Republicans the Senate. Leaders of both parties devised an electoral commission that would decide the outcome; the commission would have seven Democrats, seven Republicans, and one independent (Supreme Court Justice David Davis of Illinois). After the commission was created, however, Davis was nominated for senator and he resigned from the commission. Much to the Democrats' chagrin, and outrage, Justice Joseph Bradley, appointed by Grant in 1870, took Davis's place. The commission members voted along party lines, and all the disputed votes went to Hayes, who defeated Tilden 185 to 184. (Hayes earned the nickname "Old Eight-to-Seven" because of the commission's party-line votes.) Nevertheless, after the election the last troops were withdrawn from the South, effectively handing power to Southern whites. Whether or not this "deal" was arranged in order to mollify angry Democrats is still disputed, but the effect helped heal sectional relations among whites and ease Southerners back into a position of power in national politics.

With the so-called Compromise of 1877 the political narrative of Reconstruction largely ended. Northerners withdrew from the South and left whites, primarily ex-Confederates, in charge. Republican Reconstruction proved to be a short interlude in the long history of Democratic rule, and after 1877 the region became the "solid South" and the electoral foundation of the national party. African American voters remained a force in certain areas into the twentieth century, when "legal" disenfranchisement made Southern politics essentially all white until the 1960s. The most dramatic developments of Reconstruction were the Fourteenth and Fifteenth Amendments, accomplished in just a few years and during the height of Northern resentment over the postwar actions of ex-Confederates. Those amendments became the foundation of the modern civil rights movement of the 1950s and 1960s. Political Reconstruction ended in 1877, but the adjustment of ex-slaves to freedom, of course, was a much longer and more complicated process. For whites, military occupation and black male suffrage engendered anger that lasted for generations. "Were it not for the bitter wrongs of Reconstruction and the fatal legacy it has left us," Georgia's Eliza Frances Andrews wrote in 1908, "the animosities engendered by the war would long ago have become . . . a mere fossil curiosity."

Rhoda Childs on Violence Against African Americans (September 25, 1866)

This description of a brutal assault was given to the Freedmen's Bureau in Georgia. The woman making the report was married to a Union Army veteran, which she averred was the primary reason for the attack.

[Griffin, Ga.] Sept. 25, 1866

Rhoda Ann Childs came into this office and made the following statement:

"Myself and husband were under contract with Mrs. Amelia Childs of Henry County, and worked from Jan. 1, 1866, until the crops were laid by, or in other words until the main work of the year was done, without difficulty. Then, (the fashion being prevalent among the planters) we were called upon one night, and my husband was demanded; I Said he was not there. They then asked where he was. I Said he was gone to the water mellon patch. They then Seized me and took me Some distance from the house, where they 'bucked' me down across a log, Stripped my clothes over my head, one of the men Standing astride my neck, and beat me across my posterior, two men holding my legs. In this manner I was beaten until they were tired. Then they turned me parallel with the log, laying my neck on a limb which projected from the log, and one man placing his foot upon my neck, beat me again on my hip and thigh. Then I was thrown upon the ground on my back, one of the men Stood upon my breast, while two others took hold of my feet and stretched My limbs as far apart as they could, while the man Standing upon my breast applied the Strap to my private parts until fatigued into stopping, and I was more dead than alive. Then a man, Supposed to be an ex-confederate Soldier, as he was on crutches, fell upon me and ravished me. During the whipping one of the men ran his pistol into me, and Said he had a hell of a mind to pull the trigger, and Swore they ought to Shoot me, as my husband had been in the 'God damned Yankee Army,' and Swore they meant to kill every black Son-of-a-bitch they could find that had ever fought against them."

her
Roda Ann X Childs
mark

Quoted in Berlin, et al., eds., *Free at Last,* 537–38.

A Northern View of Southern Elections

White Democrats used violence and intimidation to reclaim power across the South. This Northern cartoon depicts ex-Confederates— armed to the teeth—forcing a freedman to vote the Democratic ticket. A middle- or upper-class Southern white turns his back on the scene, suggesting that Northerners believed poor men led the "redeemers" and perpetrated the violence. On the contrary, however, studies of the "redeemers" and the KKK suggest that those groups included Southern whites of all classes and backgrounds.

Courtesy, American Antiquarian Society.

Harriet Hernandes on Ku Klux Klan Violence
(July 10, 1871)

*Many African Americans testified to the widespread violence
that characterized Reconstruction. This statement describes
several incidents carried out, according to the witness, by
members of the Ku Klux Klan in South Carolina. It underscores
the precarious position of black women, who were often left
alone after men were killed or forced into hiding.*

* * * *

Spartanburg, South Carolina, *July* 10, 1871.
Harriet Hernandes (colored) sworn and examined.

Question. How old are you?
Answer. Going on thirty-four years.
Question. Where do you live?
Answer. Down toward Cowpens' Furnace, about nineteen miles from
here.
Question. Are you married or single?
Answer. Married.
Question. Did the Ku-Klux come to your house at any time?
Answer. Yes, sir; twice.
Question. Go on and tell us about the first time; when was it?
Answer. The first time was after last Christmas. When they came I
was in bed. They hallooed, "Hallo!" I got up and opened the door; they
came in; they asked who lived there; I told them Charley Hernandes.
"Where is he?" they said. Says I, "I don't know, without he is at the Cowpens; he was beating ore there." Says he, "Have you any pistol here?" Says
I, "No sir." Says he, "Have you any gun?" Says I, "No sir." He took on, and
says he, "Your husband is in here somewhere, and damn him, if I see him I
will kill him." I says, "Lord o'mercy, don't shoot in there; I will hold a light
under there, and you can look." I held a light, and they looked. They told
me to go to bed; I went to bed. Two months after that they came again.

Question. Go on to the second time; you say it was two months afterward?

Answer. Yes; just exactly two months; two months last Saturday night when they were at our house. . . . They came in; I was lying in bed. Says he, "Come out here, sir; come out here, sir!" They took me out of bed; they would not let me get out, but they took me up in their arms and toted me out—me and my daughter Lucy. He struck me on the forehead with a pistol, and here is the scar above my eye now. Says he, "Damn you, fall!" I fell. Says he, "Damn you get up!" I got up. Says he, "Damn you get over this fence!" and he kicked me over when I went to get over; and then he went on to the brush pile, and they laid us right down there, both together. They laid us down twenty yards apart, I reckon. They had dragged and beat us along. They struck me right on the top of my head, and I thought they had killed me; and I said, "Lord o'mercy, don't, don't kill my child!" He gave me a lick on the head, and it liked to have killed me; I saw stars. He threw my arm over my head so I could not do anything with it for three weeks, and there are great knots on my wrist now.

Question. What did they say this was for?

Answer. They said, "You can tell your husband that when we see him we are going to kill him." They tried to talk outlandish.

Question. Did they say why they wanted to kill him?

Answer. They said, "He voted the radical ticket, didn't he?" I said "Yes," that very way. . . .

Question. How old is your daughter?

Answer. She is fifteen.

Question. Is that the one they whipped?

Answer. Yes, sir. . . .

Answer. They kept threatening him. They said if they saw him anywhere about they would shoot him down at first sight. . . .

Question. Had he been afraid for any length of time?

Answer. He has been afraid ever since last October. He has been lying out. He has not laid in the house ten nights since October.

Question. Is that the situation for the colored people down there to any extent?

Answer. That is the way they all have to do—men and women both.

Question. What are they afraid of?

Answer. Of being killed or whipped to death.

Question. What has made them afraid?

Answer. Because men that voted radical tickets they took the spite out on the women when they could get at them.

Senate Report 41, part 4, 42nd Congress, 2nd Session, 1871.

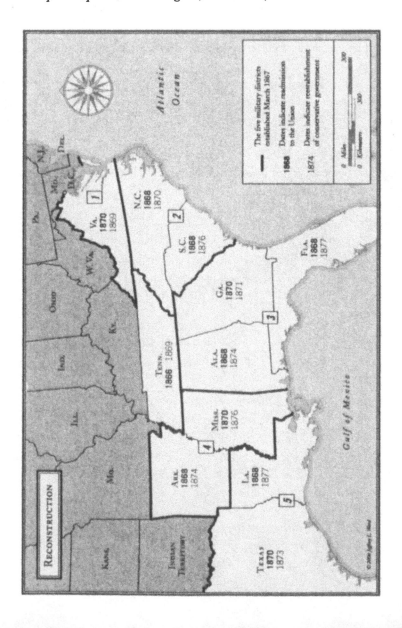

NINETEEN

African Americans and the Transition to Freedom

W HEN THE CIVIL WAR ENDED, former masters and former slaves faced each other in what must have seemed a new world. White and black Southerners had to work out their new lives by defining a new set of relationships—economic, social, cultural, and political. These dynamics were complicated further by the presence of Union troops and the arrival of Northern whites and blacks, many of whom had their own agendas that conflicted with what Southern whites or ex-slaves wanted. Nothing was certain as men and women struggled to pick up their lives and move forward in the aftermath of emancipation and the war's massive destruction and death. How would ex-slaves try to take advantage of their new economic opportunities? Would whites accept emancipation; or to what extent would they accept it? What precisely did *freedom* mean? Over time it became evident that the various constituencies in the postwar South had different answers to these questions, and different ideas about the place and roles of African Americans in public life.

Most slaves remembered forever the moment they experienced freedom. "De news come on a Thursday," Charlotte Brown recalled, seventy years after the war ended, "an' all de slaves been shoutin' an' carryin' on tell ev'ybody was all tired out. 'Member de fust Sunday of freedom. We was all sittin' roun' restin' an' tryin' to think what freedom meant an' ev'ybody was quiet an' peaceful." When the reality of emancipation sank in, many ex-slaves left their plantations and searched for family members sold away during slavery. Reconstituting families became an obsession for many African Americans. Other freedmen, particularly those with families still intact, stayed on their plantations. Some African Americans who had at least tolerable relations with their former masters also remained where they were if the situation offered economic security. Probably more typical, though, was William Mathews's experience. When Union troops came to his plantation and enforced emancipation, his master made "us git right off de place, jes' like you take an old hoss and turn it loose. Dat how us was. No money, no nothin'." Individual personality naturally played an important role: confident, ambitious men and women more likely left to seek a better life; timid or conservative people were more apt to stay put.

Ex-slaves also pursued education—systematically denied to them for so many years—with a vengeance. The Freedmen's Bureau began offering public education to African Americans during the war. Men and women from the North, funded by private organizations led by New England abolitionists, came south and taught children and adults in occupied areas. The Freedmen's Bureau continued and expanded the efforts for public education after 1865. Under Republican Reconstruction, most state governments also initiated an aggressive building campaign for public schools—rolling up a big tax bill that angered conservatives—while taking over most of the institutions founded by private groups and the Freedmen's Bureau. The Bureau and private schools enrolled both white and black students, although virtually no white children chose to attend. Even most "moderate" Southern whites opposed integrated schools. For their part, African Americans sought to establish as much independence from whites as possible, and many ex-slaves actually supported separate schools. Under slavery, of course, whites had maintained a close physical relationship with blacks as they tried to regulate every aspect of slaves' lives. It was whites, for instance, who wanted integrated church services to ensure that slaves got the "right version" of Christianity from white ministers. Thus, after 1865, African Americans initiated the movement for separation (as opposed to segregation, which whites legislated in the late nineteenth and early twentieth centuries) in public facilities such as schools and churches.

More than anything, ex-slaves wanted land, something that they believed—in the American tradition that stretched back to the earliest European settlements—would ensure independence. They also believed that it was owed to them, as payment for so many years of uncompensated labor. Radical Republicans advocated land distribution during the war, and by the war's conclusion, more than forty thousand blacks were established on forty-acre plots of land in the Carolinas and Georgia. This process started with General William Tecumseh Sherman's Field Order 15, issued in January 1865, and was the basis for the call among freedmen for "forty acres and a mule" in the immediate postwar years. In Congress the most consistent advocate of far-reaching land reform was stalwart Radical Thaddeus Stevens. "Reformation *must* be effected," he wrote late in 1865, "the foundation of their institutions, both political, municipal and social *must* be broken up and *relaid*, or all our blood and treasure have been spent in vain." He proposed "to confiscate all the estate of every rebel belligerent whose estate was worth $10,000, or whose land exceeded two hundred acres in quantity." Stevens understated when he said, "This plan would, no doubt, work a radical reorganization in Southern institutions, habits, and manners. It is intended to revolutionize their principles and feelings." Each adult freedman (as head of household) would receive forty acres; any remaining land would be sold at auction. Land redistribution would ensure the freedmen economic independence, Radicals argued, which in turn would guarantee their political freedom and power. When freedmen did acquire land, they grew anything but cotton. The allure of potential cotton profits did not entice most African American landowners, who preferred to stay clear of white bankers, merchants, and creditors. Even a small family farm allowed many black families to grow enough food to survive and meet whatever cash obligations they had.

Southern whites, on the other hand, tried to limit blacks' freedom and independent economic opportunities as much as possible. Most of all, they wanted ex-slaves to get back to work, preferably in the cotton fields of former planters who were trying to regain the prosperity and world market share they enjoyed before 1861. Given the massive labor shortage across the postwar South, African Americans should have enjoyed a strong bargaining position. Amid the depression and cash shortage that plagued the Southern economy, however, former planters and other potential employers could not afford high wages. The first attempt to regulate this fluid, even chaotic, labor market involved annual labor contracts negotiated during the war under the supervision of the Freedmen's Bureau. First used in occupied Louisiana, the annual contracts (enforced by Union troops) required black workers to stay on plantations, primarily to grow cash crops.

Although many agents tried to enforce fair agreements that helped freed-men make the transition to a wage economy, the basic problem was that ex-slaves wanted their own land and to escape field labor under white su-pervision. The annual labor contracts alienated many freedmen and made them suspicious of the Freedmen's Bureau. In time, the Black Codes at-tempted to ensure the planters' economic stability by preventing ex-slaves from moving, negotiating better jobs, or pitting employers against one an-other.

The Freedmen's Bureau had responsibilities that extended far beyond labor contracts and education, becoming almost a de facto local govern-ment during Reconstruction and serving as the representative of federal authority. Each Bureau agent confronted dozens of problems and conflicts each week, ranging from labor disputes to aggravated assault and domestic battery. Their competence and effectiveness varied greatly, and agents nat-urally drew the ire of many whites who resented them as advocates for freedmen, and a daily reminder of defeat. Other whites, however, came to respect and appreciate the agents' attempts to deal fairly with the needs of both ex-slaves and ex-masters. For their part, African Americans often ac-cused Bureau agents of siding with white landowners. When ex-slaves ap-peal to the agent, wrote one black editor in 1867, "he finds there an officer who rides with his employer, who dines with him, and who drinks cham-paign with him. He is not likely to receive impartial justice at the hands of such a prejudiced officer." White Bureau agents often shared the racism endemic in society at large, although others clearly favored freedmen over whites—perhaps out of sympathy for freedmen or hatred for white Rebels.

Annual contracts continued after the war but coexisted with other la-bor arrangements. In "share-waging," groups of ex-slaves worked for land-owners and were paid a lump sum. This appealed to whites, who organized the workers into gangs that could be supervised closely by an overseer, much as during slavery. African Americans, not surprisingly, tried to avoid share-waging since it reminded them too much of slavery and offered lit-tle or none of the daily independence from whites that they craved. The other problem was the chronic lack of capital that limited whites' ability to pay anyone in cash. Therefore, a mutually preferable solution for landown-ers and laborers was sharecropping, an arrangement in which each party received a share of the year's crop. Arrangements varied, but typically, if the landowner furnished seed and other supplies, he kept half of the crop; if workers supplied yearly provisions, then the landlord received only one-third. For African American workers, sharecropping allowed them to live and work as families, free of the gang system and overseers. White land-owners normally chose what was planted and so succeeded in restarting production of cash crops, particularly cotton, in a system that allowed them to sidestep the lack of capital. In other words, each side got some things it wanted and neither got everything.

The resumption of cotton production helped make allies of white Southern landowners and some Northern businessmen, because both groups opposed widespread land distribution. They wanted and needed ex-slaves to get back into the fields and produce the crop that had balanced American trade in 1860 and fueled the nation's growing textile industry. Any incentive for ex-slaves to withdraw their labor from the cotton fields would cripple the South's economic recovery and undermine the nation's overall growth. More widespread opposition to land distribution was rooted in American traditions that glorified hard work, thrift, and "self-help," which dictated that African Americans not be "given" anything "without working for it." All Radical efforts to overturn these prejudices failed, and by 1867, nearly all of those families settled under the terms of Sherman's Field Order 15 had been evicted and the land given back to its original Confederate owners. Thus, economic power returned to many of the same planters who had dominated the South in 1860.

Furthermore, the lack of capital spawned a vicious circle of exploitation in the crop-lien system. Rural merchants advanced farmers a year's worth of necessities against their eventual crop, often charging 50 percent (or more) as interest for the supplies. At the end of the year, most farmers could not pay what they owed and became trapped in a cycle of debt. Making matters worse, merchants began to insist that farmers plant only cotton—the most marketable cash crop. Southerners never regained their position in the worldwide cotton market, however, mainly because the British had developed alternative sources during the war. Domestic demand continued to rise, but as Southerners grew more and more cotton, the price, and the profits, inevitably fell. The regional economy was more one-dimensional, and less successful, after 1865. Although some Southern leaders advocated diversity, cotton continued to dominate the region's economy into the twentieth century. Efforts to expand railroad construction, textile manufacturing, and coal mining helped, although they contributed only more low-paying, unskilled jobs. Thus, as the nineteenth century ended, most Southerners—black and white—were stuck in an economy that offered tenant farmers and sharecroppers few alternatives to cotton and the crop-lien system; textile factory work or coal mining held little promise.

During the same postwar years, black and white Southerners developed nearly separate lives, interacting in few public settings (on court and election days, occasionally at the county store, and in clubs and businesses in which blacks served whites) and even less in private. For much of Reconstruction, most African Americans struggled to achieve economic stability and material competency. An increasingly independent culture founded on religion, family, and education evolved over time. Most of all, freedmen wanted autonomy from the constant white supervision and interference that had characterized slavery. During the postwar years some black men and women also chose to leave the South, a small number moving west to establish family farms but more gravitating to Northern cities (large-scale migration north did not begin until the twentieth century). Only after Reconstruction did African Americans develop separate, nearly complete socioeconomic hierarchies within distinct communities.

In the early 1890s, poor black and white farmers cooperated—to an extent—in the Populist movement, a political crusade aimed at breaking the economic power of large businessmen and merchants to the benefit of rural producers. The Populists' success threatened wealthy Southern leaders, who, in response, led the movement for "legal" disenfranchisement of African American voters in the late 1890s and early twentieth century. Other whites believed that by the end of the century, they sensed a new and dangerous attitude among a generation of black men who had not experienced the "proper discipline" of slavery. With this justifying excuse, whites enacted legal segregation to keep the races separate and "protect" their women. Segregation and disenfranchisement, added to ongoing, endemic violence—a wave of lynchings swept the region beginning in the 1880s—provided Southern white men with the psychological healing they needed to reclaim a sense of manhood and social leadership. Having failed to win the war, Southern white men united to subjugate African Americans as one way to reassert themselves.

Northerners let them do it. By the mid-1870s, most Northern whites were tired of Reconstruction. President Grant himself signaled a growing weariness in a famous 1874 interview, during which he expressed frustration over the continuing violence and unrest in the South. "I am tired of this nonsense. Let Louisiana take care of herself as Texas will have to do. I don't want any quarrel about Mississippi State matters to be referred to me. This nursing of monstrosities has nearly exhausted the life of the party. I am done with them, and they will have to take care of themselves." Grant's attitude seemed to characterize the feelings of many Northern whites, who expressed a conviction that African Americans needed to take charge of their own lives and assert their political and legal rights. Of course, lacking economic independence, this proved difficult, if not impossible.

Reconstruction, according to most assessments, failed. It did not fundamentally change the distribution of power in the postwar South—the men who led secession and the Confederacy, by and large, resumed leadership of the "New South" by the mid-1870s. The war years and Republican Reconstruction, in many ways, represented a brief interruption to the dominant nineteenth-century themes of localism and racism. Of course, failure is in the eye of the beholder. During Reconstruction, African Americans achieved emancipation, citizenship, and, for men, the legal right to vote. Whites denied them many of these rights for nearly a hundred years, but the Reconstruction amendments laid the foundation for the modern civil rights movement. Public schools, even though segregated and with black schools inferior to schools for whites, provided a foundation for social and economic advancement. Even so, as Reconstruction ended in the 1870s, African Americans faced decades of discrimination and random violence before legal equality became a reality; the goal of economic equality that Radical Republicans and freedmen pursued in 1865 remains unfulfilled.

An African American Soldier Appeals for More Schools
(October 8, 1865)

Freedmen relentlessly pursued education, particularly for their children. In this letter, the author, John Sweeny, appeals to an officer of the Freedmen's Bureau to establish a school in his part of Kentucky.

Sir   I have the honor to call your attention To the necessity of having a school for The benefit of our regement   We have never Had an institutiong of that sort and we Stand deeply inned of instruction for the majority of us having been slaves   We Wish to have some benefit of education To make of ourselves capable of business In the future   We have estableshed a literary Association which flourished previous to our March to Nashville   We wish to become a People capable of self support as we are Capable of being soldiers   my home is in Kentucky Where Prejudice reigns like the Mountain Oak and I do lack that cultivation of mind that would have an attendency To cast a cloud over my future life after have been in the United States service   I had a leave of abscence a few weeks a go on A furlough and it made my heart ache to see my race of people there neglected And ill treated on the account of the lack of Education being incapable of putting Thier complaints or applications in writing   For the want of Education totally ignorant Of the Great Good Workings of the Government in our behalf   We as soldiers Have our officers Who are our protection To teach us to act and to do   But Sir What we want is a general system of education In our regiment for our moral and literary elevation   these being our motives We have the Honor of calling your very high Consideration   Respectfully Submitted as Your Most humble serv^t

John Sweeny

Quoted in Berlin, et al., eds., *Free at Last*, 518.

A Group of Freedmen Asks for Land (1865)

*Besides education, African Americans wanted land above all
else. Vague promises from Union generals and politicians during
the war raised hopes among many freedmen that they would be
granted small tracts of land. In this appeal from men and
women on Edisto Island, South Carolina, the petitioners ask to
keep land previously granted to them, and contrast themselves
with former Confederates.*

To the President of these United States. We the freedmen of Edisto
Island South Carolina have learned From you through Major General O O
Howard commissioner of the Freedmans Bureau. with deep sorrow and
Painful hearts of the possibility of government restoring These lands to the
former owners. We are well aware Of the many perplexing and trying
questions that burden Your mind. and do therefore pray to god (the pre-
server of all, and who has through our Late and beloved President (Lincoln) proclamation and the war made Us A free people) that he may guide
you in making Your decisions. and give you that wisdom that Cometh
from above to settle these great and Important Questions for the best interests of the country and the Colored race: Here is where secession was
born and Nurtured   Here is where we have toiled nearly all Our lives as
slaves and were treated like dumb Driven cattle. This is our home, we have
made These lands what they are. we were the only true and Loyal people
that were found in possession of these Lands. we have been always ready
to strike for Liberty and humanity yea to fight if needs be To preserve this
glorious union. Shall not we who Are freedman and have been always true
to this Union have the same rights as are enjoyed by Others? . . . are not
our rights as A free people and good citizens of these United States To be
considered before the rights of those who were Found in rebellion against
this good and just Government (and now being conquered) come (as they
Seem) with penitent hearts and beg forgiveness For past offences and also
ask if thier lands Cannot be restored to them are these rebellious Spirits to
be reinstated in thier *possessions* And we who have been abused and op-

pressed For many long years not to be allowed the Privilige of purchasing land But be subject To the will of these large Land owners? God forbid, Land monoploy is injurious to the advancement of the course of freedom, and if Government Does not make some provision by which we as Freedmen can obtain A Homestead, we have Not bettered our condition.

We have been encouraged by Government to take Up these lands in small tracts, receiving Certificates of the same—we have thus far Taken Sixteen thousand (1600) acres of Land here on This Island. We are ready to pay for this land When Government calls for it, and now after What has been done will the good and just government take from us all this right and make us Subject to the will of those who have cheated and Oppressed us for many years God Forbid!

In Ira Berlin, et al., "The Terrain of Freedom: The Struggle over the Meaning of Free Labor in the U.S. South," *History Workshop* 22 (Autumn 1986), 128–29.

Southerners Debate Integration (May 9, 1867)

Legal segregation—the "Jim Crow" laws—did not evolve until the 1890s. Before then, many Southern towns experienced a significant degree of integration in public areas and public facilities. This newspaper editorial from New Orleans discusses the city's recent experiments with integrated trolley cars, and urges a more general movement to create a "united" city.

This experiment [integrating trolley cars] well illustrate[s] the fact that absurd distinctions are not of the essence of human society. Such discriminations may be maintained by pride, prejudices, or hatred. But as soon as they are dropped, the whole community perceive that they were not necessary, and that the social machinery works better and in a simpler way after they have disappeared; they even experience a sense of relief by the introduction of any reform that benefit the masses of the people. . . .

But now that the car question, which was a minor one, is settled, the time has come to consider the propriety, justice and simplicity of admitting all children into the public schools. The distinction kept up in the schools has no different, and therefore no better ground, than that which was made in the cars. It originated from the same source, slavery, which has now disappeared. It was kept up much more by pride than by prejudice. . . . There is not a single reason that can be given to abolish the distinction on railroads, that cannot apply as well to the abolition of a similar distinction in schools.

We do not see why the city should go to the expense of organizing twenty or thirty new schools, when she has already a sufficient number of public schools to receive all the children to be educated. Discriminations among children, on account of religion and on account of language, would certainly be better justified than a distinction based on their complexions. . . .

Even a distinction based on the social condition, occupation, or respectability of parents, would be better justified than a distinction on color. Yet nobody thinks of setting apart, in distinct schools, children of merchants and of mechanics, of tradesmen and of laborers. It is not proposed to separate bad children from good ones. Why? Because such distinctions are against the Democratic principle of American society . . .

We have to make this community one nation and one people, where two nations and two people previously existed. We had better begin at the roots, and first of all unite the children in the public schools, than to unite at once the grown persons in the city cars.

New Orleans Tribune, May 9, 1867.

★ SUGGESTED READINGS ★

The extensive number of books and articles written about the American Civil War continues to grow each year. Listed below are just a few of the most valuable secondary sources (and some Web sites) that may be helpful for further study of the Civil War era. Many of the primary documents included in this book were drawn from these sources and/or are widely available at a variety of Web sites and in multiple anthologies. Several of the collections listed below include longer or different versions of documents included here.

General Texts

Beringer, Richard, et al. *Why the South Lost the Civil War.* Athens, GA: University of Georgia Press, 1986.

Donald, David Herbert, Jean Harvey Baker, and Michael F. Holt. *The Civil War and Reconstruction.* New York: W. W. Norton & Co., 2001.

McPherson, James M. *Ordeal by Fire: The Civil War and Reconstruction.* New York: Alfred A. Knopf, 1982.

Document Collections

Berlin, Ira, et al., eds. *Free at Last: A Documentary History of Slavery, Freedom, and the Civil War.* New York: The New Press, 1992.

Escott, Paul D., et al., eds. *Major Problems in the History of the American South, Volume I: The Old South.* Second Edition. Boston: Houghton Mifflin, 1999.

Gienapp, William E. *The Civil War and Reconstruction: A Documentary Collection.* New York: W. W. Norton & Co., 2001.

Holt, Thomas C., and Elsa Barkley Brown, eds. *Major Problems in African-American History, Volume I: From Slavery to Freedom, 1619–1877.* Boston: Houghton Mifflin, 2000.

Perman, Michael, ed. *Major Problems in the Civil War and Reconstruction.* New York: Houghton Mifflin, 1991.

Antebellum Era and Secession

Barney, William. *The Road to Secession: Alabama and Mississippi in 1860.* Princeton, NJ: Princeon University Press, 1974.

Freehling, William. *The Road to Disunion: Secessionists at Bay, 1776–1854.* New York: Oxford University Press, 1987.

Gienapp, William. *The Origins of the Republican Party, 1852–1856.* New York: Oxford University Press, 1987.

Holt, Michael. *The Political Crisis of the 1850s.* New York: W. W. Norton & Co., 1978.

Kolchin, Peter. *American Slavery, 1619–1877.* New York: Farrar, Straus and Giroux, 1993.

Oakes, James. *The Ruling Race: A History of American Slaveowners.* New York: Alfred A. Knopf, 1982.

Confederate Home Front

Ash, Stephen V. *When the Yankees Came: Conflict & Chaos in the Occupied South, 1861–1865.* Chapel Hill: University of North Carolina Press, 1995.

Blair, William. *Virginia's Private War: Feeding Body and Soul in the Confederacy, 1861–1865.* New York: Oxford University Press, 1998.

Faust, Drew Gilpin. *Mothers of Invention: Women of the Slaveholding South in the American Civil War.* Chapel Hill: University of North Carolina Press, 1996.

Sutherland, Daniel E. *Seasons of War: The Ordeal of a Confederate Community, 1861–1865.* Baton Rouge: Lousiana State University Press, 1995.

Thomas, Emory. *The Confederate Nation: 1861–1865.* New York: HarperCollins, 1979.

Union Home Front

Baker, Jean. *Affairs of Party: The Political Culture of Northern Democrats in Mid-Nineteenth-Century America*. Ithaca, NY: Cornell University Press, 1983.

Bernstein, Iver. *The New York City Draft Riots: Their Significance for American Society and Politics in the Age of the Civil War*. New York: Oxford University Press, 1990.

Bogue, Allan. *The Earnest Men: Republicans of the Civil War Senate*. Ithaca, NY: Cornell University Press, 1981.

Gallman, J. Matthew. *The North Fights the War: The Home Front*. Chicago: Ivan R. Dee, 1994.

Paludan, Philip. *"A People's Contest": The Union and the Civil War, 1861–1865*. New York: HarperCollins, 1988.

Military

Hattaway, Herman, and Archer Jones. *How the North Won: A Military History of the Civil War*. Urbana, IL: University of Illinois Press, 1980.

Linderman, Gerald. *Embattled Courage: The Experience of Combat in the American Civil War*. New York: Simon & Schuster, 1987.

McPherson, James M. *Battle Cry of Freedom: The Civil War Era*. New York: Random House, 1989.

———. *For Cause and Comrades: Why Men Fought in the Civil War*. New York: Oxford University Press, 1997.

Mitchell, Reid. *Civil War Soldiers: Their Expectations and Experiences*. New York: Simon & Schuster, 1988.

Power, J. Tracy. *Lee's Miserables: Life in the Army of Northern Virginia from the Wilderness to Appomattox*. Chapel Hill: University of North Carolina Press, 1998.

Sears, Stephen. *Landscape Turned Red: The Battle of Antietam*. New Haven, CT: Houghton Mifflin, 1983.

Smith, John David, ed. *Black Soldiers in Blue: African American Troops in the Civil War Era*. Chapel Hill: University of North Carolina Press, 2002.

Wiley, Bell Irvin. *Life of Billy Yank: The Common Soldier of the Union*. Baton Rouge: Lousiana State University Press, 1993 (orig. 1943).

———. *Life of Johnny Reb: The Common Soldier of the Confederacy*. Baton Rouge: Lousiana State University Press, 1993 (orig. 1943).

Reconstruction

Edwards, Laura F. *Gendered Strife and Confusion: The Political Culture of Reconstruction.* Urbana, IL: University of Illinois Press, 1997.

Foner, Eric. *Reconstruction: America's Unfinished Revolution, 1863–1877.* New York: HarperCollins, 1988.

Litwack, Leon. *Been in the Storm So Long: The Aftermath of Slavery.* New York: Alfred A. Knopf, 1979.

Rable, George. *But There Was No Peace: The Role of Violence in the Politics of Reconstruction.* Athens, GA: University of Georgia Press, 1984.

Biographies

Cooper, William, Jr. *Jefferson Davis, American.* New York: Alfred A. Knopf, 2000.

Davis, William. *Jefferson Davis: The Man and His Hour.* New York: HarperCollins, 1991.

Donald, David Herbert. *Lincoln.* New York: Simon & Schuster, 1995.

McFeely, William S. *Frederick Douglass.* New York: Simon & Schuster, 1991.

———. *Grant: A Biography.* New York: W. W. Norton & Co., 1981.

Oates, Stephen. *With Malice Toward None: A Life of Abraham Lincoln.* New York: HarperCollins, 1977.

Thomas, Emory. *Robert E. Lee: A Biography.* New York: W. W. Norton & Co., 1997.

Web Sites

African American Civil War Memorial Freedom Foundation and Museum. http://www.afroamcivilwar.org/

The American Civil War: Forging a More Perfect Union (National Park Service). http://cwar.nps.gov/civilwar/

The Civil War (PBS). http://www.pbs.org/civilwar/

Civil War Women: Primary Sources on the Internet (Duke University). http://scriptorium.lib.duke.edu/women/cwdocs.html

The Library of Congress: American Memory. http://memory.loc.gov/ammem/

The United States Civil War Center (Louisiana State University). http://www.cwc.lsu.edu/

United States Military Academy (West Point).
   http://www.dean.usma.edu/departments/history/
The Valley of the Shadow: Two Communities in the American Civil War
   (University of Virginia). http://valley.vcdh.virginia.edu/

★ ACKNOWLEDGMENTS ★

I WANT TO THANK the many people who have helped make this book possible. My publisher, Thomas LeBien, deserves the most credit. In a casual conversation a couple of years ago I told him about the general idea I had for a Civil War book like this one. He said it sounded like a great idea and that "you should do it," then paused a couple of seconds and said, "we should do it." Since then, he has helped refine the book's overall approach and methodology, and his editorial prodding and stylistic suggestions have improved it immeasurably. Thanks also to the many other people at Farrar, Straus and Giroux who worked on the book, particularly June Kim. Jenna Dolan, who copyedited the manuscript, cleaned up many of my grammatical and usage mistakes.

Numerous friends, family members, and colleagues helped me clarify passages and prompted me to rethink entire sections. In particular, thanks to Jennifer Olsen for her typically careful reading. I also benefited from the support of my colleagues and friends at Indiana State University. As much as anyone, I want to thank the hundreds of students who have taken my American Civil War survey class over the last few years. This book is designed with them in mind, and their questions and discussions have helped organize my thinking about the war. I never cease to be amazed at how much I learn from them—or how much research they make me do. They might get tired of my pledge to "look that up for tomorrow," but I know it has made the class and, I hope, this book better.

As always, my family deserves the most thanks and credit because they remain so very supportive and interested. My (professional) historian father, Richard Olsen, and my (amateur) historian mother, Jean Olsen, inspired a love for history from an early age. My sisters, Catherine, Elizabeth, and Conny, and my in-laws, Bob and Janet Ross, are always willing to talk about this and other things I'm working on. My wife, Jennifer, is my best friend and another teacher and sometime historian; she always supports whatever I do, which is the most anyone can ask. Our children, Emma, Charlotte, and Ross, keep me grounded to the most important things in life. Finally, thanks to Franz Wahldieck and Abraham Wolf, ancestors from another century, whose Civil War discharge papers hung in our house since I was a kid and, I suspect, inspired me subconsciously.

★ INDEX ★

Page numbers in *italics* refer to documents and maps.